DREAMTIME

OVERLEAF: The Paps of Danu, Sliabh Luachra, Co. Kerry (*Courtesy Rex Roberts* ABIPP)

DREAMTIME

John Moriarty

THE LILLIPUT PRESS

Copyright © Estate of John Moriarty, 1994, 1999, 2009, 2020

All rights reserved. No part of this publication
may be reproduced in any form or by any means
without the prior permisson of the publisher.

First published in 1994.
This revised, expanded edition published in 1999,
reissued in 2009 and amended 2020 by
THE LILLIPUT PRESS
62-63 Sitric Road, Arbour Hill,
Dublin 7, Ireland
www.lilliputpress.ie

A CIP record for this title is available from
The British Library.

ISBN 978 1 901866 31 5

Set in 11 on 13 point Garamond 3
Printed in Spain by GraphyCems

CONTENTS

INTRODUCTION   vii

Ces Noidhen	3
Humanity at Bay	9
A Shudder in the Loins	13
Ollamh Fódhla	17
Fintan Mac Bóchra	21
Adventure	22
Challenge	26
The Naked Shingles of the World	32
Triduum Sacrum	35
Job and Jonah	39
Crossing the Kedron-Colorado	44
A Tenebrae Temple	46
The Wandering Christian	49
Altjeringa Rock	50
The Sword in the Stone	53
The Dolorous Stroke	56
Stone Boat	60
The Third Battle of Magh Tuired	66
Ata Dien Cecht Do Liaigh Lenn	70
Inis Fáil	71
Hawk over My Head, Horse at My Door	75
Aisling	80
Mórdháil Uisnig	83
Europe's Year One Reed	95
Ulropeans	98
Mona, Our Moses	100
Ragnarok and Ginnungagap	103
The Theranthropic	106

Kathodos	111
A Songline of the Greek Dreamtime	114
A Songline of the Hebrew Dreamtime	124
Ancient Sleep	128
Rift Man	129
Crossing the Kedron	131
Watching with Jesus	132
The New Heroism	136
Passover	144
Redeeming Our Heroes in the Light of the Triduum Sacrum	145
Healing the City	151
Holy City	155
Ragnarok	160
Bastille Day	164
Immram Eva	170
Sila Ersinarsinivdluge	174
Shaman	179
Prothalamion	182
Connla's Well	192
The Realm of Logres	195
Morgan Le Fay, Our Mayashakti	196
The Mind Altering Alters All, Even the Past	198
Missa in Nocte	201
Partholon	204
Coming Forth by Day	205
Sumer Is Ycumen In	209
Before Sheela-na-Gig Was, Danu Is	212
Mandukya Dawn over Danu's Ireland	213
Second Coming Christianity	221
A Ceiling of Sibylline Visions for the Ruined Cathedral of Clonmacnoise	221
Imagine	224
The New Gae Bolga	226
Enflaith the Bird Reign of the Once and Future King	229
Epilogue: The Last Eureka	233
GLOSSARY	265

INTRODUCTION

The first and obvious question: why the title, why 'Dreamtime'?

'Altjeringa' is a very beautiful Australian Aboriginal word. To me, at any rate, it is very beautiful. It means the Dreamtime, or the Dreaming, that was in the beginning. As Aborigines imagine it, the earth in the beginning was a featureless waste, but beings called the Altjeringa Mitjina, the Eternal Ones of the Dream, emerged, and they went walkabout, each in his or her own way, across this featurelessness; and as they did so, they dreamed with the dreaming earth, dreaming now of a river, now of a mountain, now of trees; and the rivers, the mountains, the trees, the vast variety of things they dreamed of, came to exist objectively and independently of the Altjeringa Mitjina who dreamed them. And so it was that the earth as we now know it came to be. And so it was also that the culture came to be, culture having its origin in things said and done in the beginning. It is this latter aspect of the Dreamtime that I had in mind when I chose the title.

How, structurally and thematically, does this concept of Dreamtime have a bearing on this book? In what way or ways did it help to generate it, motivate it, shape it?

We live in what Hölderlin and Heidegger would call a destitute time. And both Hölderlin and Heidegger ask, What are poets for in a destitute time? The answer implied but not overtly stated in this book is that poets must be healers—healers who, healed themselves, heal us culturally, heal us, or help to heal us, in the visions and myths and rituals by which we live, and to do this effectively they must in some sense be Altjeringa Mitjina, temporary ones, not eternal ones, of the Dream.

Do you see a part of the purpose of the book as enacting and integrating that healing?

Yes, I suppose so. The hope is that, however ethnically various it might be, there is a European Dreamtime. The hope is that Dreamtime always is, is everywhere, is now, and that there are people who have access to it. It is sometimes the case, isn't it, that individuals are healed as they are at present only as a consequence of having been healed as they were in their past?

As with individuals, so, sometimes, with a whole people. Healing in our cultural present will come as a consequence of healing in our cultural past. Out of a healed past a healed present will grow. Out of a re-realized past a re-realized present will emerge. It is as necessary that we realize a past out of which to grow as it is to realize a present and future into which to grow. Our past we have always with us. Our past we must always re-realize. And to do this we need people who can live in our cultural Dreamtime, people who go walkabout, creatively, within the old myths, people who go walkabout into the unknown. It isn't wise, I believe, to do what the originators and executors of the French Revolution did or sought to do. Seized by revolutionary fervour, they would have wiped the slate clean. Intending to hang the last king in the entrails of the last priest, they installed a statue of reason in Notre Dame. But it might be no harm to remember that just as there is an irrational misuse of the irrational, so also is there an irrational misuse of the rational, and that this latter misuse is often as terrible in its consequences as is the former.

Could you locate the book in the context of other writings in the Western tradition?

If you pull back far enough from it, I think you will see that it is an aisling. The word *aisling* is a Gaelic word that means vision, or, better perhaps, dream-vision, and in Ireland, from the eighteenth century on, it gave its name to a kind of poem that was popular among people who, religiously, politically and economically, had been dispossessed. In the typical aisling, the poet wanders in a lonely place, or falls asleep in a lonely place, and in a dream-vision he sees a beautiful woman. Invariably, the poem goes on to enumerate and lavishly describe her beauties of feature and form. Then the poet asks her who she is and she, calling herself by one or another other poetic names, reveals that she is Ireland, adding that she is in deepest sorrow and distress because she has been ousted from her rightful inheritance. Heroically, then, the poet declares that he will fight, unto death if necessary, in her cause, and the poem ends with a vision of the old order restored, of Ireland restored to her ancient inheritance, of Ireland once again having the walk of a queen.

That, briefly, is what a typical aisling might read like. In *Dreamtime*, however, it isn't only Eire who is in trouble. Europa is in trouble. Ecclesia is in trouble. Eire, Europa and Ecclesia are, as it were, three women at a Hawk's Well. Sitting there in deepest gloom, like Dürer's 'Melencolia', they are waiting for the healing waters to flow. Waters that will heal them of their Medusa mindset. Waters that will release them back into their Dreamtime.

But surely anyone who is aware of recent Irish history couldn't, in good conscience, write an eighteenth-century aisling? To do so would be to give further voracious life to the old sow that devours her farrow.

That's true. But, while I think of what I've written as in some sense an aisling, I do hope that it doesn't read like an eighteenth-century aisling. For one thing, it doesn't stand on sectarian ground, or on racial ground, or on socio-economic class ground. Twice or three times it crosses the Kedron with Jesus and stands Grand-Canyon deep in the world's karma. And, although in many pieces there is an attempt to bring together the two extremities of the Indo-European expansion, when they do come together, when they come together creatively, they do so at the heart of the Triduum Sacrum, which is Semitic. The Triduum Sacrum is the athanor of their chymical wedding.

Where does this leave Dreamtime? *If it isn't an eighteenth-century Irish aisling, what is it?*

I don't know, in any simple formula, what it is, I only know that it isn't a thesis. It resists being a thesis. It resists linearity. It is a tapestry of themes and styles, and the hope is that when we come to the end and stand back, we will see that a unified picture does indeed suggest itself. Order will be seen to emerge from chaos. And there is, in any case, an aesthetics of emergent order, just as there is an aesthetics of achieved order. And it might indeed be that in our quest for a vision by which to live, we will sometimes have to be content with an aesthetics of chaos. Waddington, who was a fine scientist, has said nature doesn't aim, it plays. And we aren't perturbed when, reading a book of poems, we find that they differ one from another in theme and form. In spite of its inner variety, such a book might yet come across as a single, if complex, vision of reality.

So, in your own experience of your own book, does it, do you think, have an architecture, a structure, an order?

I think it does. To give you a sense of what it is I will quote a passage from *Apocalypse* by D.H. Lawrence: 'To get at the Apocalypse', he says,

> we have to appreciate the mental working of the pagan thinker or poet—pagan thinkers were necessarily poets—who starts with an image, sets the image in motion, allows it to achieve a certain course or circuit of its own, and then takes up another image. The old Greeks were very fine image-makers, as the myths prove. Their images were wonderfully natural and harmonious. They followed the logic of action rather than reason, and they had no moral axe to grind. But still they were nearer to us than the orientals, whose image-thinking often followed no plan whatsoever, not even the sequence of action.

We can see it in some of the Psalms, the flitting from image to image with no essential connection at all, but just the curious image-association. The oriental loved that.

To appreciate the pagan manner of thought, we have to drop our own manner of on-and-on-and-on, from a start to a finish, and allow the mind to move in cycles, or to flit here and there over a cluster of images. Our idea of time as a continuity in an eternal straight line has crippled our consciousness cruelly. The pagan conception of time as moving in cycles is much freer, it allows movement upwards and downwards, and allows for a complete change of the state of mind, at any moment. One cycle finished, we can drop or rise to another level, and be in a new world at once. But by our time-continuum method we have to trail wearily on over another bridge ...

That I think describes the aesthetics of *Dreamtime*. It is image-thinking, and it moves in cycles. It is a kind of music, and pieces that read like repetitions are *leitmotifs*. One of these *leitmotifs* constitutes a kind of loosely structuring plot. I am thinking of the king motif. The book opens with a story from the *Mabinogion* which is re-told. In this re-telling of it, it becomes a story of a king in trouble. There is an idea, some would call it a primitive idea, that if a king is in trouble, then a people is in trouble, and the land they inhabit is in trouble.

Somewhere towards the centre of the book there are two stories, the theme of which is the healing of the Fisher King and his realm, now, as a consequence of his wound, a *tière gaste,* a wasteland. You will remember, maybe, that, according to the prose Perceval, the Fisher King lives in Ireland. He is the Maymed Kynge that we meet in Malory's 'The Tale of the Sankgreal'. He is our Riche Roi Méhaigné.

In the final story of the book a man emerges from a pre-Celtic tumulus tomb like Newgrange and walks naked towards Tara, carrying the sun-spear in his hand. He is both Pwyll and Arawn of the first story. He is king of both worlds, this world and the Otherworld. He is, very obviously of course, a type of the risen Christ, whose father also, if only iconographically, was a bird. The sun-spear he carries isn't a warrior's spear, it isn't an tsleg boi ac Lugh. Neither is it Cuchulainn's Gae Bolga. It is the spear of light that enters Newgrange at the winter solstice. Carrying that spear, a spear by which he was himself transformatively killed, he will re-establish his ancient Bird reign in Ireland. To begin with in Ireland.

As Nemglan, the Birdman in the waves, had said to him:

Bid saineamail ind énflaith.
Your Bird reign shall be distinguished.

During his Bird reign the waters of Connla's Well will flow again, the healing waters of the Hawk's Well will flow again, and Eriu, Europa and Ecclesia will come home bearing brimming water-jars on their heads.

So your book, after all, is an aisling of a kind?

Perhaps you can call it an Altjeringa aisling. It goes back to and comes forward from the Celtic, Judaeo-Christian and European Dreamtimes. As I was writing it, I had a sense that I was attempting to write a Blakean Prophecy. I am thinking of the Blake who would awaken Albion. Speaking of Blake, Kathleen Raine remarks that the myth of the king who sleeps but will one day awaken is the great and perennial British myth. She tells a lovely story: one day, taking time off from tending his flock, a shepherd was knitting a scarf. Moving himself to ease an ache in his back, his ball of thread slipped from his lap and rolled a little way down the hillside, disappearing through a cleft in the rock. Entering through the cleft, the shepherd found himself going down into a cave. There he saw a sleeping king and on a table beside him a sword and a horn. The shepherd took this sword and struck the table. The king opened his eyes and raising himself said: You should have blown the horn. Reclining again, he went back to sleep.

That's it, I suppose. *Dreamtime* attempts to blow the horn.

Conaire has awakened.

Conaire, whose Bird reign will be distinguished, is walking naked to Tara. And, corresponding to the *claidheamh solais* of the Celtic Dreamtime, the spear he is carrying is a *tsleg solais*, for Conaire isn't only a type of Christ coming forth from the tomb—he is also Plato's Philosopher King coming forth from the cave.

Walk on Conaire.
Bid sameamail ind énflaith.

It is time to sing,

Tá na bráithre ag teacht thar sáile's iad ag triall ar muir.
The friars are coming over the brine and journeying on the sea.

They are bringing Second Coming Christianity. They are bringing Upanishads and Sutras and the Tao Te Ching. They are bringing the Mandukya Om.

Our Carraig Choitrigi is our new Carraig Donn, our new Carraig Om.

We have a centre that will hold.

DREAMTIME

Animum debes mutare, non caelum

CES NOIDHEN

Towards the end of the last century, Yeats and Lady Gregory spent many days together collecting folklore in the countryside around Coole in the west of Ireland. In the course of their work they discovered that

When we passed the door of some peasant's cottage we passed out of Europe as that word is understood.

The Europe they here have in mind is of course official Europe, the Europe that continues to have its cultural origins in Hebrew prophecy, Greek philosophy and science, and Roman law.

And now at last a door, and we lift the latch, and the voice that says come in could be the voice of Fintan Mac Bóchra. It could be the voice of Merlin or Taliesin. It could be the voice of Morgan le Fay.

And how strange it is to stumble on the path that takes us to that door. And how strange it is to lift that latch. And how strange it is to hear that voice. And how strange it is to discover we were always so near home.

Coming again the next day, that path might not be there.

There, but not there for us.

Not there for us because now again we have no eyes for it.

Our eyes are for seeing hard facts.

Hadrian's Wall is a hard fact.

First, it fenced us into a world of hard facts.

Now, stronger than ever, it fences us into a world of manufactured hard facts, it fences us into official Europe. And we don't even wail at it. Nor do we take a sledge to it. It is within a great prison we are unconscious of that we celebrate our Bastille Day.

Almost from the beginning, the wall that Hadrian had built across the north of England became an inner wall. A defensive wall, it has served its sundering purpose only too well, and we, its prisoners, we have gone on building it, deepening it, widening it, filling up cracks in it. Fortunately no crack was wide enough, not even the crack we call Romanticism was wide enough, to let Merlin walk through.

From before a foundation stone of it was laid, Aristotle had a hand in it. More recently, Descartes had a hand in it. On a morning when he celebrated Christ's nativity, Milton had a hand in it, forced his Saviour, infant though he was, to have a *dredded* hand in it. Locke had a hand in it. Indeed, all rationalist and empirical philosophers had a hand in it. Hardly an eighteenth- or nineteenth-century scientist but had a hand in it.

We have gone on building your wall for you, Hadrian. Building it inwardly and outwardly against shamanic Eurasia. Building it inwardly and outwardly against Faerie. Building it inwardly and outwardly against our Dreamtime.

> Against Merlin, Taliesin and Morgan le Fay.
> Against Boann, Badb and Cailleach Beara.
> Against Ollamh Fódhla.
> Against Fintan Mac Bóchra.
> Against Pwyll, Prince of Dyfed.

It wasn't by sitting at home, waiting for a turn in the weather, that Pwyll came to know where a stag hunt might lead if it led to Glen Cuch.

It wasn't by sitting at home, waiting for the spring run of salmon in the river, that Pwyll found the crone and the crone found the well where he slept for nine nights, on nine hazel wattles, seeking a vision his people could live by.

It wasn't by sitting at home, waiting till his minstrel had come to the end of his winter cycle of stories, that Pwyll rode back one day, his banner of lordship in the Otherworld streaming behind him.

Pwyll in our world meant the heraldry of the Otherworld in our world. Streaming from tower and outer wall, they would brighten a sad day in Dyfed.

It was the time of year when Pwyll and his men-at-arms rode to his court in Arberth. The sun picking out great braveries of armour and ornament, they rode four abreast and, to a man, they had the look of men who lived in hill-forts and worshipped in henges.

Theirs was a world that had genius in every stone and bush of it, and it wasn't by incantation that a bush would enchant you, leaving you helpless, your hand halt, and your sword hanging idle at your thigh. Rough men though they were, and intent on adventure, not one of them but knew when to rein in his horse. Riding together or alone, riding at nightfall in desolate places, not one of them but knew when to rein in his instincts.

It was that kind of world. A man who had won everlasting renown in a long war might die coming home when a hare who wasn't a hare of this world put an eye that wasn't an eye of this world upon him. Upon him and his horse.

To die in circumstances such as these was, more often than not, to be called away to a glorious life in a glorious elsewhere.

Of such a man his companions and neighbours would say that he had been swept. By whom they would, in awful reverence, rarely say. Any yet everyone knew that it was the Aes Shidhe.

The world he had gone into wasn't far away. Nights there would be when people would hear overhead the hosts of the air go riding by and someone who had second sight would recognize the dead man, glorious now on a glorious steed, riding among them. And it was well known that a woman who loved a swept man could, in a ritual performed at a crossroads, induce him or even compel him to come back.

It was that kind of world.

It was a world of worlds, all of them one world, all of them a world in which there was coming and going between worlds. As often as not, Pwyll Prince of Dyfed was called Pwyll Pen Annwn, Pwyll who was Head of the Otherworld.

Like all of us, although in our case at an unknown or unrecognized depth of ourselves, Pwyll was a Lord in two worlds. Had the banners of two worlds flying from his towers.

Every year, at leaf-fall, Pwyll and his men rode to Arberth. Riding through a valley five valleys from home they were like an old story Taliesin would tell. And they had it in them to go with the story. They had it in them, living now, riding now to Arberth, to be a tale told by a fireside in the far past, to be a tale told by a fireside in the far future. And they would say, would sometimes say, that their only reason for being in the world was to give the world a chance to live out its own strangeness, its own danger, and its own wonder in them. And this year, reaching Arberth, that's what they looked like. They looked like men who had survived. They looked like men who had come through a dream that Ceridwen, having drunk a new brew from her cauldron, had of them.

After meat and good cheer in his hall the next day, Pwyll announced, as though something had come over him, that he would now go out and sit on the throne mound. At his bidding, a score of men, and they the bravest, accompanied him.

Famous in all worlds, even in worlds we rarely cross into, the throne mound in Dyfed was called Gorsedd Arberth. A thing of crags and swards, of furze and whitethorns, it was lair to a man's own fear of it. It was lair to his fear of himself. In some of its moods, horses, in screeching refusal, would rear at it. And so, it wasn't in ignorance of its perils that Pwyll climbed it. Today, sitting there, he knew that one or another of two adventures would befall him: either he would endure wounds and blows or he would see a wonder.

It was Teyrnon Twyrf Liant, Lord of Gwent Is Coed, who first saw it: in fields all about them not a horse but had stopped grazing and was looking intently, as if in a trance, towards the wood.

Pwyll was of the impression that they were looking into a depth of themselves and into a depth of the world that only the most privileged of us have ever walked in.

Persons so privileged, Pwyll was aware, had rarely come back.

Although he could never afterwards say how or why, Pwyll had come back, a pennant and banner of the Otherworld streaming above him in the January wind.

And as he once came home having slept for nine nights on the nine hazel wattles, so now he came home with a boon for his people. He had news for his people: the Otherworld is a way of seeing this world, it is a way of being in this world.

And still the horses were entranced.

And sure by now that it wouldn't be blows and wounds, Pwyll expected a wonder.

And a wonder, yes, a wonder she was.

She was riding a roan horse.

The roan horse she was riding had red ears.

As soon as she had fully emerged from the wood, the horses of this world neighed.

And the horse the high woman was riding, the horse with red ears, she neighed.

And then it happened.

Not a man on the mound but was utterly helpless, utterly struck down. It was with each one of them as it is with a woman in labour.

> And it went on.
> And it went on.
> And it went on.

They had come to defend Pwyll. But not a hand let alone a sword could any one warrior lift.

And it went on.

And it went on.

And then as mysteriously as they were afflicted they were released.

When at last they could come to their feet and had vision for things outside themselves, they looked and saw that she was gone. And strangest of all was how utterly like its old self the world was. As if nothing had happened, a robin was singing.

As if nothing had happened, the horses were grazing.

On each of the three following days things fell out as they had on the first. Pwyll and his men went to the mound.

In fields all about them the horses stopped grazing and, standing there in a trance of vision, they looked towards the wood.

The woman emerged.

Two worlds, one of them our world, neighed to each other.

And then, more frightful every day, more frightful because more intense, the labour pains of Pwyll and his warriors.

In a vision they would have of it, in their moment of deepest affliction, the throne mound in Dyfed was a red mound. It suffered as they suffered. In the way that Pwyll suffered the crags suffered, the furze suffered, the thorns suffered. For as long as it lasted, this suffering was the ground of their oneness with each other. For as long as it lasted, Pwyll might as well have been a thorn, red with haws, on the side of a hill.

It was strange.

A power against which spear and shield and sword were useless had emerged among them. And what, as warriors, they would most instinctively resist, that was happening to them.

Being warriors though, they would see it through to the end. They would go everyday to the mound. And even if it meant that he would indeed end up as a bush, too haunted and too dangerous for anyone to approach, too haunted and too dangerous for anyone to pick haws from— even if by doing so that is what would happen to him, Pwyll would nonetheless go everyday to Gorsedd Arberth. He would sit where all previous kings of Dyfed had sat. He would sit in the chair, called the Dragon's Lair, between the crags. It was only in the engulfing danger of this chair that he could do what he was born to do. It was only in a willing self-sacrifice of all that he was in all worlds that he, Pwyll Pen Annwn, could mediate between them.

The burden of Pwyll's destiny was simple, and dreadful: a world that is cut off from other worlds will soon die.

Come what may, therefore, Pwyll must go to Gorsedd Arberth.

It was late on the sixth day when Pwyll and his men recovered their eyesight for things outside themselves. Wondering what it might portend, they saw that instead of turning her horse and riding back into the wood she had slackened rein and was coming along the road that passed beneath them.

At Pwyll's request, Teyrnon Twryf Liant rode, as courteously as he could manage it, to meet her.

But how can this be, he thought reaching the road, how can it be that she who rides so slowly and at such an even pace has already gone past?

Putting spurs to his horse, he gave chase.

In a shore while he was riding at full stretch, and yet, even though she continued in her unhurried, slow pace, the distance between them continued to lengthen.

Soon she was out of reach and, discomfited in the way we sometimes are in our dreams, Teyrnon gave up and rode back to the mound.

Pwyll and his men, their arms at ease, returned to the court.

Again the next day, after meat and carouse, they went to the mound.

It was as they expected. In fields near and far there was not a horse but had stopped grazing. As in previous days they were looking enraptured at the wood.

Anticipating what would happen, Pwyll had asked his best rider to fetch the bay, his best horse, from his stables. He was on the mound, mounted and waiting, when she emerged. He rode to meet her.

Great was his wonder when, reaching the road, he saw that she had gone past.

He gave chase.

In a while he was riding at five times, six times, seven times her pace, and yet, she never changing demeanour or motion, the distance between them continued to grow.

On the day following, Pwyll was alone on the mound. Mounted and waiting, he showed spurs to his horse as soon as he saw her.

But no!

When he reached the road she had gone past.

He gave chase.

Never did a horse know so well what was expected of her.

Never had a horse such heart for hard riding.

Never did a horse yield so at length to her rider's desire.

But no! No!

It was all in vain.

The echoing hills carried his call

> Stay for me
> Stay for me
> In the name of him you best love, stay for me.

On a crag, looking down at him, she waited.

Who are you, he asked? Who are you and what is your errand?

My names are many, she replied. There are those who call me Epona, those who call me Macha, those who call me Rhiannon. But by whichever name they know me, they know me only as a woman who rides a roan horse. A horse with red ears. You, however, you have seen the enraptured horses.

You have seen my demeanour and motion. So you know who I am. I am who you feared, yet hoped, I might be.

And your errand? Pwyll asked.

You've already suffered it, you and your men.

And must we continue to suffer it?

That is for you to choose. It's by choice from now on.

Turning her horse, she rode away, and soon she was out of sight, gone into another way of being in our world.

And that's how it happened.

That's how, after long ages, the Horse Goddess came to us, bringing us the terrible yet perfect gift of suffering her labour pains with her.

She foals on May Eve. But for anyone who at anytime chooses to endure them, her labour pains are a door between ways of being in the world.

Will you walk through it Hadrian?

And you Europa, will you walk through the labour pains of the Horse Goddess into our Dreamtime?

HUMANITY AT BAY

One morning, not enchanted, no spell at work in me, no recurring dream having forced my hand, I was rowing a first boatload of saplings across a clear lake. Looking at the mirrored mountains I marvelled at the lake's hospitality to things as they are. Such sight, unfalsifying and unafraid, is the only second sight I would ever ask for. I didn't ever ask for it, because ancient life in me has ancient needs, has ancient ways of seeing things.

Some nights an old story would be my element. Living in it, letting it live in me, I'd draw big waking and big dreaming from it. I drew big dreaming and big waking from this old story, one of the many stories a mabinog, an apprentice bard, must know:

Pwyll, prince of Dyfed, was minded one day to go hunting. There was more to the world in those days than there is now. In those days the world had many marvellous elsewheres in it. Suddenly, the hunt at full stretch maybe, a horse would rear, and rear, and rear again, wouldn't be mastered, would refuse most savagely to go forward. Sooner than his rider sometimes a horse would sense entry into another world.

It was into this world of many worlds, his hounds, like himself, scenting sirloin, that Pwyll, prince of Dyfed, rode one day.

The chase and the dangers of the chase, wherever it would be, lured him on. Five rivers from home the world was darker and wilder than he had ever known it to be.

Some valleys he rode through were an exasperation of crags and woods and waterfalls.

In the narrowest valley of all, overhung by great draperies of mist and light, the world kept its craggy, mountainous mind to itself.

He had heard about such places. He had heard about rock walls that wouldn't even send back an echo.

Today, Pwyll had ridden farther into the world than was his wont.

In Glyn Dhu he saw only a stooping hawk.

In Glyn Cree he saw cast antlers.

In Glyn Cuch he heard howling. He heard baying coming closer. Coming suddenly into view, then suddenly turning, a stag stood at bay in a clearing below him. Hounds that snapped at him were like none he had ever seen. In colour they were white with red ears.

Riding down to them, mastering his horse in tighter and tighter circles among them, he drove them off.

Baiting his own pack he was when someone, in person and poise most kingly, came riding towards him.

You do me great discourtesy, the kingly stranger said.

How so? asked Pwyll, fronting him, not aggressively, but inquiringly, with his horse.

You are baiting your hounds on a stag my hounds have pursued since noon.

Pwyll was abashed. You will favour me greatly, he said, if you will let me know in what way or ways I can make amends.

Arawn is my name, the stranger said. I am king of Annwn. And Annwn, as you know, is the farthest yet also some days the nearest of otherworlds. Like this world, it is sometimes in some places other than itself. In some places, sometimes, it is its own otherworld.

And yes, he said, yes, there is for you a way to make amends. In Annwn, were it not for Hafgan, there would be peace and plenty. Hafgan is most cruel. He comes every night from beyond a deep river raiding our country with fire and sword. You would make amends and you would furthermore win our friendship forever were you, by killing him, to bring to an end the hurt and the terror we suffer at his hand.

Gladly will I assay the killing of him, Pwyll replied. But how best may I encompass it?

To that great end will I instruct and assist you, Arawn said.

I will in this regard, submit most happily to your good counsel, Pwyll averred.

So be it. In this wise, with your consent, shall we proceed. First and foremost, you and I must be friends. From faithful and strong friendship between us much good will follow. As for the rest, with regard, I mean, to the task you are willing to undertake, this is what I propose: leaving here you will go to Annwn in my stead. You will go not in your own appearance and shape but in mine, which I have power to make manifest in you. Assuming your appearance and shape I will go to Dyfed. Arrived there, I will be as you would be, I will do as you would do. In Annwn, when you come there, you will do as I would, you will hunt, you will feast, you will preside, moving in a royal progress from one to another, in my many duns and castles and courts, you will play chess with the chief seneschal, you will listen to wandering minstrels and resident royal bards, you will sleep every night in our bed with my wife who, I am bold to say, is fairer in looks, in her ways and walk, than any woman you have so far seen. A year from today you must ride out to joust with Hafgan at the ford. If it be in your power to do so, and I am sure that it is, see to it that you wound him mortally and unseat him in the first violent charge. In a show of most woeful pain, he will plead with you to end his life, but do not strike him. A second blow to Hafgan revives him, and be in no doubt about it, Hafgan revived is an altogether more awful opponent. Hafgan revived will win the day.

And so, good friendship between them avowed, they parted, Pwyll in the image and likeness of Arawn, its king, going home to Annwn, Arawn in the image and likeness of Pwyll riding home with his hounds from the hunt to Dyfed.

Great was the welcome for both, but great above all was the welcome for Pwyll when he arrived in the Otherworld.

Everything was as it would be were it Arawn himself who had come home.

From the moment, however, that he crossed its borders coming into Annwn, he had to cope with huge surprise. Like leaves that fall from a tree in autumn, his beliefs about Annwn fell from Pwyll, prince till today in Dyfed, leaving him bare.

The secret of Annwn, whatever it was, that he never revealed. His eyes opening as he crossed into it, he saw maybe that life in Dyfed was a forgetting.

It is only, maybe, when the forgetting of Dyfed falls from our eyes that we come into Annwn.

In Annwn we are awake to the Great Life. In Annwn we see.

Awake and with eyes to see in Annwn, Pwyll lived as Arawn would have lived. In only one thing did he not live like him. In bed every night he offered no tenderness or caressings of love to Arawn's wife. However cold towards her it must have seemed, he would always lie on his right side facing the wall.

Images of himself he saw on that wall.

Images of himself as a wounded Bull, a wounded Birdman.

And so it was one autumn morning that his days and nights in Annwn were almost at an end.

There remained only one thing to do. And that he did. Riding to the ford, he encountered and killed Hafgan.

But the Hafgan within himself, the Hafgan impulses he would sometimes see, lying awake, on the wall—that was another story, and he rode out of Annwn one day not knowing the beginning or the end of it.

Riding in Glyn Cuch to his tryst with Arawn, he heard his own hounds, the hunt coming towards him. Out of a wood it burst, the stag suddenly turning, standing at bay. Riding into it he dispersed the pack.

Baiting the Otherworld hounds he had hunted all year with he was, when someone who looked like Pwyll, prince of Dyfed, approached. He was seeing himself for the first time. He was seeing himself with wide, Annwn eyes and that first humbling but healing vision of himself, he would never forget.

And there was worse: it was clear to him now, looking at himself outside himself, that during the year and a day he had spent in Annwn his appearance, borrowed though it was, had become his identity. His disguise had become his deepest guise. His disguise had become his destiny.

He dismounted.

Standing there. Stripped of disguise and guise, Arawn looking down at him from his high horse, he experienced his own nothingness.

So that was it. He saw it now. Pwyll, prince of Dyfed, had ridden out with his hounds to hunt in Glyn Cuch. Himself he alarmed. Himself he pursued. Himself he ran down. And turning at last, and facing his hounds, Pwyll, prince of Annwn, prince of Dyfed, stood at bay.

That's an old story.

It is one of the many stories a mabinog must know.

I often listen to it.

Every time I listen to it, it runs me down.

Every time I listen to it I stand, like Pwyll, at bay.

But standing at bay, like Pwyll in Glyn Cuch, isn't the end of the story. The story moves on. Or it will move on, beyond Annwn and Dyfed. And that's why, every morning for months, I rowed a boatload of saplings across the clear lake. That's why I planted a forest. The story might one day move into it. It moved into it in India and it emerged as Upanishads. It emerged as the Mandukya Upanishad, a classic text of Advaitavendata. Imagine it, the Mandukya Om chanted in a forest by the Bay of Bengal, chanted in a forest by Galway Bay.

Imagine it: the Mandukya Om chanted at the two extremities of the Indo-European expansion.

Hari Om.

A SHUDDER IN THE LOINS

Had he, under tutelage, disciplined the savagery that was in him, and the generosity that was in him, Crunncu might have been a great warrior. As it turned out, he ended up alone, discovering once to his cost that he hadn't, like his cattle, lost his wildness.

Afterwards, as much as he could, he avoided fairs. And assemblies of his people at Bealtaine and Samhain, and assemblies in honour of Crom Dubh, them also he stayed away from.

His four unbroken horses coming down the hillside after her, she came.

His door was open.

I'll be a woman to you, she said, going to the fire and putting fresh logs on it.

Wild though she was, one of the horses put her head through the door.

Not wishing to give the impression that his house was a stable, or that he lived with his animals, Crunncu went towards her, threatening her.

She didn't move.

The horse and the woman looked at each other.

They looked a long time at each other.

At exactly the same moment, nothing overtly happening between them, the woman turned to her work, the horse backed away, and realizing he was out of his depth, Crunncu asked no questions.

Unsure of himself, he went out.

He stayed out all day, gathering his dry cattle and herding them to higher grazing ground.

The higher view didn't help him.

Heights today didn't mean elevation of thought or of feeling. Being higher than the highest wild goat, being higher than a peregrine falcon bringing wool to her nest, to Crunncu up there looking down on his life's work that meant, not delight, but defeat. Bracken and furze had all but taken over his world. Yet, even now, when last year's bracken was tinder dry, he wouldn't fire it. The fired bracken would fire the furze, but he thought of all that wildness going up in smoke, that was a price he wouldn't pay. Wild nature outside him, letting it be, that was his sacrifice of appeasement to wild nature inside him. Religiously, in ways such as this, Crunncu coped.

Shoulder deep in furze, flowering now, he walked back to his house.

A changed house it was.

Nothing had been altered, nothing disturbed, not even the five cobwebs in the five hanging bridles had been molested. And that re-assured him. In firelight, now as always, they looked like death masks. Masks of something dead in himself, he sometimes thought.

No, in outward appearance nothing had changed. And yet, particularly at threshold and hearth, it was as if the house had undergone rededication. But to what he didn't know.

Who is she? he wondered, watching her skimming the evenings milk.

Had she come bringing last year's last sheaf of corn, he'd have thought she was the Corn Caillech.

Had she come, walking tall and naked, and holding a spear, he'd have thought she was Scáthach.

Had she come, a lone scaldcrow calling above her, he'd have thought she was Badb Catha.

Had she, having come, opened her thighs and showed her vast vulva he'd have thought she was Sheela-na-Gig.

Awake, he wondered.

Asleep, he wondered.

Who is she? he wondered, watching her rear like a horse in his dreams.

And the horse that so regularly came to stand in their door? Shoulder deep in the morning, eyes deep in the evening, what did that portend?

There was, he sensed, something he knew about her. But he knew it only where it was safe to know it, in dreamless sleep.

And he wasn't a man to her yet. And in the way that a woman is sometimes a woman to a man, she had so far showed no sign that she wanted to be a woman to him in that welcome way.

And how could any man be a man to a woman like her? How, he looking at her, and she looking at him, could he lay a desiring hand upon her? Would she, showing her teeth, rear like a horse as she did in his dreams?

Sitting across from her by the fire one evening, something dawned on him: Until she came his house had sheltered him, but only as a shed might shelter a cow. Like a religion now, it sheltered him inwardly. Like a religion that was there from the beginning, like a religion that had grown with the growing world, it sheltered him in his difficult depths.

It was strange.

> A horse, and she not broken, standing shoulder deep
> In his door every morning
> A horse, and she not broken, standing hip deep
> In his door every evening.

From hip deep in his nature the dream came: walking high moors he was when he came upon it, the tall standing stone. Taller than a man, it was a man's member, or a god's member, and it was suffering. As a woman in labour suffers, it was suffering. And then, up from the roots a shuddering came, upwards it shuddered, upwards it surged into a long releasing scream that awakened Crunncu, and lying there he knew that in some strange way he had been a man to the woman who was lying beside him.

Welcome to the great world, she said.

Terror of what had happened was shaking Crunncu.

Till dawn it continued, shaking the shaken foundations of old established mind in him, of old established mood in him.

I'm ruined, he said.

Walk through the ruins, she said.

Walk through the ruins you've already walked through.

Walk in the great world you've already walked into.

It's a nothing, a nowhere, I've walked into, he said.

No more marvellous place than that nothing, that nowhere, she said. It's God, she said. It's the Divine behind God, behind all gods, she said. It's the Divine out of which the gods and the stars are born, she said.

My name is Macha, she said.

For the first time since waking Crunncu opened his eyes, opened them in anger, in dangerous, frightened anger.

We should never call anyone Macha but Macha, he blazed.

Do you hear me? We should never call anyone Macha but Macha. Macha's name is a holy name. It belongs to no one but Macha. To no one, no one. To no one but Macha.

His anger became religious indignation, he fixed her in a cold stare: your name isn't Macha! In this house it isn't Macha. I keep horses for Macha. In honour of Macha, in praise of Macha, in thanksgiving to Macha, I never, not even in a moment of greed, I never attempt to bridle them, I never attempt to break them in. Wild on the hills, neighing on the hills, their manes and their tails streaming in the hills, they are the glory of Macha. They are the nearest we can ever come, safely come, to a vision of Macha.

> In her nature Macha
> In her name Macha
> Sharing neither nature nor name with anyone, that is Macha.

Taking Macha's name you have sinned against Macha. Taking Macha's name you aren't safe to sit with, you aren't safe to eat with, you aren't safe to live with, to lie with. What I cannot understand is why our cow hasn't run dry, is why our well hasn't run dry. In my house, no! In my house your name is not Macha.

By what name then shall I be known?

By the name of my neighbour's nag.

What's her name?

She has no name. Nag is her name. And it's your name. Until you find favour with Macha, it is your name. Nag is your name! Nag!

And how might that be? How might I find favour with Macha?

That's for Macha to decide. She might never decide. Macha's heart can be hoof hard. And her head! No! Macha's holy head has never been bridled. Cobwebs blind the bridles we would bridle Macha with. The bridles we would bridle Macha with are masks of our own terror. Attempt to bridle Macha as you'd attempt to bridle an ordinary horse, attempt it, just that, and your face will fall in, into nothingness, into emptiness, into your own empty skull looking back at you as the bridle you'd have bridled her with.

> Macha is lovely
> Macha is ugly
>
> Macha is gentle
> Macha is vicious
>
> Macha has arms
> Macha has hooves
>
> The most beautiful of women is Macha: she opens her thighs
> and you see a mare's mouth.
>
> Macha is Life
> Macha is Death
>
> Bigger life than the life we live is Macha
> Bigger death than the death we die is Macha
>
> With no ritual have we bridled Macha.
> With no religion have we broken her in.
> In no temple to Macha have we stabled Macha.

> Everything in the world that we aren't able for, that's Macha.
> Everything in ourselves that we aren't able for, that's Macha.
> Everything religion isn't able for, everything culture isn't able for,
> That's Macha.

> Stories we have that can cope with Crom Dubh.
> No story we have or ever will have can cope with Macha.

Search our stories, our Tains and Toraiochts, and in them you'll find not a hoof-mark of Macha, in them you'll find not a shake of her tail.

No! No! Neither Tain nor Toraiocht has covered Macha. Rising on its hind legs like a stallion, our Aill at Uisnech hasn't covered Macha.

Living in a world as wild as this one is, the only goddess or god I leave a door open for, and leave a fire on for, is a goddess or god who hasn't submitted to our sanctimonies and sacraments, who hasn't submitted to religion. And that's Macha.

> For Macha I leave my door open.
> For Macha I leave my fire lighting at night.

> Macha hasn't been covered by culture.
> Macha hasn't been covered by religion.

Who or what could cover Macha? he asked.

You have covered Macha, she replied.

Outraged and afraid, he was on the floor pulling on his clothes and his boots.

Hearing her walk away, he looked up.

Hearing hooves on the yard, he went to the door.

It was May morning and Crunncu knew, too late he knew, that it wasn't his neighbour's nag who neighed from the hills.

OLLAMH FÓDHLA

As is the case with all other rivers, our river has its source in Nectan's Well. And that is why we learn to speak. To learn to speak is to learn to say:

> Our river has its source in an Otherworld well

and anything we say about the hills and anything we say about the scars is a way of saying.

A hazel grows over the Otherworld well our river has its source in.

Our time being so other than Otherworld time, it isn't often, in our time, that a hazel nut falls into Nectan's Well, but when it does it is carried downstream and if, passing from current to current, it is brought to your feet and you eat it, then though in no way altered, sight in you will be pure wonder. Then, seeing ordinary things in the ordinary way you had always seen them, sight in you will be more visionary than vision.

To know, and to continue to know, that any well we dip our buckets into is Nectan's Well is why we are a people.

We are a river people.

Exile for us is to live in a house that isn't river-mirrored.

Our river isn't only a river. It is also the moon-white cow who will sometimes walk towards us, but not all the way towards us, on one or another of its banks.

The river and the cow we call by the same name. We call them Boann.

Boann, the moon-white cow.

Boann, the gleaming river.

In dreams I know it as cow.

Awake I know it as river.

And my house isn't only river-mirrored. It is mirrored in Linn Feic, its most sacred pool. And this is so because, by difficult and resisted destiny, I am ollamh to my people. They call me Ollamh Fódhla. In their views of me, Boann, the gleaming river, has carried a hazel nut to my feet.

As these things often do, it began in sleep, in dreams in the night: standing in my door I'd be tempted to think he was only a short morning's walk away, and yet it would often be nightfall before I'd at last turn back, not having made it. A sense I had is that the man I was seeking to reach was myself as I one day would be. In the most frightening of all the dreams I dreamed at that time a man who had no face came towards me and said, you are worlds away from him. When he next came towards me he had a face and he said, you are as far away from him as waking is from dreaming. In the end it was my own voice, more anguished than angry, that I heard: it isn't distance, measurable in hours or days of walking, that separates you from what you would be. It is states of mind, yours more than his.

Defeated, I settled back into my old ways. At this time of year that meant that one morning I'd pull my door shut behind me and drive my cattle to the high grazing ground between the Paps of Morrigu.

My father who quoted his father had always assured me that there was no sacrilege in this. According to the oldest ancestor we had hearsay of, it was in no sense a right that we claimed. Fearfully, it was a seasonal rite we were called upon to undergo. This I took on trust, allowing that there was something more than good husbandry at stake.

Up here, summer after summer since I was a boy, we shook off the vexations and the weariness of winter enclosure.

Up here the gods were not fenced in.

Up here, when we heard him neighing, we knew that the horse god couldn't be cut down to cult size, couldn't be made to serve religious need.

Up here there is a rock. It so challenges our sane sense of things that I long ago capitulated to the embarrassment of crediting what my father and his father before him used to say about it, that every seven years, at Samhain, it turns into an old woman driving a cow.

Sensing my difficulties, my father was blunt: if in the eyes of the world you aren't embarrassed by your beliefs about the world then you may conclude that the wonder-eye which is in all of us hasn't yet opened in you.

That's how it was with me in those days. No sooner had I learned the world and learned my way in it than, standing in front of a rock or a tree, I'd have to unlearn it. I'd hear a story and think that's it, that's how the world is, that story will house me, but then there she'd be, the old woman driving her cow in through my front door and out through my back door, leaving me homeless yet again.

And it wasn't just anywhere I was homeless. I was homeless on the high grazing ground between the Paps of Morrigu, and it wasn't by hearsay that, however red-mouthed she was, Morrigu was divine, all the more divine in my eyes because, like the horse god who neighed only at night, she would never submit to religious servility. Though a people prayed to her she wouldn't send rain in a time of drought or stand in battle with them against an invader.

Worship of Morrigu, of red-mouthed Morrigu, had to be pure.

And that's what I did up here.

Up here every summer I lived between the breasts of a goddess who, in her form as scald crow, called above me everyday, circled and called, searching for afterbirths, searching for corpses, searching for carrion.

The contradiction ploughed me. It ploughed me and harrowed me. 'Twas as if the breasts of the mother goddess had become the Paps of the battle goddess. And to live between the Paps was to live in trepidation of the divine embrace.

Sometimes hearing her call as a scald crow calls I would hear a demand: you must be religious but in being religious you must have no recourse to religion.

So that is it, I thought. That is the seasonal rite. To be religious up here is to fast from religion.

These were heights I wasn't continuously able for. Always by summer's end I'd have lost my nerve, and now again I would pull a door shut behind me and I would go down, me and my cattle, my cattle going down to the shelter of the woods and swards along the river, and I going down to the shelter of traditional religion and story.

Here, as well as being a moon-white cow, the goddess is Boann, the gleaming river.

Down here, we are river-mirrored. And since it is the same sacred river that mirrors us, we are a people.

My house is mirrored in Linn Feic.

In a sense therefore I sleep in Linn Feic, I dream in Linn Feic.

At a sleeping depth of me that I'm not aware of, maybe I am a salmon in Linn Feic, and maybe I swim upstream every night, all the way up into the Otherworld, all the way up into Nectan's Well. At that depth of myself, maybe the shadows of the Otherworld hazel are always upon me. Are always upon all of us, letting wisdom and wonder drop down into us.

Could it be that we are safer in our depths than we are in our heights? Or, could it be that we will only be safe in the heights when we already know that we are safe in our depths?

This time the old woman didn't drive her cow through the conclusion I came to. This time, bringing a six years' solitude in the Loughcrew hills to a sudden end, it was like a stroke, it was like waking up from waking. During an endless instant, all heights and depths had disappeared, leaving only a void, or what seemed like a void.

Twenty-six years later, sitting in my house by Linn Feic, I was able say, it is in Divine Ground behind all depths and heights that we are safe.

That summer, sitting in my reconstructed hut between the Paps, I was able to say, it is from Divine Ground behind and within them that we become able for our depths and heights.

Coming down, at a turn on the path where I was only a short morning's walk away from them, I felt I was able for the sense that people had of me. I felt I was able to be their ollamh. Opening my door, knowing that I was mirrored by the sacred river, I felt that in that depth of me that is overarched by the Otherworld hazel I had consented to be Ollamh Fódhla.

FINTAN MAC BÓCHRA

The geography of my mind is the geography of the world I walk in. In the geography of my mind and therefore also in the geography of the world I walk in are Glyn Cuch, Linn Feic, Gorsedd Arberth and Connla's Well. And if you ask me about life, about what we haven't eyes for in this life, I will talk to you about Gorsedd Arberth and the paths to Glyn Cuch. And the stars, if you ask me about the stars I will tell you that only they who have seen them mirrored in Linn Feic have knowledge of them, only they who have seen them mirrored in that divine deep within themselves can call themselves astronomers. And Connla's Well, at Connla's Otherworld well it was I first realized that being human is a habit. It can be broken. Like the habit of going down to the river by this path rather than that, I broke it. And so it is that, although I always know who I am, I can never be sure that what I am going to sleep at night is what I will be when I wake up in the morning. In me the mutabilities of sleep survive into waking. What I'm saying is, my shape depends on my mood. In one mood, as you can see, I'm an old man, old in the way weather-lore is old, old in the way old stones are old. In another mood I'm a salmon in Lough Derg. In a mood that lasted from the coming of the Partholon to the coming of the Milesians I was a hawk in Achill.

Yes, that's how it is. You only need to break the habit once, the habit of being human I mean, and then you will be as you were between death and rebirth. Between death and rebirth our bodies are mind-bodies, and that means they are alterable. Alterable at will. We only have to will it and it happens, we flow from being a swan in Lough Owel into being a hind on Slieve Bloom into being a hare on Beara.

If for some reason he crosses into our world, the hare will have one red ear.

That's how it is.

What's possible for all of us there is possible for some of us here.

Mostly, though, we've forgotten all this, but folktales remember. Folktales aren't afraid. On its way to the well at the world's end, a folktale will stop by a rock and tell you that every seventh year, at Samhain, it turns into an old woman driving a cow. On its way to Linn Feic, a folktale will sit with you under a bush and, where a bard might tell you the history of your people awake, that bush will tell you the much more serious history of your people asleep.

And the folktale knows what so many people no longer know. It knows how to walk the path to Glyn Cuch. In Glyn Cuch the world has shaken off the habit of being worldly. In Glyn Cuch we come to see that the world's habit of being worldly is not in the world, it is in our eyes.

As the folktale sees I see.
As the folktale lives I live.
And the path to my door, that too is a folktale.

Coming here, you either undergo what people undergo in a folktale or you'll never lift my latch.

> Little wonder I so rarely hear my latch being lifted.
> Little wonder I so rarely hear my latch being lifted.
> Little wonder I so rarely hear my latch being lifted.

ADVENTURE

D.H. Lawrence has this to say:

To me it is important to remember that when Rome collapsed, when the great Roman Empire fell into smoking ruins and bears roamed in the streets of Lyon and wolves howled in the deserted streets of Rome, and Europe really was a dark ruin, then, it was not in castles or manors or cottages that life remained vivid. Then those whose souls were still alive withdrew together and gradually built monasteries, and these monasteries and convents, little communities of quiet labour and courage, isolated, helpless, and yet never overcome in a world flooded with devastation, these alone kept the human spirit from disintegration, from going quite dark, in the Dark Ages. These men made the Church, which made Europe, inspiring the martial faith of the Middle Ages.

In the same vein, he says:

The flood of barbarism rose and covered Europe from end to end. But, bless your life, there was Noah in his ark with the animals. There was young Christianity. There were the lonely fortified monasteries, like little arks floating and keeping the adventure afloat. There is no break in the great adventure in consciousness. Throughout the howlingest deluge, some few brave souls are steering the ark under the rainbow ... If I had lived in the year 400, pray God, I should have been a true and passionate Christian. The Adventurer. But now I live in 1924, and the Christian venture is done. The adventure is gone out of Christianity. We must start on a new venture towards God.

When we come to or see the end of some great thing we will tend, almost inevitably, to remember its beginnings. As Yeats imagined them, Christian beginnings were stupendous:

> *The Roman Empire stood appalled.*
> *It dropped the reins of peace and war*
> *When that fierce virgin and her Star*
> *Out of the fabulous darkness called.*

Calling us, Lawrence, calling us to a new adventure towards God.

Calling us, as Noah was called, to build a new nave.

And how glorious a thing it was. How glorious was the nave we did, in the end, build. Standing in Chartres Cathedral we might, for the moment, be forgiven for wanting to believe that the call was indeed a call godward from God, and it had been heard.

And there are logbooks.

This is Suso, who calls himself The Servitor, speaking of an experience he had:

> In the first days of his conversion it happened upon The Feast of Saint Agnes, when the Convent had Breakfasted at midday, that the Servitor went into the choir. He was alone and he placed himself in the last stall on the prior's side. And he was in much suffering, for a heavy trouble weighed upon his heart. And being there alone, and devoid of all consolations—no one by his side, no one near him—of a sudden his soul was rapt in his body, or out of his body. Then did he see and hear that which no tongue can express. That which The Servitor saw had no form neither any manner of being; yet he had of it a joy such as he might have known in the seeing of the shapes and substances of all joyful things. His heart was hungry yet satisfied, his soul was full of contentment and joy: his prayers and hopes were all fulfilled. And the Friar could do naught but contemplate The Shining Brightness; and he altogether forgot himself and all other things. Was it day or was it night? He knew not. It was, as it were, a manifestation of the sweetness of Eternal Life in the sensations of silence and rest. Then he said, 'If that which I see and feel be not The Kingdom of Heaven, I know not what it can be: for it is very sure that the endurance of all possible pains were but a poor price to pay for the eternal possession of so great a joy ... This ecstasy lasted from half an hour to an hour, and whether his soul were in the body or out of the body he could not tell. But when he came to his senses it seemed to him that he had returned from another world. And so greatly did his body suffer in this short rapture that it seemed to him that none, even in dying, could suffer so greatly in so short a time. The Servitor came to himself moaning, and he fell down upon the ground like a man who swoons. And he cried inwardly, heaving great sighs from the depths of his soul and saying, 'Oh, my God, where was I and where am I?' And again, 'Oh, my heart's joy, never shall my soul forget this hour.' He walked, but it was but his body that walked, as a machine might do. None knew from his demeanour that which was taking place within. But his soul and his spirit were full of marvels, heavenly lightnings passed and repassed in the depths of his being, and it seemed to him that he walked on air. And all the powers of his soul were full of these heavenly delights. He was like a vase from which one has taken a precious ointment, but in which the perfume long remains.

Teresa of Avila was many times *in periculo maris*. Many times, standing to starboard, she had foreknowledge of safe haven:

> I saw an angel close by me, on my left side, in bodily form. This I am not accustomed to see unless very rarely. Though I have visions of angels frequently, yet I can see them only by an intellectual vision, such as I have spoken of before. It was The Lord's will that in this vision I should see an angel in this wise. He was not large, but small of stature, and most beautiful—his face burning, as if he were one of the highest angels,

who seem to be all of fire: they must be those whom we call Cherubim ... I saw in his hand a long spear of gold, and at the iron's point there seemed to be a little fire. He appeared to me to be thrusting it at times into my heart, and to pierce my very entrails; when he drew it out, he seemed to draw them out also and to leave me all on fire with a great love of God. The pain was so great that it made me moan; and yet so surpassing was the sweetness of this excessive pain that I could not wish to be rid of it. The soul is satisfied now with nothing less than God. The pain is not bodily, but spiritual; though the body has its share in it, even a large one. It is a caressing of love so sweet which now takes place between the soul and God that I pray God of his goodness to make him experience it who may think that I am lying.

For Pascal one night there was neither larboard nor starboard, and no wake to suggest that there had been a voyage:

L'an de grâce 1654.
Lundi, 23 novembre, jour de Saint Clément, pape
et martyr et autres au martyrologe
Veille de Saint Chrysogone, martyr, et autres,
Depuis environ dix heures et demi du soir jusques environ minuit et demi
Feu.

Dieu d'Abraham, Dieu d'Isaac, Dieu de Jacob,
Non des philosophes et des savants.
Certitude. Certitude. Sentiment. Joie. Paix. (...)
Oubli du monde et de tout, hormis Dieu, (...)
'le monde ne t'a point connu, mais je t'ai connu.'
Joie! joie! joie! pleurs de joie.

There they are. Entries in the Christian logbook.

Like lighthouses in our night they are: Pascal's night of Divine Fire, Suso's noon of Heavenly Lightnings, and Teresa's Transverberation.

It isn't a universally happy logbook, however.

Not all faggots of sticks brought into Barcelona or Cologne were used to boil a first mate's or a second mate's mess of potage.

Heavenly Fire there was, yes. But there was also *auto-da-fé* fire.

There were Christian master-mariners who ran a tight ship. Too tight maybe.

To have refused to look through Galileo's telescope, calling it a devil's tube, and, furthermore, to have refused initially to sail out into heavy southwesterlies as the *Beagle* did, these refusals, singly and together, have had their consequences. It might be that they amount to a refusal of the Gethsemane experience in its modern form. And whenever, or wherever, Christianity refuses Gethsemane, the Gethsemane of its contemporaries, then, and there, it is in trouble.

Meanwhile, whatever its provenance, Galileo's tube is now a Trojan Horse in our Christian city. And, returned from its voyage, the ten-gun brig is in our bay.

Our Hadrian's Wall has collapsed.

The cosmologies and geographies our minds were moored to are with the four winds.

Our biblical immune system isn't able to cope.

And, coming to us out of the Gethsemane we have refused, a voice of great fear:

Le silence éternel de ces espaces infinis m'effraie.

The voice of someone in the Gethsemane of our time and place. The voice of someone Christianity isn't watching with. It is a voice we cannot not hear.

Hearing it, the Christian empire stands appalled. Hearing it, the Christian empire drops the reins.

The empire might die. But a Christianity without an empire isn't a Christianity without hope. A politically destitute Christianity isn't a dead Christianity.

A Christianity, destitute though it be, that crosses the Kedron with Jesus is giving itself to adventure, the greatest there is.

A Christianity that watches with Jesus in Gethsemane, that watches with him on Golgotha—
A Christianity that watches with him all the way to Jesu Apsusayin,
All the way to Jesu Anadyomene.

That Christianity can watch with anyone, whatever his or her chalice might be, or whatever his or her cup of trembling might be.

And yes, Lawrence, you are right. We must start on a new adventure towards God.

And God's adventure cowards us! Who knows what God's adventure towards us will be!

A transverberated Universe? A Universe transverberated in every atom?

A Universe whose ultimate intuitions or atoms are memorials of a Night of Fire?

A Universe whose first and last intuitions or atoms are an *oubli du monde et de tout hormis Dieu?*

Maybe.
Maybe.

It might be that what happened to Pascal can and will happen to every atom of every universe.

Religiously, everything is enfranchised. Religiously, the highest possibility, the possibility of blissful transcendence, is available to everything.

Pascal's night of fire is available to every atom and galaxy.

Suso's noon of heavenly lightnings is available to every atom and galaxy.

Teresa's transverberation is available to every atom and galaxy.

What happened to Pascal can happen to everything. It can happen to the universe. Let us enfranchise the universe.

And one thing is sure: the Triduum Sacrum is a great frontier. And persons undergoing the Triduum Sacrum aren't only at a frontier, they are a frontier, of human seeking. They seek not to colonize, rather to be colonized, recolonized by soul, by God. Than that there is no greater adventure.

Our new adventure towards God can begin within Christianity. It can proceed with the help of Christianity.

Meanwhile, lying open at its last entry, at Pascal's entry, the Christian logbook has no end of clean pages yet remaining.

The name of our nave until now was Evangel.

Its name from now on is Evangelanta.

Balefully Nietzsche lived the consequences of the death of God. Anyone who now experiences himself or herself to be a 'little compendium of the sixth day' can begin to live the consequences of the divine aliveness of all things, can begin to adapt to the transverberating aliveness of stone and star.

Back to our Evangelanta Ark, bringing news of a moon of heavenly lightnings, comes the raven.

Back to our Evangelanta Ark, bringing news of a night of fire, comes the dove.

Good reason to not be afraid of whatever looms to larboard, of whatever looms to starboard.

Good reason to keep the adventure afloat.

CHALLENGE

Francis Bacon was much concerned to splay and display a sure means of acquiring knowledge. Pursuing his quest in as many directions as seemed to him needful, he turned his attention to the human mind, and in it he found what he called idols or false notions, some innate, some acquired. They were of four kinds: idols of the tribe, idols of the cave, idols of the marketplace, and idols of the theatre.

As he sees and understands them, idols of the theatre are acquired. He says this of them:

> Lastly there are idols which have immigrated into men's minds from the various dogmas of philosophers, and also from wrong laws of demonstration. These I call idols of the theatre; because in my judgement all the received systems are but so many stage-plays, representing worlds of their own creation after an unreal and scenic fashion.

There are many who think that Christianity is such a stage-play, a purely fictitious world projected onto the real world. And speaking of it, Nietzsche says that it is

> distinguished from the world of dreams, very much to its disadvantage, by the fact that the latter mirror actuality, while the former falsifies, disvalues and denies it.

As though the Europe he grew up in was a purely idolatrous Mexico and he a Cortez who had come ashore, Nietzsche proceeded to smash and roll Christianity down the steps of its own pyramid temples. In its place he set up actuality, eternal recurrence, and will to power.

Pleased with himself as a great conquistador, he is happy, looking back on his work, to say:

> Christianity has been up till now mankind's greatest misfortune.

And followers of Christ should know that

> What was formerly merely morbid has today become indecent—it is indecent to be a Christian today.

This is a far cry, a far, very loud and bitter cry, from Tertullian's claim that the human soul is naturally Christian. *Anima naturaliter Christiana* is the phrase.

The human soul is not naturally Christian in the sense that it naturally knows that God is a unity and trinity of divine persons.

The human soul is not naturally Christian in the sense that it naturally knows that Jesus of Nazareth was a hypostatic union of divine and human nature.

The human soul is not naturally Christian in the sense that it naturally knows that the world we live in will one day pass away and be replaced by a new heaven and a new earth.

So, is there a sense in which the soul is naturally Christian?

I think there is.

It is as natural for a human being to undergo the Triduum Sacrum as it is for an insect to undergo metamorphosis.

The Triduum Sacrum is the Gethsemane experience, the Good Friday experience and the Easter experience.

In Gethsemane we are offered the cup of all our karma. Drinking it, we know what Sir Thomas Browne knew:

There is all Africa and her prodigies in us.

Drinking it, we know what Jacob Boehme knew:

In man lies all whatsoever the sun shines upon or heaven contains, and also hell and all the deeps.

Drinking it, we discover what Nietzsche discovered:

I have discovered for myself that the old human and animal world, indeed the entire prehistory and past of all sentient being, lives on, works on, loves on, hates on in me.

Drinking it we discover what Joseph Conrad discovered:

The mind of man is capable of anything—because everything is in it, all the past as well as all the future.

In Gethsemane we integrate what we discover, we integrate what we phylogenetically are, and since so much of what we phylogenetically are is so fearfully archaic, it is appropriate that we call the process of integrating it an agony.

On Golgotha, which literally means the place of the skull, we undergo Tenebrae. In the course of it we come to resemble Christ looking down into Adam's, and therefore into his own, empty skull.

Eckhart is unambiguous:

God expects but one thing of you, and that is that you should empty yourself in so far as you are a created human being, so that God can be God in you.

St John of the Cross is unambiguous:

And when he shall have been brought to nothing, when his humility is perfect, then will take place the union of the soul and God, which is the highest and noblest estate attainable in this life. This consisteth not in spiritual refreshments, sweetness or sentiments, but in the living death of the cross, sensually and spiritually, outwardly and inwardly.

Fenelon is unambiguous:

God felt, God tasted and enjoyed is indeed God, but God with those gifts that flatter the soul. God in darkness, privation, forsakenness and insensibility is so much God that it is so to speak God bare and alone.

De Caussade is unambiguous:

As long as these crucifying operations last, everything—spirit, memory and will— exists in a terrifying void, in sheer nothingness. Let us cherish this mighty void, since God deigns to fill it; let us cherish this nothingness, since God's infinity is to be discovered in it.

It is as if the skull at the foot of the cross was speaking to us, reassuring us, telling us to fear not.

Its appearance notwithstanding, the Golgotha skull is a glory. A glory when it speaks. An even greater glory when it is silent, for, as the Tao Te Ching tells us:

> He who speaks does not know.
> He who knows does not speak.

And it doesn't only speak in a Christian way to Christians. Of no matter what people you are, of no matter what age or place, it will speak to you in your language and out of your tradition.

Listen to the Kena Upanishad:

There goes neither the eye, nor speech, nor the mind; we know it not; nor do we see how to teach one about it. Different it is from all that is known, and beyond the unknown it also is.

Listen to the Heart Sutra:

Therefore, O Chariputra, in emptiness there is neither form, not feeling, nor perception, nor karmic formation, nor thinking.

Listen to Chuang-tzu:

Ch'i is empty, yet all things depend on it. Tao gathers in emptiness alone. Emptiness is the fasting of the mind.

Listen to his God talking to Niffari:

Between Me and thee is thy self-experience: cast it away, and I will veil thee from thyself.

Listen to Al Hallaj:

Between me and Thee there is an 'I am' that torments me. Ah! Through thy 'I am' take away my 'I am' from between us both.

Whether we call it fasting from mind or dereliction, Christ looking down into Adam's empty skull could one day come to be seen, could one day come to be inherited, as our final evolutionary transition, not just by Christians but by humanity. A humanity that has come this far can call itself sapient.

In his dereliction Christ cried out:

> My God, my God, why hast thou forsaken me?

God's absence or our experience of his absence is now in a most marvellous way a mode of God's presence. Although God has disappeared as object of awareness, He nonetheless abides as Ground, as Divine Ground, of our being. But until, beyond all empirical means and modes of apprehension, we apprehend this, we are derelict. And the dereliction is stupendously real. Everything that could walk out on Christ walked out on him. It might even be that in the end his cross walked out on him. It might even be that his sufferings walked out on him. For where there are sufferings there is something to hold on to.

Tauler must have known something of this when he said:

Everything depends on a fathomless sinking in a fathomless nothingness.

And Marguerite Porete must have known something about it when she talked of:

The Souls' fall from love to nothingness.

But just as the emptiness that mystics talk about isn't a negative emptiness so also is the nothingness they talk about not a negative nothingness. It is an infinitely rich nothingness. And it ever and forever heals us of nihil, of nihilism.

But who, experiencing it for the first time, will not cry out as Christ cried out.

We haven't yet come to know what Fenelon came to know, that

God in darkness, privation, forsakenness and insensibility is so much God that He is to speak God bare and alone.

What a great religion Christianity is, the Religion that has given Religious respectability to a pleroma of agony in Gethsemane, to a pleroma dereliction on Golgotha.

We come through because, apprehend it or not. God abides as ground of our being.

We come through because both pleromas are pleromas of grace.

We come though because, having surrendered, we are taken through.

And then—and what a *then* it is—God's final favour. We call it Easter.

The Easter that happens only secondarily in the Garden of the Sepulchre.

The Easter that happens in the ground of our being.

Eckhart exults:

Oh, wonder of wonders, when I think of the union the soul has with God! He makes the enraptured soul to flee out of herself, for she is no more satisfied with anything that can be named. The spring of Divine love flows out of the soul and draws her out of herself into the unnamed Being, into her final Source which is God alone.

Marguerite Porere jubilates:

Being completely free and in command of her sea of peace, the soul is nonetheless drowned and loses herself through God, with him and in him. She loses her identity, does the water from a river—like the Ouse or the Meuse—when it flows into the sea, and the same is true of the soul. Her work is over and she can lose herself in what she has totally become: Love. Love is the bridegroom other happiness enveloping her wholly in his love and making her part of that which is. This a wonder to her, and she has become a wonder ...

Suso jucundates:

When the good and faithful servant enters into the joy of his Lord, he is inebriated by the riches of the house of God for he feels, in an ineffable degree, that which is felt by an inebriated man. He forgets himself, he is no longer conscious of his selfhood; he disappears and loses himself in God, and becomes one spirit with him, as a drop of water which is drowned in a great quantity of wine. For even as such a drop disappears, taking the colour and the taste of the wine, so it is with those who are in full possession of blessedness.

Pascal weeps with joy:

Year of grace 1654
Monday, 23 November, day of St Clement, pope
and Martyr, and others in the martyrology
Eve of St Chrysogonus, martyr, and others,
From about half past ten in the evening to half past midnight
Fire

God of Abraham, God of Isaac, God of Jacob,
Not the God of philosophers and scholars
Certainty, certainty, emotion, joy, peace (...)
Forgetfulness of the world and of everything, outside God (...)
The world has not known you, but I have known you
Joy, joy, joy, tears of joy.

No Nietzsche. It is not indecent to be a Christian.

No, Nietzsche. Christianity is not a misfortune. Nor is it a stage-set of fictions and idols that should be rolled away much as Cortez rolled the religion of the Aztecs away.

A religion that grows out of the Triduum Sacrum, a religion that is therefore able to sponsor and foster the Triduum Sacrum in us in the way that nature sponsors and fosters metamorphosis in insects, such a religion is as necessary to us as water is to fish.

A religion that fosters the Gethsemane experience, the Good Friday experience and the Easter experience in us is a religion that is fostering the evolving Earth, is a religion that is fostering a seed of great growing in the evolving stars.

Since we should hear what he has to say more as a challenge than as a lament, it is time that we listened to a modified version of something Kierkegaard has said:

The kind of men and women Christianity has in mind no longer exist.

THE NAKED SHINGLES OF THE WORLD

'No coward soul is mine', Emily Brontë says, 'No coward soul is mine, / No trembler in the world's storm-troubled sphere.'

Nothing, she declares, can disturb her faith:

> *Though earth and man were gone,*
> *And suns and universes ceased to be,*
> *And thou wert left alone,*
> *Every existence would exist in thee.*
>
> *There is not room for Death*
> *Nor atom that his might could render void*
> *Thou—thou art Being and Breath,*
> *And what thou art may never be destroyed.*

Listening to 'the grating roar of pebbles' on Dover Beach, Arnold isn't so sure:

> *The sea is calm to-night.*
> *The tide is full, the moon lies fair*
> *Upon the straits;—on the French coast the light*
> *Gleams and is gone; the cliffs of England stand*
> *Glimmering and vast, out in the tranquil bay.*
> *Come to the window, sweet is the night-air!*
> *Only, from the long line of spray*
> *When the sea meets the moon-blanched sand,*
> *Listen! you hear the grating roar*
> *Of pebbles which the waves draw back, and fling,*
> *At their return, up the high strand,*
> *Begin, and cease, and then again begin,*
> *With tremulous cadence slow, and bring*
> *The eternal note of sadness in.*
>
> *Sophocles long ago*
> *Heard it on the Aegean, and it brought*
> *Into his mind the turbid ebb and flow*
> *Of human misery; we*
> *find also in the sound a thought,*
> *Hearing it by this distant northern sea.*
>
> *The Sea of Faith*
> *Was once, too, at the full, and round earth's shore*
> *Lay like the folds of a bright girdle furl'd;*

> *But now I only hear*
> *Its melancholy, long, withdrawing roar,*
> *Retreating, to the breath*
> *Of the night-wind, down the vast edges drear*
> *And naked shingles of the world.*
>
> *Ah, love, let us be true*
> *To one another! for the world, which seems*
> *To lie before us like a land of dreams,*
> *So various, so beautiful, so new,*
> *Hath really neither joy, nor love, nor light,*
> *Nor certitude, nor peace, nor help for pain;*
> *And we are here as on a darkling plain*
> *Swept with confused alarms of struggle and flight,*
> *Where ignorant armies clash by night.*

I think I know what you mean, Matthew: I was lying on a rock at the edge of a lake one day. There was a thin wind, blowing onshore. Inwardly run aground, I was listening to the laplap, lap, laplaplap—lap, laplaplap of the water on the rocks. Wondering whether I was carrion, a scald crow circled above me. His voice, like my mind, had no silver lining in it. That's it, I thought. That's it. My educated, European head is in trouble. With it, and emptily in it, I can only hear the godless logos of lake water and scald crow.

I stood up and, in a seizure of half-blind lostness, I walked or stumbled across the bog. Religiously and culturally, I was out of doors. I was the thing itself, the bare forked animal. A hare broke from before my feet. Instantly and without thinking, I dropped to the ground and I eased my head into the warm form in the heather. Thinking of it to begin with as a poultice, I asked it to suck my education out.

Then I imagined it to be an egg, a wild ovum, an ovum of heather and grass and one day, reborn in my oldest and deepest instinctive and mental depths, I would be able for the splendour and terror and danger and wonder of a world everywhere and in everything eruptively Divine.

I asked it to evolve me backwards into the Pleistocene, backwards into the commonage consciousness of an Aurignacian shaman, a nomad pitching his tent among the herds between Altamira and Lascaux.

I imagined a totemically sheltered man, a man whose headgear was a hare's form.

I imagined Hareman. Hareman dancing. Hareman dreaming, being dreamed, in his Pleistocene tepee. Dreamed by the dream that dreams codes and stars.

But no! Walking home that evening, I could see by my shadow that I wasn't Hareman. I wasn't, I could see, totemically sheltered. A modern European. I was heir to Matthew Arnold's trouble.

Arnold turned away, seeking refuge in his marriage.

Darwin sailed out into heavy south-westerlies and the ring of his geological hammer on the beach at Punta Alta is our modern Angelus, an Angelus which, for so many, announced the death of their God.

> Have you not heard of the madman who lit a lantern in the bright morning hours and ran to the market-place crying incessantly 'I seek God! I seek God!'? As many of those who did not believe in God were standing around just then, he excited considerable laughter. Have you lost him then? said one. Did he lose his way like a child? said another. Or is he hiding? Is he afraid of us? Has he gone on a voyage? Or emigrated? Thus they shouted and laughed.
>
> The madman jumped into their midst and pierced them with his glances. Where has God gone? he cried. I shall tell you. We have killed him—you and I. We are all his murderers. But how have we done this? How were we able to drink up the sea? Who gave us the sponge to wipe away the entire horizon? What did we do when we unchained this earth from its sun? Whither is it moving now? Away from all suns? Are we not perpetually falling? Backward, sideward, forward, in all directions? Is there any up or down left? Are we not straying as through an infinite nothing? Do we not feel the breath of empty space upon us? Are we not colder? Is not night coming on darker and more dark? Must not lanterns be lit in the morning? Do we not yet hear the noise of the grave-diggers burying God ...

Modern Western humanity come to Dover Beach.

Modern Western humanity come to the beach at Punta Alta.

Modern Western humanity listening to the naked shingles of the *res extensa* world.

Modern Western humanity listening to the naked shingles of Ulro.

Modern Western humanity listening to the ring of Darwin's geological hammer echoing within its Medusa mindset.

The fossilized skull of *Megalonyx* reduced to shore shingle. And, a geological epoch or two from now, the fossilized skull of *Homo sapiens,* similarly reduced, perhaps.

Matthew's trouble:

> *The Sea of Faith*
> *Was once, too, at the full, and round earth's shore*
> *Lay like the folds of a bright girdle furl'd,*
> *But now I only hear*
> *Its melancholy, long, withdrawing roar*
>
> *Retreating, to the breath*
> *Of the night-wind, down the vast edges drear*
> *And naked shingles of the world.*

Emily's faith:

> *Though earth and man were gone*
> *And suns and universes ceased to be*
> *And thou wert left alone,*
> *Every Existence would exist in thee.*

> *There is not room for Death*
> *Nor atom that his might could render void:*
> *Thou—thou art Being and Breath,*
> *And what thou art may never be destroyed.*

Emily, our Cordelia, come to Dover Beach.
Emily, our Cordelia, come to the beach at Punta Alta.
Singing it within, and with, the grating roar, she sings her Song of God on Dover Beach, she sings her Bhagavad Gita at Punta Alta.

> Come to the window, Matthew.
> No. Come out of doors.
> Come with your wife.

> Can ye see her?
> Can ye hear her?

> Can ye see that the shingles aren't naked?
> Her song is their song.

> The Universe is a Mantraverse.
> In all its shingles and stars, it is a Mantraverse.
> Its mantra is the Mandukya Om.

TRIDUUM SACRUM

Metamorphosis in insects, Triduum Sacrum in human beings.

In insects, metamorphosis is of two kinds: it is complete or incomplete.

In human beings, the Triduum Sacrum is of two kinds: it is complete or incomplete.

Metamorphosis in insects is a change of form: a caterpillar becomes a butterfly, a nymph becomes a dragonfly. The Triduum Sacrum in human beings is a going beyond form. It is ego-centred form losing itself in the Formless Divine.

Persons undergoing the Triduum Sacrum, persons engulfed and swallowed up in it, will sometimes feel that, body and soul, they are evaporating. Like a saucepan of water over a fire, they sometimes feel that, body and soul, they are being boiled away, saucepan and all.

Only it isn't like that. It isn't like a saucepan of water over a fire—a saucepan of clear well-water over an ordinary fire, over a turf fire. No, it isn't like that. I feel like a cauldron of unregenerate dark energies over a Ragnarok fire. I am boiling away. A steam of nightmares and dreams condenses on my bedroom window.

I wake every night at the hour of the wolf. Recording another kind of time in another kind of way, my clock always says it is twenty to four. My room is thick with moral pollution.

As the peoples of northern Europe imagined it, Ragnarok was something that happened to the world. But whoever I am, it can happen to me.

Ask not for whom the bell tolls ...

Ask not for whom Fenrir howls or Fjalar crows ...

But, fear not, fear not, O nobly born.

For look at his shadow. Even as he howls his Ragnarok howl, look at Fenrir's shadow—it is the Abhaya Mudra.

And look at Fjalar's shadow. Even as Fjalar crows his shadow is the Abhaya Mudra.

> Fjalar crows,
> Goldencomb crows,
> Rustred crows.

When Rustred crows at the bars of Hel his shadow too is the Abhaya Mudra.

And Ragnarok itself? Even as it comes, cataclysms coming before it, even as it comes engulfing all worlds, what else but the Abhaya Mudra is Ragnarok?

Fjalar has crowed.

Announcing Chasm Time, Fjalar, Goldencomb and Rustred have crowed.

> Chasm Time,
> Quake Time,
> Time of Earth Yawnings.

> Cup of Trembling Time,
> Wine of Astonishment Time.

> Hell is naked before me Time,
> Out of the Depths have I cried to Thee Time,
> I am a brother to dragons and a companion to owls Time,

> I am come before the King of Terror's Time,
> I am sore Broken in the place of Dragons' Time,
> Tempest and waters steal me away Time,
> Terrors take hold on me Time,
> Fearfulness and trembling are come upon me Time,
> Horror hath overwhelmed me Time,
> Spirits move before my face Time,
> Hair of my flesh stands up Time,
> He breaketh me with breach upon breach Time.
>
> A Wide Breaking in of Waters Time,
> A Wide Breaking in of Waters Time,
> A Wide Breaking in of Waters Time.
>
> A Wide Breaking in of the Waters of Nun Time.
>
> A Wide Rushing in.
>
> Tohu Wavohu.
>
> Tehom.
>
> Ginnungagap.

But throughout it all, and after it all, the bow, the Abhaya Mudra, in the cloud.

Abyssus abyssum invocat (Deep calls unto deep).

> In my nothingness is my only hope
> In my nothingness is Divine hope

May I be as out of your way awake, God, as I am in dreamless sleep.

I can't sense you or know you or commune with you, God, I can't find you inside me or in the world outside, but I still want to be your servant, God.

Jesus turned to cross the Kedron. But the Kedron he would cross was Colorado-river deep in his own and in the world's karma.

And how well protected were you, Jesus?

Were your garments inscribed with coffin texts? Was the great red robe you were wearing inscribed, on its inside, with The Tibetan Book of the Dead, on its outside, with the Papyrus of Ani? Were the scraps of your sandals inscribed, on the inside, with The Book of Gates, on the outside, with The Book of Caverns? Were the soles of your sandals inscribed, inside, with Upanishads, outside, with Sutras?

Did you ask all the praying of ancient Egypt and Mesopotamia to go down with you?

Were you wearing the world's praying?

All the praying of Incas, Eskimo, Yoruba, Aranda, Yakut? And the praying, not yet, of Christendom and Islam?

Was the praying of all peoples, in all places, in all times—was this praying an immune system in you against the terror you must surely walk into?

Or were you destitute?

Did you only have your destitution and dereliction to wear?

How well provided, in his awful going down, Ani was.

How well provided for underworld faring Atreus was.

How well provided for oceans unknown the Sutton-Hoo chieftain was.

And your chosen companions didn't watch with you.

> They were willing in spirit
> But, incarnate, they were weak.

And we don't watch with you. We can't.

Even now, after centuries of Christian praying, we can't. To watch with you is not to observe. It is to undergo what you are undergoing on all the old karmic floors of the psyche, on all the old karmic floors of the earth.

On the heaved-up trilobite seafloor you have gone down into. On the black, pink-flamed firefloor well below the last depth in which it is possible to be alive biologically.

The spirit is willing but the flesh is weak. Willing initially to watch with you, we protect ourselves by falling asleep.

> Sleep on now.
> Sleep, Chasms. Sleep, Canyons.
> Sleep, Sun. Sleep, Moon.
> Sleep Taurus. Sleep Ursa.
> Sleep on now.

> His God walks out on him.

Even his cross, even his sufferings, walk out on him.

Dreaming walks out on him. Waking walks out on him.

He is in the Dark that was before world was, before psyche was.

Out of Adam's empty skull, empty of dreaming, of waking—speaking comfortably to him out of that skull He hears His own divine Voice:

> Yatra na anyat pasyati na anyat
> srinoti na anyad vijanati sa bhuma!
> (Where nothing else is seen, nothing else is heard
> nothing else is thought about, there's the fullness!)

O Dichosa Ventura.
(O happy lot.)

And, on the mountain, Jivanmukta Jesus. And how beautiful upon the mountain are the feet of him who comes to us out of the Triduum Sacrum.

His time has come,
He comes down.

Our teacher comes down from the Hill of the Koshaless Skull.

Watching him, we know there is Palm Sunday before the Triduum Sacrum and Palm Sunday after it. On the Palm Sunday after it, the writings of Christian and other mystics are the palms we wave welcoming him back into Christianity.

JOB AND JONAH

A question early Christians asked with passionate urgency was: who in his nature, who in his being, in his substance, was Jesus? A very Aristotelian question to which, at Chalcedon, there was given a very Aristotelian answer.

There is, however, another, not less passionately urgent question these same seeking Christians might have asked: who, as experiencer, is Jesus? Who as experiencer who has crossed the Kedron, is Jesus? Is he, having crossed the Kedron, utterly unique, utterly without analogy to anyone or anything, so that we cannot, as a consequence, talk about him? Or, given the fullness of humanity in him, can we not assume that there are archetypes to which, if only partially, we can assimilate him, seeking to know. We mustn't assume, a priori, that the most hospitable archetypes will be biblical.

Maybe there is no room in the archetypal Middle-Eastern inn. No room, maybe, in the archetypal Mediterranean inn, in the archetypal European inn, in the archetypal Christian inn.

A lonely man.

A man sore amazed.

A man whose intuitions and experiences caused him to be archetypally unaccommodated, archetypally unassimilable?

A man religiously and culturally out at heel, out at elbow, out at medulla, out asleep, out awake.

A man with whom, philosophically or mythologically, his culture couldn't watch.

As the fourth Evangelist, had he so perceived it, might have put it: made flesh, The Word was verbally unhoused.

There are persons whose vision of things isn't culturally validated, isn't, in their lifetimes, culturally assimilable. Of itself, their vision of things excommunicates them.

If the gospels say sooth, however, experiencing himself archetypally disenfranchised wasn't a sorrow the Man of Sorrows was acquainted with.

On the contrary, it is, Christians believe, his willingness, in obedience, to be the Archetype he was and knew himself to be that most characterizes him. It is his willingness to stupendously enact, to stupendously endure, the stupendous consequences of being the Incarnate Archetype he was that so religiously appals, so religiously delights, them.

And Jesus returned in the power of the spirit into Galilee: and there went out a fame of him through all the region round about. And he taught in their synagogues, being glorified of all. And he came to Nazareth where he had been brought up: and, as his custom was, he went into the synagogue on the Sabbath day, and stood up for to read. And there was delivered unto him the book of the prophet Esaias. And when he had opened the book, he found the place where it was written, The Spirit of the Lord is upon me, because he hath anointed me to preach the gospel to the poor; he hath sent me to heal the broken hearted, to preach deliverance to the captives, and recovering of sight to the blind, to set at liberty them that are bruised, To preach the acceptable year of the Lord. And he closed the book, and he gave it again to the minister, and sat down. And the eyes of all them that were in the synagogue were fastened on him. And he began to say unto them, This day is this scripture fulfilled in your ears. And all bare him witness, and wondered at the gracious words that proceeded out of his mouth. And they said, Is not this Joseph's son?

He was Joseph's son. Sure, he was. But placating a neighbour whose gate was lying there uncompleted didn't preoccupy him now:

Then certain of the scribes and the Pharisees answered, saying, Master, we would see a sign from thee. But he answered and said unto them, an evil and adulterous generation seeketh after a sign; and there shall no sign be given to it but the sign of the prophet Jonas: For as Jonas was three days and three nights in the whale's belly; so shall the Son of man be three days and three nights in the heart of the earth. The men of Nineveh shall rise up in judgment with this generation, and shall condemn it: because they repented at the preaching of Jonas; and, behold, a greater than Jonas is here.

Greater than Jonah.

Greater not just as a prophet, we presume. Greater, also, in that, when his time comes, he will be more able than Jonah was for the Jonah initiation.

Out at sea, in a tempest, Jonah was thrown overboard. Swallowing him, a whale turned flukes and sounded, carrying him down under the roots of the mountains, under the roots of psyche and universe, not under them as two realities, under them as one reality, because, at root, at centre, and at summit, psyche and universe are one and the same.

Jonah was carried down into the Great Deep under experienceable reality. He was carried down into the Great Deep that was before the psyverse was. The Great Deep. Hebrews call it Tehom. Hindus call it Turiya. Turiya is Nirguna Brahman, the Brahman without attributes, the Divine Ground that is groundless, and out of which, in playful delight, the psyverse emanated, back into which, sensing bliss, it will return.

For all its emanative vastness, the psyverse hasn't left, hasn't emerged from, the Divine Ground it is emanating from. When it wakes from the dream of its emanations, it will know that it never left home.

And when he returns, the raven that Noah sent out will bring Good News.

To Christians, Muslims, Jews, to all peoples who don't yet know, the raven, returning, will announce

Tehom is Turiya.

Carried down under the roots of the mountains, carried down, subjectively that is, under the roots of awareness-of, the weeds of the Great Deep, of Nirvikalpasamadhi that is, were wrapped about Jonah's head.

And Jesus, Joseph's son, says of himself that he is greater than Jonah. Clearly, an immense spiritual breakthrough is at hand.

Greater than Jonah.

Greater than Job. More able than Job for the Job initiation.

Job and Jonah are rites of passage. In Jesus, these initiations, these rites, were sanctified. In Jesus, in him, and through him for us, these rites, these initiations, became religiously available, religiously safe.

Job was a good man. Civically and domestically, he was rock solid. So habituated in an unquestioning, unconscious way was he to conventional living that there was little or no trace of irrational, first or pristine nature in him. From his core out, calmly and contentedly, Job was honourable, acceptable civic second nature. At evening, Job would sit in the big city gate, being wise, conventionally. He was much given to proverbs.

Suddenly, as if in the night while he slept there had been a wide breaking-in of waters, civic, domestic living was swept away, and Job awoke, his proverbs no use to him now, at the frontier.

Job had come before himself.

The self he had come before was a King of Terrors.

Nights now when Job was a brother to dragons and a companion to owls.

Nights now when Hell was naked before him; when, before him, within him, Destruction had no covering.

Nights now, when, like it or not. Job must drink the wine of astonishment. Nights now when, drinking it to its dregs. Job must drink the cup of trembling.

A man inwardly clairvoyant to all that he inwardly was, behemothically. A man sore amazed.

A man sore expectant of what had already come to pass: a man sore expectant of abyss and beast irruptively from within.

A man sore broken in the place of dragons.

His religion couldn't watch with him. Wise only in the wisdom of its city gates, civilization couldn't watch with him.

Job was in trouble. Job was at the frontier.

The untameable God of all untameable frontiers, inner and outer, a theologically untameable God, a God before whom Hebrew prophecy and Greek philosophy were without arraignable resource, a God who, whatever else he was, was Pashupari, Lord of animals—this terrifying Lord of all untameable frontiers, this Lord of animals, this Lord of Abyss and Beast, confronted Job, commanding him to take stock of himself, as a man, before daystars, abyss and beast.

Job's biblical bluff was called. With unlobotomized mind, with unlobotomized eyes. Job beheld the unlobotomized Earth.

When they passed before him in Eden, Adam named the animals.

When, more brutally but also more bounteously, they passed before Job, Job, falling silent, shook dust and ashes on his biblically betrayed, biblically blessed head.

For recovering of sight to the blind, Jesus came.

For us, as for Job, this means the falling away like scales from our eyes, the falling away like *idola tribus* from our eyes, of verses twenty-six and twenty-eight of Genesis, chapter one.

Jesus, Joseph's son, came to set at liberty them that are bruised epistemologically by their naïve realism.

It was claimed for Jesus, Joseph's son, that, genetically, he was of the royal line of David.

Crossing the Kedron, his genetic ancestry doesn't count for particularly much.

His ancestors now are Job and Jonah.

It is to Job and Jonah, in the fullness of their de-vast-ating experiences, that he will be experientially assimilated.

And because he is greater than Job, greater than Jonah, the Job and Jonah rites of passage will enact themselves more comprehensively and more inwardly in him than we have been biblically prepared for in the biblical versions of the Job and Jonah initiations.

The names 'Job' and 'Jonah' aren't only names of two fictional characters in the Bible. Like the name 'Osiris' in ancient Egyptian religion, they are generic names. They are the names of all those people who, while they are undergoing them, undergo the Job and the Jonah anagnorises.

Nowadays, in many societies, it is expected of persons that they will become inimitable, unique individuals. There have been and are societies, however, where a contrary outcome to our growing was or is desirable. Archetypalization not individuation is the goal. In medieval Christendom, for instance, there were persons who, in the hope of becoming an Alter Christus, another Christ, attempted, sometimes with fierce ascetic determination, to suppress or eliminate what was unique and individual in them. And in ancient Egypt, a person, having died, was sacramentally assimilated into the image and likeness and post-mortem destiny of Osiris. So complete was the assimilation, that the person was sometimes referred to as the Osiris.

Having crossed the Kedron, Jesus, while remaining uniquely himself, is also, in experiential assimilation, a Job who is greater than Job, a Jonah who is greater than Jonah.

Rites of passage enacted themselves in Job and Jonah.

In plenary realization of their inherent possibilities, these rites of passage re-enacted themselves in Jesus, and in him in whom there was sorrow but no resistance, they opened out into a continuous way through into the bliss of self-loss in Divine Ground.

We are heirs, if we choose, to this way through.

And, as a consequence,

> We are, most humbly, heirs with Hindus to Upanishads.
> We are, most humbly, heirs with Buddhists to Sutras.
> We are, most humbly, heirs with Taoists to the
> Tao Te Ching.
> We are, most humbly, heirs with Christians to
> Evangel and Evangelanta.
> We are, most humbly, heirs with Jews to heard of and unheard of
> Books of Splendour.
> We are, most humbly, heirs with Sufis to Bezels of Wisdom.
> We are, most humbly, heirs with Navajo to sacred circles and songs.
> We are, most humbly, heirs with Siberian, Inuit and Aboriginal shamans
> to sacred songs.

Jesus crossed the Kedron.

There is a way through for us, when we are ready.

When they are ready, for stars.

CROSSING THE KEDRON-COLORADO

To cross the Kedron seeking phylogenetic and chakrad awakening and integration in oneself, to cross it seeking moksha for or from oneself, is one thing. To cross it as Lamb of God, and for Lamb of God reasons, as Christians claim Jesus did, is altogether another thing.

To cross the Kedron as Lamb of God, for Lamb of God reasons, is to cross it where it is Colorado-river deep in the world's karma, it is to absorb willingly that karma, all of it, into oneself, and to climb with it, carrying it to an abyssal summit of Moksha Mountain called Golgotha.

> Lamb of God who absorbs the world's karma, walk with us.
> Lamb of God who absorbs the world's karma, walk with us.
> Lamb of God who absorbs the world's karma, guide us, climbing,
> to the abyssal summit.

There is Holy Thursday in the Garden of Olives. And there is Holy Thursday in Gethsemane.

There is Good Friday, reconcilingly, on Calvary. There is Good Friday, advaitally, on Golgotha.

Golgotha means the place of the skull. Elaborating, we might say, it is the place of the empty skull. Remembering the acosmic dark that prevailed from the sixth to the ninth hour, we might go yet further and say, Golgotha is the no-place, beyond space and time, of the empty skull.

Golgotha is the no-place, beyond space and time, of total kenosis.

'God expects but one thing of you', Eckhart says, 'and that is, that you should empty yourself insofar as you are a created human being, so that God can be God in you.'

On Golgotha where, from the sixth to the ninth hour, abyssal emptiness prevailed, Adam's skull was empty.

The skull of the First Adam. The skull of the Second Adam.

A process of self-emptying which began in heaven had its end, most triumphantly, here.

The triumph isn't visible. It isn't visible to someone who might look for it with ordinary eyes. It isn't visible to someone who might look for it with Easter eyes.

On Golgotha we are beyond the dream division, the dream wound, that opened in the beginning between seer and seen. In the gulf that yawns between Good Friday on Calvary and Good Friday on Golgotha, rock of faith becomes abyss of faith. Veda gives way to Vedanta in that gulf. Evangel gives way to Evangelanta.

Could it be that the Second Coming which Christians expect and pray for will be a new understanding of what has already happened?

> Dying, You destroyed our death.
> Rising, You restored our life.
> Lord Jesus, come in glory.

Could it be that the glory will be a glorious understanding of Good Friday on Golgotha?

Could it be that the Second Coming happened simultaneously with the First?

Could it be that the Second Coming is a mystical opening within the First?

Are we waiting for something that has already happened?

> Crossing the Kedron
> into
> Holy Thursday in the Garden of Olives,
> Good Friday on Calvary,
> Easter Morning in the Garden of the Sepulchre
> into
> Holy Thursday in Gethsemane,
> Good Friday on Golgotha,
> Nirvikalpasamadhi.

Good Friday on Golgotha: Dereliction Day on an abyssal summit of Moksha Mountain.

Day deeper than day, than night.

Day when I see that, conscious and unconscious, psyche is the blind not the window.

Day when, conscious and unconscious, psyche is the veil that is rent.

Day when I see that psyche in me isn't Ground in me, isn't Ground of me.

Day when I see that awareness of self and other-than-self isn't Ground in me, isn't Ground of me.

> Dereliction Day,
> Dis-illusioning Day,
> Dis-identification-with-illusion Day,
> Dereliction Day: Divine Ground Day,
> Coming home unobstacled by awareness-of-self
> And other-than-self to Divine Ground Day.
> Day which, from the beginning, is.

Day which, from the beginning, the First and the Second Comings have been waiting for.

Day which, from the beginning, the First and Second Comings have been preparing us for.

Dereliction Day: Divine Ground Day,
Call it
Good Friday.

A question comes to mind. But who is big enough to ask it? Who is morally big enough to assume moral responsibility for asking it? I am not. And yet in fear and trembling I ask it: Is Easter as we have traditionally understood it a satisfactory answer or finale to Good Friday? Is Good Friday itself the only adequate answer to Good Friday? Is an advaitavedanta understanding and experience of Good Friday the only adequate outcome to Good Friday?

Must we, given the fact of Good Friday, be open to the possibility that, as in Hinduism, there is Veda and Vedanta, so, in Christianity, there is, or there ought to be, Evangel and Evangelanta?

Pondering the varieties of religious experience, William James concluded that 'there should be no premature closing of our account with reality'.

Have we Christians closed our account prematurely with what crossing the Kedron might mean?

A TENEBRAE TEMPLE

Inland but a little from the upper reaches of the Shannon there is a lake called Lough Key. It has many wooded islands and on one of them there was a castle which was of more than passing interest to Yeats:

> I planned a Mystical Order which should buy or hire the castle, and keep it as a place where its members could retire for a while for contemplation and where we might establish mysteries like those of Eleusis or Samothrace, and for ten years to come my most impassioned thought was a vain attempt to find philosophy and to create, a ritual for that order.

It is interesting to think of Yeats as the new St Benedict, the new St Kieran, the new St Kevin. It is interesting to imagine that a Protestant Irishman whose given name was William might have reversed the dissolution or destruction of the monasteries of Duiske, Muckross and Mellifont.

But instead of regretting what he didn't do we should of course rejoice in what he did do: he founded the Abbey Theatre.

Nights there were when this theatre was an abbey. It was an Eleusis in which the curtain opening was a veil opening, and we were epoptai, seeing sacred showings.

Seeing through our psyches into our souls, we saw the Great Herne. Seeing through our psyches into our souls, we saw a hawk dance at the Hawk's Well. Seeing through our psyches into our souls, we saw the Walk of a Queen. How, having seen these mysteries, can we ever afterwards settle for the greasy till? How, having seen these mysteries, can we ever afterwards settle for the cold eye?

But the visionary is one thing, the mystical something else altogether, and Yeats knows it, no where more explicitly perhaps than in a poem of his called: 'A Dialogue of Self and Soul':

> *My Soul*: I summon to the winding ancient stair;
> Set all your mind upon the steep ascent,
> Upon the broken, crumbling battlement,
> Upon the star that marks the hidden pole;
> Fix every wandering thought upon
> That quarter where all thought is done:
> Who can distinguish darkness from the soul?

What better philosophy than this for a mystical order? Summoning us to:

> Fix every wandering thought upon
> That quarter where all thought is done.

The Kena Upanishad will witness for him:

There goes neither the eye, nor speech, nor the mind, we know it now, nor do we know how to teach one about it. Different it is from all that is known, and beyond the unknown it also is.

The Chandogya Upanishad will witness for him:

Where nothing else is seen, nothing else is heard, nothing else is thought about, there's the Infinite.

Eckhart will witness for him:

So long as something is still the object of our attention, we are not yet one with the one. For where there is nothing but the One, nothing is seen.

St John of the Cross will witness for him:

Therefore, rising above all that may be known and understood, temporally and spiritually, the soul must earnestly desire to reach that which in this life cannot be known, and which the heart cannot conceive, and leaving behind all actual and possible taste and feeling of sense and spirit, must desire earnestly to arrive at that which transcends all sense and all feeling.

But Yeats didn't only need a philosophy for his order, he needed a ritual for it. Strangely, the most mystical ritual that humanity is heir to was already there for him, ready to hand, but because perhaps it was so near to him, he didn't see it. Called Tenebrae, it takes its name from the Latin version of the Passion narratives:

Erat autem fere hora sexta, et tenebrae factae sunt in universam terram usque in horam nonam. Et obscuratus est sol; et velum templi scissum est medium.

In English it reads:

And it was about the sixth hour, and there was a darkness over all the earth until the ninth hour. And the sun was darkened, and the veil of the temple was rent in the midst.

As Christians enact it, Tenebrae is a journey into the darkness and dereliction of Good Friday.

A candle rack, triangular in shape, is set up in the sanctuary. Called the Tenebrae harrow or the Tenebrae hearse, it has sockets for seven candles on each of its ascending sides and, coming to fifteen in all, a socket at its apex.

As we would expect, given its provenance, Tenebrae is performed during Holy Week. In medieval times, it was performed in the dead of night.

In solemn Gregorian mode the great tragic texts of the Bible are antiphonally chanted. Every now and then, at prescribed intervals, a candle is extinguished. In the end only the candle at the apex is still lighting. The climactic moment comes when this is removed, taken round behind the altar and entombed there. And so it is that, in ritual re-enactment, the darkness of Good Friday prevails. In our senses prevails. In our minds prevails. In our souls prevails.

With Yeats, at this stage, we might sing:

> Who can distinguish darkness from the soul?

But that isn't the whole story. Neither for Jesus nor for Yeats is it the whole story.

Let us return to 'A Dialogue of Self and Soul':

> *My Soul.* Such fullness in that quarter overflows
> And falls into the basin of the mind
> That man is stricken deaf and dumb and blind,
> For intellect no longer knows
> *Is* from the *Ought* or *Knower* from the *Known*—
> That is to say, ascends to Heaven;

> Only the dead can be forgiven;
> But when I think of that my tongue's a stone.

Eckhart is more assured:

> Comes then the soul into the unclouded light of God. It is transported so far from creaturehood into nothingness that of its own powers it can never return to its faculties or its former creaturehood. Once there God shelters the soul's nothingness with his uncreated essence, safeguarding its creaturely existence. The soul has dared to become nothing and cannot pass from its own being into nothingness and back again, losing its own identity in the process, except God safeguarded it.
>
> Oh, wonder of wonders, when I think of the union the soul has with God! He makes the enraptured soul to flee out of herself, for she is no more satisfied with anything that can be named. The spring of Divine Love flows out of the soul and draws her out of herself into the unnamed Being, into the first source which is God alone.

Yeats, with the help of others, founded a theatre. Completing his dream, maybe we should build a Tenebrae Temple.

Then once again, the falcon will hear the falconer. Then once again we will have a centre that will hold.

THE WANDERING CHRISTIAN

Silence, silence, and the next night a silence so loud I thought 'twould destroy me.

Since he had come, coming in out of the insect-singing desert, he had done nothing, had said nothing.

Whatever else, I would live canonically.

I said matins.

Between matins and lauds I broke. I spoke: Bushes burn in this desert, I said. They burn and they are consumed.

In a dazed, half-tranced sort of way, I was looking at his feet.

Of goat's hide, he said, my sandals. Of the hide of last year's scapegoat. That's why they are still so raw looking.

I said lauds, aloud. As I did so, he leafed through my Bible, leaving it open. There was silence again.

It was a stubborn silence. It was a silence waged between two people.

I said nones, concluding aloud,

Keep back thy servant also from presumptuous sins, let them not have dominion over me: Then shall I be upright, and I shall be innocent from the Great Transgression.

Are you that? I asked, looking fixedly at him.

Am I what?

Are you the Great Transgression? You look like it.

The hump on my back is a camel's hump, he said. It's a hump of bad cosmologies. Cosmologies like yours that hurt the earth. Living as I do in this desert, it is all I have to draw on. In times of starvation and drought, it is all I have to draw on.

But you have no hump, I said.

No. Not that you can see.

Standing in my cave door, his back to me, he continued, Like the Wandering Jew, I wander. I'm the Wandering Christian. Till the bush that burns is consumed, I must wander.

I watched him go. Already now, it being noon, the mountains he walked between were desert deliriums.

He had left my Bible open at Leviticus, chapter sixteen. I read it through, returning to linger, or malinger, with verses twenty-one and twenty-two:

> And Aaron shall lay both his hands upon the head of the live goat, and confess over him all the iniquities of the Children of Israel, and all their transgressions in all their sins, putting them upon the head of the goat, and shall send him away by the hand of a fit man into the wilderness.
> And the goat shall bear upon him all their iniquities unto a land not inhabited: and he shall let go the goat in the wilderness.

The stars don't seem so hurt these nights. And I think I know why. An image I have of him walking away. He was who he said he was. In lands not inhabited he wanders, bearing upon him and within him all our cosmologies that hurt or inhibit or darken the stars.

ALTJERINGA ROCK

Then came the children of Israel, even the whole congregation, into the desert of Zin in the first month: and the people abode in Kadesh; and Miriam died there, and was buried there. And there was no water for the congregation: and they gathered themselves together against Moses and against Aaron. And the people chode with Moses and spake, saying, Would God that we had died when our brethren died before the Lord! And why have ye brought up the congregation of the Lord into this wilderness, that we and our cattle should die there? And wherefore have ye made us to come up out of Egypt, to bring us in unto this evil place? it is no place of seed, or of figs, or of vines, or of pomegranates: neither is there any water to drink. And Moses and Aaron went from the presence of the assembly unto the door of the tabernacle of the congregation, and they fell upon their faces: and the glory of the Lord appeared unto them. And the Lord spoke unto Moses, saying, Take the rod, and gather thou the assembly together, thou, and Aaron thy brother, and speak ye unto the rock before their eyes: and it shall give forth his water, and thou shalt bring forth to them water out of the rock: so thou shalt give the congregation and their beasts drink. And Moses and Aaron gathered the congregation together before the rock, and he said unto them, Hear now, ye rebels: must we fetch you water out of this rock? And Moses lifted up his hand, and with the rod he smote the rock twice: and the water came out abundantly, and the congregation drank, and their beasts also.

Legend has it that this rock followed and nourished the children of Israel during all their wanderings in the wilderness. A great and terrible wilderness it was. A wilderness wherein were fiery serpents and scorpions and drought.

There were times in this wilderness when the people felt their souls were dried away. Then, sitting disconsolate in the doors of their tents, they would remember the fish which they did eat in Egypt freely. They would remember the cucumbers and the melons and the leeks, and the onions and garlic.

Their souls were dried away. But their God, He of the mighty hand and the outstretched arm, He was with them. His mountain sometimes was all on fire. Sometimes it quaked greatly, so that, in holy dread, the people would remove themselves and stand afar off. Near and afar, stiff-necked though they were, they were learning to submit to their God's intentions for them. Such a God: earth-quakingly awful, yet loving. A God who had 'assayed to go and take him a nation from the midst of another nation, by temptations, by signs, and by wonders, and by war, and by a mighty hand, and by a stretched out arm, and by great terrors'.

Surrounded, assaulted almost, by such spectacularly numinous, momentous events, the people were beginning to lose their capacity and appetite for ordinariness. This was a tragedy. The precedent was set. Here in this wilderness of scorpions and fiery serpents we had, as it were, been given religious permission to seek for spiritual authenticity in signs and in wonders —wonders and signs Gautama, the Buddha, would have sought to wean us from.

A capacity for ordinariness is an Easter-Morning gift.

Meanwhile, the extraordinary! A rock perceived to be extraordinary. The rock that followed and nourished the children of Israel in the wilderness.

Europeans also. We also have come up out of somewhere into a desert of Zin. We most certainly have come up out of the commonage consciousness of Altamira and Lascaux into a great and terrible *res extensa* desert of Cartesian clarities. This place we are in, it is no place of Earth oracles, of God-haunted gorges, of holy wells, of Paps mountains, of Uffington horses, neither, on Hallowe'en night, do we leave our doors on the latch.

The Oracles are dumm,
No voice or hideous humm
Runs through the arched roof in words deceiving.
Apollo from his shrine
Can no more divine,
With hollow shriek the steep of Delphos leaving.
No nightly trance, or breathed spell,
Inspires the pale-ey'd priest from the prophetic cell.

...

Nor is Osiris seen
In Memphian Grove or Green,
Trampling the unshowr'd Grasse with lowings loud;
Nor can he be at rest
Within his sacred chest,
Naught but profoundest Hell can be his shroud,
In vain with Timbrel'd Anthems dark
The sable-stolèd Sorcerers bear his worshipt Ark.

He feels from Juda's Land
The dredded Infant's hand,
The rayes of Bethlehem blind his dusky eyn;
Nor all the gods beside,
Longer dare abide,
Not Typhon huge ending in snaky twine:
Our Babe to shew his Godhead true,
Can in his swadling bands controul the damnèd crew.

So when the Sun in bed,
Curtain'd with cloudy red,
Pillows his chin upon an Orient wave,
The flocking shadows pale,
Troop to th'infernall jail,
Each fetter'd Ghost slips to his severall grave,
And the yellow-skirted Fayes
Fly after the Night-steeds, leaving their Moon-lov'd maze.

In Europe, the human psyche has undergone a Miltonic-Cartesian clean sweep.

Everything except conscious high noon, fixed forever at the zenith, has been banished to th'infernall jail.

Our souls are dried away.

The children of Israel chode with Moses: 'And wherefore,' they complained, 'wherefore have ye made us to come up out of Egypt, to bring us unto this evil place? it is no place of seed, or of figs, or of vines, or of pomegranates, neither is there any water to drink.'

'And Moses lifted up his hand and with the rod he smote the rock twice: and the water came out abundantly, and the congregation drank and their beasts also.'

I imagine that, on our wilderness wanderings also, we are being followed by a rock, the last surviving, fine-grained fragment of a Precambrian sea floor. And now at last, withered within, mummified within, by the terrible blaze of cogito consciousness, we turn, reluctantly, to it, careful that our Gorgon perception of it, that our Cartesian perception of it, won't turn it into yet another *res extensa* rock, into yet another, unechoing Ulro rock.

Hammer and chisel in hand, the young, adolescent girl who most recently dreamed of the rock goes towards it. Putting the chisel to it, she raps it, lightly, once. Released, could it be, from the bondage of our cogito consciousness of it, the rock transforms itself effortlessly into an image and likeness, almost alive, of Anantashaya.

Our Altjeringa rock. Our Dreamtime rock. Rock that dreams the Anantashaya dreams of a new beginning.

THE SWORD IN THE STONE

All time is once-upon-a-time Time. At all stages of their evolution and involution, all worlds are once-upon-a-time worlds. All things are once-upon-a-time things. The bucket I take to the well is a once-upon-a-time bucket. I never know, till I've hauled it, what beckonings might be in it.

Once-upon-a-time Time thinks us. Asleep and awake, it dreams us, it lives us. When once-upon-a-time Time thinks you, dreams you, lives you, you are, being a man, Merlin, you are, being a woman, Morgan Le Fay.

It was Whitsunday in Camelot.

Entering the punctiliously timbered hall of all high heraldries, a squire, himself trumpet-announced, announced a great marvel: in the river below a great stone and in it, to its hilt, a sword.

News such as this some had been expecting. For, in Camelot, on this great day, it was a custom, venerably observed, that the king and his knights would not sit down to meat till an adventure had been achieved.

In procession, religiously resplendent, no one showing a gaudy will to win, they went down to the river.

Setting his hand to it, Arthur sought to draw out the sword.

Gawain did likewise.

And Lancelot, in tournament tremendous, and gorgeous withal, he set his hand to it.

Hand after hand of great renown in lands neighbourly and Outremere were set to that sword that day, but, of knights long notorious for strength and valour, there was none could draw it out.

It was a man newly emerged from nature, a man who, later that morning, would sit, unmischiefed, in Syege Perelous, it was he, Galahad, who drew it out, effortlessly, so that all who saw it marvelled.

He drew our petra-fying perceptions of it, so hurtfully hilt deep in it, out of the rock.

Liberated, the rock blossomed into a linga and yoni, and in his beast-impotent, plant-impotent, rock-impotent world far away, the Maymed Kynge was healed.

Healed, he could see that his sexual wound was an impulse to sexually wound. An impulse he dreaded.

Sometimes he would, wide-awake, imagine that this impulse to wound had reified itself anatomically. It had, he would imagine, become a weapon in his phallus.

So long unconscious, this impulse to sexually wound could only generate a wound. But now, four hundred and fifty and four years after the passion and death of Christ was accomplished, the Maymed Kynge could see, seeing clairvoyantly, that it wasn't only out of the stone that Galahad was drawing the sword. He was drawing it out of his phallus.

When, healed at last, the Maymed Kynge came to Camelot, the jousting stopped. Troubled and disturbed, everyone could see how like King Arthur he was.

Troubled and disturbed, every knight, his sword hanging from his hip, could see how like himself he was.

Something of themselves, something hitherto hidden, hilt-deep, in their psyches, had been drawn out.

Taking precedence, the Maymed Kynge entered the hall, grail-brightened, grail-fragrant, since Whitsunday.

He sat, unmischiefed, in Syege Perelous.

A great day, the day the Grail King came to Camelot.

Keeper of the Grail as heavenly vessel, he is, in Camelot, a keeper of it also as Lapsit Exillas, as ordinary, earthly stone, as stone below in the river which, in one of its blossomings, is Divine Linga and Divine Yoni.

And now that the stone has been released, now that we have been released, we can build a Bhuvaneshvar Temple to this blossoming.

Architecturally, in some of its moods, this temple will say:

> The Earth is a state of mind called Mayashakti.
> The Earth is a state of mind called Merlin.
> The Earth is a state of mind called Morgan Le Fay.

Manifesting a call to adventure hitherto unheard of in Camelot, it will seem architecturally to suggest that pia mater is pia maya.

From Fata Morgana to Moksha is the Great Queste.
Drawing the sword out of the stone.
Drawing our petra-fying perceptions of it out of it.
Drawing our hurtfully reductive perceptions of it out of it. Drawing our Gorgon gaze, so hurtfully hilt-deep in it, out of it.
Drawing out the sword.
Drawing out the sword we see there is no such thing as matter.
When we look at a mountain and see matter it is our own Medusa mindset, not the mountain we are seeing. The mountain is mind in hibernation.
Matter is mind in hibernation.
In every mountain and mote of it, in every black hole of it, the universe is psyverse.
In every mote, mountain, moon and megagalaxy of it, the universe, being a psyverse, is alive.
In every mote, mountain, moon and megagalaxy of it, the universe draws breath.
In every more, mountain, moon and megagalaxy of it, the universe breathes Brahman.

So as they stood spekynge, in corn a squyre that seyde unto the kynge,
 Sir, I brynge unto you mervaylous tydynges.
 What be they? seyde the kynge.
 Sir, there is here bynethe at the ryver a grete stone whych I saw fleete abovyn the watir, and therein I saw stkynge a swerde.

Our Big-Bang cosmology is the sword in the stone. Our Medusa mindset is the sword in the stone.

But we must not be downcast. From deep among mountains that breathe Brahman he comes. In our time, which is once-upon-a-time Time, Galahad will come to Camelot.

THE DOLOROUS STROKE

Time was when the world was as full of surprises in our waking experience of it as it is now, sometimes, in our dream encounters with it. Is there anything at all, Gawain must have often wondered, is there anything at all, be it bird call or bush, that is docile to our commonsense understanding and expectation of it?

Come home to Camelot, knights noble and chivalrous would relate their adventures:

... opening his door the churl invited me in. I learned too late, having crossed it, that the threshold was as rich in world openings as Aaron's rod ...

Like a mind asleep the world sprouted adventures and at Camelot it was a custom, reverently observed, that, on Whitsunday, the knights would not sit down to dinner until a great adventure had been achieved.

On Whitsunday four hundred and fifty and four years after the passion and death of Christ, a squire, too excited to wait deferentially upon occasion, burst into the august yet courteous presence of King Arthur:

Sir, seyde the squyre, I brynge unto you mervaylous tydynges.
What be they? seyde the kynge.
Sir, there is here bynethe at the ryver a grete stone whych I saw fleete abovyn the watir, and therein I saw stykynge a swerde.

An adventure had presented itself. And, adventure being their element, Arthur and his knights proceeded towards it, descending to the river with great, yet courteously contained, delight.

Besought so to do by Arthur, Gawain assayed to draw out the sword, but for all his virtue, moral as well as physical, he might not stir it. Neither, for all his gracious radiance, could Perceval stir it. And this being so, there was no other knight, no matter how valiant, who would dare put his hand to it.

In the end, however, the adventure didn't want for a knight who was adequate to it.

Up out of the restraining maternities of nature, he came, out of them emerged into such clarity of decisive, high, white riding that, seeing him, you would think that worldly causes alone couldn't explain him. Indeed, it might well be that it was from that depth below worldly causes in all things that he came. And so, it was he, Galahad, only he among all other knights, who could sit, unmischiefed and unperturbed, in Syege Perelous, the vacant vajra chair at the round table. And it was he who, descending to the river, drew the sword from the stone and sheathed it in a scabbard that had been hanging, waiting for it, at his side. It was Whitsunday at Camelot and a great adventure had been achieved. But that wasn't all. After evensong at the minster, Arthur and his knights went again to the great hall, this time to supper. Hardly were they seated at table when they heard a cracking and crying of thunder and a light of the highest heaven, pentecostally plenteous, entered the hall, transfiguring them. As though the last trump had sounded, it also dumbfounded them. And then a marvel of marvels, a great and glorious thing, its glory veiled, entered the hall, filling it with heavenly odours and, passing among them, it gave of its bounty to each knight the food and drink that he best liked.

Suddenly, the glorious thing departed and, able now again to speak, Arthur gave thanks to Lorde Jesu Crysts for what he had shown them and given them on this high feast of Pentecost four hundred and fifty and four years after his passion and death.

Rising to his feet, Sir Gawain spoke:

'Now', seyde Sir Gawayne, 'we have been servyed thys day of what metys and drynkes we thought on. But one thyng begyled us, that we might not see the Holy Grayle: hit was so preciously coverde. Wherefore I woll make me here a vow that to-morne withoute longer abydynge, I shall laboure in the queste of the Sankgreall, and that I shall holde me onte a twelve-month and a .day or more if nede be, and never shall I returne unto the course agayne tyle I have sene hit more opynly than hir hath bene shewed here. And if I may nat spede I shall rerurne agayne as he that may nat be ayenst the wylle of God.'

This coming to his feet by Gawain, this vow of his to ride out in quest of The Grail, was valorous example and precedent to many another knight, and on the morrow 'they toke their horsys and rode thruw the strete of Camelot. And there was wepyng of ryche and poore, and the kynge turned away and myght nat spek for wepyng.'

Each of these knights we might follow. Or only those knights most likely to succeed we might journey with. But for our intentions here nothing so copious is required. It is required of us only to know that, along some of its reaches, not all of them night reaches, the road to the Grail Castle will, almost inevitably, be a road that will sometimes engulf us, as it did Galahad, as it did Gawain, into its awful initiations and adventures. For altogether longer than a twelve-month and a day there will be no worldly tidings of us and few indeed will be they who will eventually cross the drawbridge into the strangely silent, waiting castle, the land all around it, to all horizons, being a wasteland.

These being journeys in the Celtic Christian Dreamtime, it is not surprising that, having been welcomed into it, no two knights will have the same experiences in this castle. Often, however, there is an old white-haired man who has been in agony for a long time. Dressed in a long scarlet robe, he lies on a couch before a great fire. He has many names:

King Pelles,
Amfortas,
The Maymed Kynge,
The Rich Fisher King,
Le Riche Roi Méhaigné.

By whatever name we know him and be he ever so white-haired and so old, he is the Grail King, and he entertains the questing knight, hoping that through him he will find healing for his great hurt. And until this, his great hurt, is healed, the land will be a desert desolation, a festering waste in which nothing germinates, sprouts or breeds.

There are what are called hallows in the castle. There is The Grail itself, the blessed holy vessel that entered the hall at Camelot, filling it with heavenly odours. There is a bleeding lance. Sometimes these hallows are carried in silent procession, liturgical in appearance and bearing, through the halls. Another older man, the father maybe of the Fisher King, is glimpsed through an inner, open door. The maiden who, in the procession, carries The Grail gives him a eucharistic host. And it might be that this one host which he receives once a day is his only food.

If, seeing all this, the knight who is being entertained will ask a particular question, then the king and the land will be healed. If, however, he doesn't ask the question he will be shown to his sleeping quarters. And when in the morning he awakes he will find that, in hall after hall, the castle is empty. Groomed and harnessed and ready, his horse will be waiting for him in the stable yard. And when he rides out the drawbridge, going up, will close shut behind him.

And that, more or less, is where one version of the legend leaves us.

A handsome legend it is: handsome and strange. And dreadful maybe, full of dread, the holy dread that Jacob experienced when on his way from Beersheba to Harran, he lay down one night on hard nomadic ground and having stones of that place for his pillows, he slept and he dreamed:

And Jacob awaked out of his sleep, and he said. Surely the Lord is in this place; and I knew it not. And he was afraid, and said. How dreadful is this place! this is none Other but the house of God, and this is the gate of heaven.

But how self-exiled we nowadays are from all great gates, great openings into other worlds, great openings into this world. Nierikas, the Hoichol Indians call them. How exiled we are from that stupendous Whitsunday at Camelot when the sword was drawn from the stone; when, able now to sir unharmed in it, a knight newly dubbed sat in Syege Perelous; when, thunder cracking and crying, a transfiguring, heavenly light entered the hall; when, covered in white samite, The Grail passed through the hall; when, coming to his feet, Sir Gawain, like Mary, accepted the gracious and the terrible consequences of the heavenly hail.

Looking at the varieties of religious experience, William James concluded that 'there should be no premature closing of our account with reality'.

Maybe there is a heavenly hail.

Maybe there is a Grail Castle.

Maybe there are higher worlds.

Tibetan Buddhists believe that there are vajrasattvic worlds and maybe they sent tidings of themselves, rays of themselves, essences of themselves, to King Arthur and his court at Camelot on Whitsunday.

Vajrasattvic Sunday, we might call it. Sunday when there was heard a cracking and a crying of vajrasattvic thunder.

Between our realm and the grail realm, between our world and the vajrasattvic world, a nierika had opened. And, on the morrow, mounted and armed, a hundred and fifty knights rode out of Camelot. And well indeed might Arthur weep. Seeing them go, seeking higher things, he knew that the world of the round table, his world, was now at an end.

But while Arthur sleeps, there is, I sometimes think, something that we should be doing. We should be seeking to appropriate imaginatively the stupendous fact that the sword of our Gorgonizing perceptions of it has been drawn out of the stone. And that means that the hard, *res extensa* wasteland we have been living in, that the Ulro we have been living in, is now Uluru. Now again therefore we can emerge from our soak or slough of despond and go walkabout, as Kunapipi did, as Injuwanidjuwa did, their pillows being Uluru not Ulro stones.

And there is something else we can do. Now that a nierika has opened into that world, we can re-enter Lascaux and, going down into the crypt, we can put our hand to the bleeding lance and draw it out, out of sexuality in the Bull, out of sexuality in the Birdman, out of sexuality in the Fisher King, out of sexuality in Galahad, Gawain, Perceval and Lancelot, out of sexuality in us all, out of sexuality in our God.

Older than Logres,
Older than Christianity,
Older than Europa's Europe,
Older than Stonehenge
Older than metallurgy,
Older than domesticated plants and domesticated animals.
Old as the woolly rhinoceros,
Old as the crypt in Lascaux,
Old as *Homo habilis*, older, older.

> What a dolorous stroke it was,
> Maymed Bull,
> Maymed Kynge,
> Maymed Male.

Maymed by the spear in his phallus. Maymed by an impulse to wound in his sexuality, for, as Leroi-Gourhan suggests, there is a psychological assimilation of phallus to spear, of vulva to wound.

The crypt in Lascaux is the oubliette in the dungeons or underworld of the Grail Castle. And down into it, the grail hero going before him, the Maymed Kynge must go.

A dream rite, a healing rite, will enact itself there, the bleeding spear or lance will be drawn out, and in the end, standing between the Bull and the Birdman, standing between the healed Bull and the healed Birdman, the human male, in the person of the Rich Fisher King, will walk free, and the Wasteland will flourish.

The Grail Quest accomplished, our quest for this world, the world we were born into, will begin.

> Come White Bison Calf Woman, come.

STONE BOAT

I

On Aran there is a famous stone. Sitting shoreward on this limestone island, it is obviously metamorphic, obviously erratic, brought here from the south Connemara coast during the Ice Age. Reasonable it might be to search for a certain kind of lichen on it, or for a tuft of sea pinks in a crevice of it, but it would be not a little odd, given its igneous metamorphic origins and history, to search for fossil crinoids or carboniferous sea-shells in it. And yet, there is, it is claimed, something odd, even something miraculous, about this rock. In Ireland's Dreamtime or should we say, in Ireland when it was Christian Dreamtime in it, this stone, transforming itself, would be a boat for the wonder-working, big, strong saints, strong in muscle and mind, who came and went between the islands, who came and went, miracles happening everywhere about them, between the islands and the mainland.

So why not seek for crinoids, alive and gently waving, in this rock? Why limit it, looking at it with Gorgon eyes, to the hard geological face of it. The universe, Haldane said, is queer. It is queerer, he said, than we can imagine. But isn't it we who are queer? Queer above all in that, after a few years in it, we begin to take the world for granted?

Certain it is that empirical, economic everydayness is an enchantment. Co-operating unconsciously with it, hypnotically with it, we maintain it with multifarious, immense energy.

Lir was a king in Dreamtime Ireland. A Dreamtime King in Dreamtime Ireland. He had three daughters by his first wife. Envious, his second wife cast a spell on them, turning them into swans. She doomed them to spend three hundred years on Lake Derravaragh, three hundred years in the wild sea of Moyle between Ireland and Scotland, and three hundred years in the Western Ocean. Only when they heard the first Christian bell coming to them across the waves out of Ireland could they at last swim ashore, drop their swanforms, and be human persons again.

Isn't it time, after centuries of uncharted exile, we ourselves came home.

Isn't it time, coming in our Dreamtime stone boats, that we came home to Dreamtime Ireland.

Isn't it time, dropping our purely biological understanding of ourselves there on the shore, that we walked inland, following a salmon-broken, rock-broken river into Fódhla.

>Fódhla is Dreamtime,
>Fódhla is Stone Boat Time.

And all the rivers of Fódhla have their source in an Otherworld well. The Well of Connla it is called, and every now and then the hazel that grows over it drops a kernel of wisdom into it.

Under Ireland's fields is Fódhla. Before Ireland's fences is the Great World.

Ireland and the Great World are distant from each other by only a single footstep. But in that footstep are perilous journeys. In it are initiations. In it are caves and transformations. In it is the road whose two sides come together. In it is being challenged, in a suddenly changed place, by Cúroi Mac Dara. In it are eachtras. In it are immrams.

We sometimes think we will never reach home. And in one sense of course we don't, for the person who set out isn't the person who,

> Lifetimes later,
> Fish lifetimes later,
> Bird lifetimes later,

the person who set out isn't the person who, precariously human, comes shoreward home in his stone boat.

II

Like a dew, the fields and fences of Ireland had lifted, dispersing.

In my eyes also, and in my mind, a mist had dispersed, and there it was, before me, Fódhla, the Great World.

Before me, but not yet open to me.

During this last immram I came to know, I survived only because I came to know, that it is only when we consent to be dreamed by something that we can cross into the Dreamtime.

Dreamed by a rock or an ant or a star or a sea.

Sometimes it is only when we consent to be dreamed by the Nothing that was before anything was that we can cross into it.

Crossing into it, my voyage became an immram.

Sitting on a rock, my back to the sea, I waited, consenting to be whatever the rock dreamed me to be.

Setting out I knew that any deep river I came to I would, going down into it, became an otter. Any wood I came to I knew that, going through it, I would be a fox. On the sides of wild mountains I would be a deer. On icy, precipitous summits I would be sure-footed. Up there I'd have a goat's head for heights.

How blue, in the valley below, was the smoke from Fintan Mac Bóchra's chimney.

His threshold was of bog oak.

I sat by his fire.

In a chair of bog oak.

By a fire of bog oak.

Five fires had died before he looked at me.

You've come in, but you aren't inside, he said.

Five fires later he came in, having, yet again, carried out the ashes.

He sat down.

I stood awhile by the river, he said. A salmon leaped. Out through my mirrored heart he leaped, falling back, splashing back through my mirrored head.

That explains it, he said.

That's why I am salmon bright, salmon strong, he said. As the fire faded, his salmon brightness faded.

He looked at me.

You've come in but you aren't inside, he said. It is only through a story that you can come in.

I told a story:

Once upon a time there was a man who lived alone. Every day, even on bad winter days, he went into the forest, hunting. Coming home one evening he saw some clothes of his hanging out to dry. Going inside, he was surprised to see how clean and tidy his house was. There was a freshly made fire, and a hot meal on the table. Again the next evening there was a fire and a meal, steam rising from it. And his clothes, washed and dried, were beautifully mended. He left, as usual, for the forest early next morning. But he didn't go all the way. Curious to know who it was, he turned back, hiding himself in some bushes not far from his house. After a while he saw a fox trotting towards his door. The fox went in. And not long after the hunter went in. There was a woman, making the fire. There was a fox skin hanging on the back of the door.

I'm your wife now, the woman said.

They lived together happily.

One night the man complained of a bad smell in the house.

A fox smell, he said. I can't stand it, he said.

The woman got up and went to the door. Taking down the fox skin. she put it on. A fox again, she trotted away into the wilderness.

> Gradually, as I told the story, his salmon brightness came back.
>
> And I knew I was inside, because now, for the first time, I could go out. I stood by the river. A salmon leaped. Out through my mirrored heart he leaped, falling back, splashing through my mirrored head.
>
> You are salmon strong, Mac Bóchra said.
>
> Till he spoke I wasn't aware he was standing beside me.
>
> You are salmon strong, salmon bright, he said, now you can go there.
>
> Where?
>
> Now you can go to Connla's Well.
>
> But Connla's Well is in the Otherworld.
>
> This World and the Otherworld are the same Great World. It is in the Great World, a hazel growing over it, that Connla's Well is.
>
> I didn't know I wanted to go to Connla's Well, I said.
>
> Whoever comes this far must want to go that far. Having come this far you must, to avoid calamity, go that far. The salmon has leaped. So now you must go. It is in the Otherworld. A hazel grows over it. And all the rivers of the Great World have their source in it. Rivers of the Great Life outside us. Rivers of the Great Life inside us.
>
> Was it in a river inside or in a river outside that the salmon leaped? he asked.
>
> He didn't expect, or wait for, an answer. He crossed its bog-oak threshold into his house.
>
> And I will be here, he says.
>
> I will be here, sitting under bog-oak rafters, by a bog-oak fire, when, his journey having become an eachtra, or, his voyage having become an immram, someone else will come this way.
>
> And, awake but yet being dreamed, and reaching the icy, precipitous summit, the person who comes, looking down, will say:
>
> How blue, in the valley below, is the smoke from Fintan Mac Bóchra's chimney.

III

I was standing on an outcrop. Before me was a wide water, flat and black. Coming towards me, across it, it came, a spear as long and as black as a winter's night. It went through me. It opened a wound as big as a door in me and I walked through it, into the same, everyday world, but how different it all was, how strange it was. And now, on the shore below of the wide water, there was a boatman and a boat.

Yes, he would row me over.

In the dark my salmon brightness died.

There was no shadow or image of oars in the water.

There was no image or shadow of us in the water.

There was only the creaking of the oars in their thole holds.

The creaking of the oars in their thole holds was impermeable to mind.

They weren't hospitable, even externally, to mind.

There was no door in them through which mind might enter and find night lodgings.

They wouldn't be roost to mind.

They wouldn't collude with mind, not even to the extent of pretending that reality is possible.

They wouldn't be an object to mind.

On that wide water, flat and black, mind was on its own, having only its own hallucinations to lay its head on.

Were he a cliff, the boatman would echo my words.

He didn't echo my words.

He was impermeable to my words.

No word of his or mine came back to me bringing evidence of a world.

Imagining died.

Hallucinating died.

There wasn't in the end anything within mind with which mind could go mad.

Mind died.

Like birth-cries now, hospitable to hearing, the oar creaking receded across the wide water.

How unworldly the world was.

A spear as long as the world had killed worldliness in me.

Like birth cries the stars are.

How real rocks are.

In this unworldly world how wet river water is.

River water is.

On the sides of wild mountains I am a deer.

On precipitous icy heights I am a goat.

And how blue, in the valley below, is the smoke from Fintan Mac Bóchra's chimney.

He was waiting for me mirrored in the river.

I don't remember that wood, I said.

No, he said, that is a wood in the Great World, you hadn't eyes for it then.

Invite me into it, he said.

In it, I saw it was my wood.

Beyond it were my fields and my house.

I invited him in.

The wooden water bucket was empty. It was standing where I'd left it a few days ago.

I'll go to the well, I said.

Looking down into it, I saw the mirrored hazel. My own well was Connla's well.

Watching him re-enter the wood that evening I realized it: Paddy Fitz my neighbour, the man I cut turf with and save hay with, Paddy Fitz my neighbour is Fintan Mac Bóchra. He lives beside me, yet he lives in Fódhla, he lives in the Dreamtime.

Coming up out of a valley in the hills one evening I saw smoke from my chimney and clothes hanging out.

I was glad.

Able for nature in me now, I had been praying that she would come back.

IV

A metamorphic erratic on the shore of a limestone island, a geologist would say.

During the Christian phase of Ireland's Dreamtime, it was, local legend would say, a stone boat.

Then as now a boulder, it would in the Dreamtime open out and be a boat, sea-worthy in all weathers, on all seas, supernatural and natural.

Mullán Cholm Cille.

A reminder that Ireland also had its Dreamtime.

A reminder that under Iceland's fields is Fódhla.

A reminder that an ordinary journey can become an eachtra.

A reminder that an ordinary voyage can become an immram.

A metamorphic erratic, a dreaming lobe of Dreamtime Ireland,

Mullán Cholm Cille.

Reminding us that Ireland is transitory, Fódhla is forever.

V

Across the waters from Aran comes a boat-song, a Dreamtime boat-song:

> The sword has been drawn from the stone.
> Our Medusa Mullán is Mullán Colm Cille.

Hearing it, René says: The erratic is norm.

Hearing it, Sir Isaac says: The stone the builders of Europe rejected is paradigm.

Hearing it, Matthew says: Ulro is Uluru. Hearing it, Michelangelo's Captives walk free.

THE THIRD BATTLE OF MAGH TUIRED

Tócauhar a malae dia deirc Baloir.
Cath Magh Tuired

Hovering in my doorway, darkening it, a scald crow called, once. Her call was a screech, piercing and bald. There was something human in it.

A red man walked through my dreams that night.

It's the Third Battle of Magh Tuired, he said.

Fighting itself in you, he said.

Even his words were red.

I woke. But the dream didn't fade. There was aggression in the room, an aggressive smell of boar badger in it. And that confirmed an impression I had of him. He looked as though it was only occasionally he was human.

Again the next day, in the hills, I saw the scald crow. Eating an afterbirth, a sheep's, she was. And that reminded me of a dream I had: a hag knee deep in a river washing my modern mind: downstream, in pool after pool, the fish died.

It didn't surprise me that I dreamed such a dream. I was often at odds with my modern head. Its modern way of seeing things hurt things.

In the end I had no choice. I gave in to the grain of strange growing in me. I came home to my valley.

Somedays the blue of the mountains was flush with the mountains. Somedays it was here in my house, it was in my well. Tempted one day, I took off my clothes and I let it clothe me.

I went out into the bogs. It's my ghost shirt I thought, walking in heather. The blue of the mountains is my ghost shirt, and I starred dancing, ghost-dancing its mentality out of my mind,

> Ghost-dancing Genesis chapter one verses twenty-six and twenty-eight out of it,
> Ghost-dancing Aristotle's principle of non-contradiction out of it.
> Ghost-dancing its bubonic perfections out of it.
> Ghost-dancing its Medusa mindset out of it.

Wondering would I die as the fish had died I drank, coming home, from the river.

It didn't kill me.

It was later that day though that the scald crow screeched in my doorway. How piercing it was. How bald. It frightened me back into the discarded sanities of shirt and trousers and socks and boots. The socks size ten. The boots size ten. The laces long enough for a bow knot.

It didn't work. The red man walked through my dreams that night, and in the hills the next day there was no lamb. The sheep had given birth to an afterbirth only.

To ease her udder I milked her morning and evening. Looking into her eyes as she turned to go the last time I milked her, it occurred to me that dominated nature was in trouble.

Meaning also my mind, I said to myself.

> Meaning also my mind ...
> Meaning also my mind ...

Meaning also my mind ... it was like a mantra. Meaning also my mind. I let my farm go back to the wild.

As I imagined it, spores came on every wind. Passing undigested through the gizzards and intestines of blackbirds and thrushes the seeds of hawthorn, bilberry, briar and mountain ash came. Never again, seeking to curb it, would I set fire to furze.

I didn't dream the dream. The dream dreamed me:

My pillow either side of my head was savagely sliced. As a ham might be sliced, as bread might be sliced, sliced inwards from both ends towards my head. The precision and speed of the slicing, the slices falling sideways away, that was frightful. It was frightful to think that it wasn't the pillow, it was my head was meant. And I saw no one, no weapon, no hand. I saw only the slicing. Of two things all day I was sure. I had ghost-danced myself into trouble. Depths of my psyche inaccessible to me, hostile to my conscious ambitions for me, had taken over.

By nightfall there was something else I knew. The totemic protection I had recently sought and found wasn't helping me. It wasn't helping me now to be dressed in the colours of the scald crow, grey and black.

Even if the trilobite was my totem, it wouldn't have helped. The trilobite's jurisdictive writ didn't run deep enough.

I envied Orpheus. He with his music could assuage what was savage or beastly in him.

I was learning the hard way. I was a paleface. The ghost-dance would harm, maybe havoc, me. And like it or not, the paschal lamb, a lamb slain or sliced from before the foundation of the world, that lamb was my totem.

And the supper of the lamb ...

But there was no lamb in the hills that day. The sheep gave birth to an afterbirth only. And in her form as scald crow, Badhbh, the war hag, ate it.

Badhbh had come back. She had darkened my doorway.

I recalled her encounter with Cuchulainn:

Cuchulainn beheld at this time a young woman of noble figure coming toward him, wrapped in garments of many colours.

Who are you? he said.

I am King Buan's daughter, she said, and I have brought you my treasure and my cattle. I love you because of the great tales I have heard.

You come at a bad time. We no longer flourish here, but famish. I can't attend to a woman during a struggle like this.

But I might be a help.

It wasn't for a woman's backside I took on this ordeal.

Then I'll hinder, she said. When you are busiest in the fight I'll come against you. I'll get under your feet in the shape of an eel and trip you in the ford.

That is easier to believe. You are no king's daughter.

But I'll catch and crack your eel's ribs with my toes and you'll carry that mark forever unless I lift it from you with a blessing.

I'll come in the shape of a grey she-wolf, to stampede the beast into the ford against you.

Then I'll hurl a sling-stone at you and burst the eye in your head, and you'll carry that mark forever unless I lift it from you with a blessing.

I'll come before you in the form of a hornless red heifer and lead the cattle herd to trample you in the waters, by ford and pool, and you won't know me.

Then I'll hurl a stone at you, he said, and shatter your leg, and you'll carry that mark forever unless I lift it from you with a blessing.

Then she left him.

Red-mouthed Badhbh had screeched in my doorway. I was in trouble. Cut down to a stump of a head on a stump of a pillow, I was having bad dreams. The deepest lobes, the most clenched lobes, were opening.

On Michaelmas Eve, having quenched my lamp, I took out my baptismal candle and I lit it.

I had always felt there were depths in me my baptism hadn't reached. And even if it did reach them it wouldn't or couldn't aggrandize them into its blessedness. It couldn't or wouldn't beatify them.

It was a calm night, there were no draughts, so it wouldn't gutter.

There was, I imagined, an hour's light left in it.

Lighted at my baptism from the paschal candle, it was therefore a wounded light.

The paschal candle has five wounds in it, four of them spike wounds, one a spear wound. And they are real wounds. They bleed. It's a red religion I've been baptized into.

What can I make of it? Wounded light?

The candle burns. Burns and gutters.

Wounded wax. Wounded wick. Wounded light.

Totemically one with the wounded wax, wounded wick, wounded light. Totemically one with the slain lamb, the lamb sliced wafer-thin from the foundations of the world. What can I make of it?

A Paleface, I'm not able maybe for the religion of the Plains Indians.

A Paleface, a Celt of the Celtic Dreamtime, I'm not able maybe for my own religion.

I'm not able maybe for the dreams that dream me. And as she said she would, here she comes, the hornless red heifer leading her red-horned herd.

The Battle goes on in my guttering house.

It's the ghost-dance of the wounded candle.

It's the ghost-dance of a candle going out.

It's the ghost-dance I so suddenly am in the depths of my mind.

> I am able to ghost-dance.
> I am able to ghost-dance.
> I am able to ghost-dance.

I am ghost-dancing its modern mentality out of my mind.

I am ghost-dancing the forms of my European sensibility and the categories of my European understanding out of my mind.

The forms of my European sensibility and the categories of my European understanding are a Balor's eye in me, and I am dancing it, I am ghost-dancing it, out of sight and out of mind in me.

ATA DIEN CECHT DO LIAIGH LENN
(We have Dien Cecht as our physician.)

Searching for the site of the Second Battle of Magh Tuired I was, when I heard it, all the peoples of Ireland, all who had come here and had settled here, all of them chanting

>Ata Dien Cecht do liaigh lenn
>Ata Dien Cecht do liaigh lenn
>Ata Dien Cecht do liaigh lenn.

A hare, sitting unscared by my coming, sang it.

And then, having a hare's eyes myself, I saw Dien Cecht. In him, from his depths out, was the glamour of wild things.

A crisis of seagulls screeched above me. I woke up. Lying there, I had a sense of awful miscarriage. Never did I so regret waking prematurely from a dream.

At work, footing turf the next day, the chant I heard chanted itself like a mantra in me.

>Ata Dien Cecht do liaigh lenn,
>Ata Dien Cecht do liaigh lenn,
>Ata Dien Cecht do liaigh lenn.

>do liaigh lenn,
>do liaigh lenn,
>do liaigh lenn,
>Ata Dien Cecht do liaigh lenn.

As it chanted itself in me, it was healing me of a sickness I didn't know I suffered from. It was healing me of narrowness of vision.

His mantra was eyes to me. Eyes with which I saw him crossing the bog coming towards me.

I heal people now with metaphors, he said. I heal them with Upanishads and sutras. I heal them in their mythological, historical past.

At Magh Tuired last night, in the midst of the remembered battle, I spoke a great Gita.

Magh Tuired last night was our Kuruksetra.

In Magh Tuired last night the two extremities of the Indo-European expansion came together on religiously equal terms.

Tell them that, he said. For now tell them only that.

He turned and walked away, our physician, our sage, our dhyani Dien Cecht, going back to his forest.

It occurred to me, walking home that evening, that the crisis of seagulls screeching above me was a blessing. I wasn't ready for the full revelation. I wasn't ready to be an Irish Arjuna listening to an Irish Krishna.

But, gone down into my foundations, the mantra I had heard in my dream, it was chanting itself in me:

>Ata Dien Cecht do liaigh lenn
>Ata Dien Cecht do liaigh lenn
>Ata Dien Cecht do liaigh lenn
>
>liaigh lenn
>liaigh lenn
>liaigh lenn
>Ata Dien Cecht do liaigh lenn.

INIS FÁIL

> 'Until the Battle of the Boyne Ireland belonged to Asia.'
> W.B. Yeats

Whether, when the evidence is canvassed, this statement stands or falls isn't perhaps the issue.

The issue is this: it is now three hundred years since the Battle of the Boyne and, like it or not, it is beginning to be obvious that the ancient Mediterranean logbook of Hebrew prophecy, Greek philosophy and science, Roman engineering and law—this log-book, this mariners' manual, isn't guiding us, isn't helping us, as it used to, so what do we do, where do we turn to?

Are there other, altogether different logbooks to hand? Asiatic logbooks? Logbooks that tell of other voyages to other shores?

It is time maybe that we boarded a ship whose sails are Sutras.

It is time maybe that we boarded a ship whose sails are Upanishadic Mahavakyas.

Belonging to Asia? The very thought of it induces a kind of vertigo.

But let us imagine it.

Let us imagine an Ireland that is culturally hospitable to the commonage consciousness of the shamanic north, to the disillusioning insights of the Upanishadic south, to the wei wu wei of the Taoist in-between.

But it wasn't for this, no, it wasn't for an Asiatic Ireland that

> *the wild geese spread*
> *The grey wing upon every tide.*

It wasn't for an Asiatic Ireland that

> *Edward Fitzgerald died.*

There are books that people read, books a generation of readers are influenced by, but, as Pascal reminds us, there is sometimes a book that shapes a people. We think of the Bible. We think of the Koran. And it isn't at all impossible that people living in Ireland will one day allow themselves to be shaped by the Tao Te Ching, will allow themselves to be shaped by the Upanishads, the Mandukya Aum being an Irish morning mantra.

And who knows! Maybe Yeats is himself a wild goose now. Maybe Yeats is a white wild gander now, a paramahamsa winging his way out of eternity into time.

> A wild swan of Coole
> A white wild gander on the Boyne.

Surrendering to a fancy, I see him putting off his perfection. Like a ghost in a Noh play, he revisits the battlefield. He is standing between two kings, William and James.

He is planting two Hindu parables into the bitter, blood-soaked soil. As he plants them, the kings, ghostly themselves, sing them antiphonally:

In the holy long-ago before our age, there lived a man whose name was Narada. Surrendering to immortal longings that awakened in him, he retired to a hermitage. So altruistically serious was he in his quest, so beyond all bounds were his patience and humility, that one day Vishnu, the great God, was moved to come down from his heaven and stand in his doorway.

So great and continuing is my admiration for you, the God said, that it will please me to grant you any boon you might desire.

The boon I would most graciously ask of you, Narada answered, is that with your help I would come to know the secret of your maya.

Seeking to dissuade him Vishnu smiled, enigmatically.

Narada didn't change his mind.

So be it, said Vishnu, the enigmatic smile not fading.

Let's walk, he said.

By mid-morning they had left the forest.

By noon they were walking in a terrible, red desert. Vishnu languished.

Saying he could go no further, he sat on a rock.

East of them, shimmering far away, almost out of sight, on the horizon there seemed to be a green world.

Sufficient strength remains to me, Narada said. I will bring you water.

I will await you here, Vishnu said.

I'll be back before nightfall, Narada said. He set out.

There were times when he feared for his physical integrity, and for his inner integrity, in that red rage. But he did, in the end, emerge from it and how happy he was feeling the cool green shade of the village he was walking into.

He knocked on the first door.

So enchanted was he by the young woman who opened it that he altogether forgot why he had come. He forgot his hermitage, his meditations, his quest. He walked into the house and sat down as though he had just come back from the fields. And the family too, they sat with him, ate with him, and talked to him as though he had just come back from the fields. And he did go into the fields the next day. And he ploughed and he sowed and when harvest time came he reaped and when the reaping was done, the year's work done, he asked the old man for the hand of the enchanting young woman, his daughter, in marriage.

It was a colourful wedding. Women in red and yellow saris, mirrored in it, brightened the river, brightened the boisterous, firelit night.

A child, a girl, was born to them, and as she grew older, yes, everyone said so, she looked like Narada.

In time his wife and his daughter and his two young sons would go into the rice-fields with Narada.

The old man died. Narada became head of the household.

They prospered. Not once did a serious disease or illness come to their door.

One year the monsoons came early. They came violently. More torrentially than any-one remembered. Rivers overflowed their banks. There were mud slides in the hills. It was clear that the village would soon be engulfed, not just by water falling but also by water erupting. Seeking the safety of higher ground, Narada and his wife and children went out into the night. On earthworks they were walking in the lee of opened river-banks. An onslaught of water, slow at first, fell on them, carrying them away. Narada came to consciousness in a red desert. He heard footfalls behind him, and then a voice: did you bring the water? You've been gone for almost an hour.

> Like a ghost in a Noh play, revisiting remembered ground, Yeats planted that story. And this story also he planted, the kings, his ghostly chorus, singing antiphonally:

A man was walking home late one evening. He had been working in his rice paddies all day. He was weary, as much from the heat as from the work. He was thinking only of the cool of his small thatched house and of the meal that his wife would have prepared for him. Suddenly, out of the corner of his eye, he caught sight of a deadly threatening coil on the side of the road. In spasms of terror he leaped backward, leaped backwards again, and again. Imagining himself to be at a safe distance, he opened his eyes and looked towards the venomous thing. To his great relief it wasn't a snake at all. It was a coil of rope which his son, who had gone on ahead of him in an oxcart, had lost.

> Narada I am, disillusioned I am. King William says.
> Narada I am, disillusioned I am, King James says.

> The snake we project into the rope. King William says.

The changing world we project into the unchanging, eternal Brahman, King James says.

Ya evam veda, Yeats says. Ya evam veda.

>
> Cessair came,
> Partholon came,
> Nemed came,
> Firbolgs came,
> Tuatha De Danann came,
> Fomorians came,
> Celts came,
> Christians came,
> Vikings came,
> Normans came,
> English came.

And let us imagine it:
An Ireland to which the story of Narada has come.
An Ireland to which the rope-snake parable has come.
Ireland conquered epistemologically by a story.
Ireland conquered epistemologically by the rope-snake parable.
Narada coming, like Conaire, naked to Tara.
When Narada touches it, the Lia Fáil will screech.

> Lia Fáil

> Linga Fáil.

The rope-snake coiling itself about Linga Fáil. The rope-snake expanding its seven hooded heads in a fierce half-canopy about Linga Fáil. Let us imagine it:

> Linga Fáil.

And, everywhere regenerated, Ireland rediscovering a long lost sense of itself as

> Inis Fáil.

> Ireland is and has been a foreign country,
> It is a country we are exiles in,
> It is a country we are all dispersed wild geese in.
> The Battle of Kinsale was lost by both sides.
> The Battle of the Boyne was lost by both sides.
> We are all O'Neills and O'Donnells,
> We are all Owen Roes exiled overseas in Ireland.

Imagine it, imagine King James, King William and Yeats on the Boyne battlefield: they are all Owen Roes exiled overseas in the Ireland or Britain they fought for.

King William was a wild goose too.

Going into exile in England he spread a grey wing on the Irish sea.

At home here in Ireland Yeats was an exiled Owen Roe.

Yeats, like Owen Roe, is buried in a foreign country.

But we'll disinter you William and we'll bring you home, over the exiling seas we will bring you, and reciting the Upanishads you helped to translate, we will bury you in Inis Fáil.

> Inis Fáil in India,
> Inis Fáil in England,
> Inis Fáil in Ireland.

We will bury you William in Chandogya Inis, since

> At stroke of midnight soul cannot endure
> A bodily or mental furniture.

We will bury you in the Mandukya Upanishad.

> Speed, bonny boat, like a bird on the wing,
> The Mandukya boat that brings us home,
> All Owen Roes come home in that boat.
> The boat whose sails are slokas,
> The boat whose boat songs are Mahavakyas.

Bringing William Butler Yeats from Ireland, bringing him home, a lone piper playing, to Inis Fáil.

Have you brought the water, William? Hawk's Well-water? The kings would drink it.

HAWK OVER MY HEAD, HORSE AT MY DOOR

That's what I dreamed. I dreamed of a hawk over my head, of a horse at my door. In the dream I saw that Fintan Mac Bóchra was my neighbour.

Cosmologies of cause and effect fell from my eyes, seeking and finding fell from my life, and then I found it, the path to his door, three hawk feathers, two of them thigh feathers, falling onto it.

That was my mind, I said to myself.

That was my mind moulting its modern mode of perception and thought.

Knowing he would know I was coming I didn't knock, I just lifted the latch and went in.

The moment I saw him I woke from my dream. But he didn't vanish. His house didn't vanish. I crossed the floor to a chair by the fire which didn't, when I sat in it, vanish.

He saw my distress.

You have walked between the hawk feathers falling, haven't you? Her thigh feathers, falling either side of you, that was your doorway into this depth of yourself, into this depth of the world. At this depth, dreaming and waking share the same sense of things.

> Hawk feathers falling.
> Thigh feathers and a breast feather.

Did you bring the breast feather?

I didn't, no.

I did, he said, showing it to me.

So you were the man I met on the path. You were the tramp whose conscience was mouldering.

No answer came from a downdraught of smoke that covered him.

I waited for him to emerge.

What ails you, I asked, what troubles you?

Irish sleep says of me that I am an antediluvian. It says of me that in antediluvian times I came to Ireland from the East. But that isn't saying very much, is it? And it isn't saying anything at all unless you hear it saying, Mythology is the country I came from, and, from the Paps of Danu in the south to the blind salmon of Assaroe in the north, Mythology is the country we came to.

Like toadstools that need a wood, we need mythology. But we also need clearings in it. Clearings such as a Buddha, preaching his first and his last sermons, might effect.

The Paps of Danu and, in a bend of the Boyne, the Paps of the Morrigan.

Mythology was the country I came to.

Mythology the country Cuchulainn was conceived in, born in, fought in.

You remember Cuchulainn's encounter with Morrigan, don't you?

All the warriors of Ulster were suffering the labour pains of Macha, the Horse Goddess, at the time. Only Cuchulainn wasn't, and he was defending the province, fighting an invading army at a ford.

Cuchulainn beheld at this time a young woman of noble figure coming toward him, wrapped in garments of many colours.

Who are you? he said.

I am King Buan's daughter, she said, and I have brought you my treasure and my cattle. I love you because of the great tales I have heard.

You come at a bad time. We no longer flourish here, but famish. I can't attend to a woman during a struggle like this.

But I might be a help.

It wasn't for a woman's backside that I took on this ordeal.

Then I'll hinder, she said. When you are busiest in the fight I'll come against you. I'll get under your feet in the shape of an eel and trip you in the ford.

That is easier to believe. You are no king's daughter.

But I'll catch and crack your eel's ribs with my toes and you'll carry that mark forever unless I lift it from you with a blessing.

I'll come in the shape of a grey she-wolf, to stampede the beast into the ford against you.

Then I'll hurl a slingstone at you and burst the eye in your head, and you'll carry that mark forever unless I lift it from you with a blessing.

I'll come before you in the shape of a hornless red heifer and lead the cattle herd to trample you in the waters, by ford and pool, and you won't know me.

Then I'll hurl a stone at you, he said, and shatter your leg, and you'll carry that mark forever unless I lift it from you with a blessing.

Then she left him.

Such things happen in our world. In the world I came from. In the world I came to.

In the world we are in, it can happen that one day going out a man will encounter the horse with a red ear. And he won't come home to his house that night. The trout his wife has cooked for him will go cold, but, in times to come, told after Samhain at a thousand firesides, some great adventure will be known by his name.

Such is our world. Dreaming and waking are one state of mind. And that state of mind isn't in the mind only. It is in the wells, it is in the rocks. That state of mind is the substance of all things, of mountains and case antlers, of the whitethorn bush growing alone.

And why so long after sunset was the lake so flagrant?

And my mind flagrant? And my thoughts?

I knew, looking into my mind, looking into the lake, that Cuchulainn had died.

A hornless red heifer.

Can you see her?

Hornless and red, herding a thunder of hooves against Cuchulainn, hound in many a fight, she-wolf and hound, the hound on his back showing his neck to the wolf at the end of his fighting.

And yes. Sometimes yes. In dangerous places inside our own minds our only foothold is an eel. The eel angry.

> The Paps of Danu,
> The Paps of the Morrigan.

Have you drunk from them?
Have you drunk from their shadows on May morning?

> The hornless red heifer
> And the Horse Goddess, neighing.

Have you heard her neighing? Have you suffered her labour pains? I have. And I still do. Every year, on May eve, I lie in, suffering the labour pains of the Mare.

And so, if you hear a neighing where there is no horse, you will know what that means.

Will I tell you a story about the Horse Goddess? It has no beginning. And it has no end. But you won't mind that. Cosmologies of cause and effect have fallen from your eyes. You wouldn't have come this far if they hadn't.

In her form as woman, when her name was Rhiannon, the Horse Goddess suffered great humiliation.

As a horse would be tied to it, she was tied to the horseblock outside the great gate of a great castle. But that wasn't all. That wasn't the only shame she had to endure. She must ask every visitor who came that way to mount her, so that, walking on all fours, a horse collar on her, she might carry him into the castle.

She suffered didn't she, humiliation and shame, and she a great Goddess, the Celtic Horse Goddess,

I suffer her shame and her humiliation with her. But I didn't choose them, no.

No, I didn't choose the labour pains and the shame of the Horse Goddess. They attacked me first on the side of Sliabh Fuait. They were in the world, wild in the world, seeking someone who would endure them.

So now you know. You know now why I wear this horse collar.

> I live her myth. Her myth lives me.

What myth do you live? What myth lives you? Do you suffer the labour pains of a world seeking to be reborn?

A hornless red heifer going one way, lowing, lowing, lowing
A horse with one red ear going another way, neighing, neighing.

And this story also, it has something to do, hasn't it, with the Horse Goddess:

Teyrnon Twyrf Liant was Lord of Gwent Is-Coed. If peril or dragonish pestilence in the land called for it, Teyrnon could be a mighty man. He was a generous man. He stood in his truth the way mountains or a clear morning stand in theirs. Teyrnon had a mare, and the pride of life that was in her, you could even see it in her hoof tracts. She foaled every May eve, but every May morning when he went to her stable, Teyrnon would find her foal was gone. One year, ready for terror or havoc, Teyrnon stayed awake, waiting, in the stable. The mare, as he expected she would, cast a fine foal. Hardly had he been dropped when he stood up seeking his mother's paps. Reaching through the window a claw seized him. Vigilant and alert, his sword at the ready, Teyrnon severed the claw at the elbow. Claw and foal fell to the ground. Outside there was a terrible scream, and tumult. Teyrnon rushed out. He saw nothing, heard nothing. In the morning there was a baby, a boy it turned out to be, lying at the stable door.

Can you imagine it, a night long ago in the Celtic World when, willingly, even yearningly, everyone and everything suffered the labour pains of the Horse Goddess? The blind salmon of Assaroe suffered them. The hornless red heifer suffered them. Cast antlers on the side of a mountain suffered them. The Paps of Danu suffered them. The whitethorn bush growing alone suffered them. And there the next morning the infant was. There the next morning the new world was.

It's true, isn't it? We must always be fostering some great thing.

It's true, isn't it? We are only in harmony with the world when we are growing from its greatness.

But that isn't the whole story.

I went one night to the well. I climbed down the five stone steps. I couldn't, as I descended, see the hart's-tongue ferns in the crannies, but I knew they were there, taking a rest maybe from being green. Turning below on the bedrock, I groped my way to the stone lip which always felt harder because it was so polished by the constant, small overflow. Just as I was going to sink the bucket, I saw the mirrored stars, six, seven, maybe nine of them, a constellation of them. Instantly, and without thinking, something older than eyesight in me perceived them to be ecstasies. They were standing, outside space and time, in Divine Ground.

That's all.

I came home without water, I came home without me—

The bucket was empty. I was empty. I was empty of me.

Three nights later there was a soft shoving at my door. I went to it and opened it. It was a horse, her bridle and reins picked out by the firelight. With a knowing not mine I knew that her name was Epona. For a moment that was an eternity she looked at me, seeming to wait. A depth of refusal seized me. She sensed it I think. She turned and walked away. As she did so, raising her head, the reins shimmered, shaking off a last reach of firelight. Like a flicker of conscience it was reaching after a lost opportunity.

I didn't ride out. And you know why, don't you? But maybe you don't. I will tell you. The selfhood that had been dislodged, under pressure from an eternal moment, at the well, that selfhood had reconstituted itself And not only that. Now that its long reign in me was threatened, it had reconstituted itself more contractedly and more ferociously. Threatened selfhood is a terror.

I didn't reach for the flaming reins.
I didn't ride out.

And now again, her opportunity to be Kanthaka lost, Epona went back to the horseblock.

Where she remains, waiting.

AISLING

It was early morning and as I happened to be passing that way, and had time on my hands, I thought I'd cross into the near field and stand on the floor of the hut Owen Roe was born in. Since it wasn't for the first time or the second time or, indeed, for the tenth time that I walked through this gap, I knew or assumed I knew what I'd find, a green ruin, level very nearly with the field and, in a corner where the hag-bed would have been, a clump of briars.

It was late May, so I fully expected that the sole, surviving thorn would be conjured to whiteness, and that, when I first looked up, is what I thought I was seeing.

It wasn't.

As I came closer, hesitating at last to go any further, I didn't need to ask who she was. The only thing I didn't know was by which of her ancient names she might wish to be known, Banbha, Fódhla or Éire.

I didn't speak.

I didn't smile.

And, the wonder was, I didn't turn and go.

Flaming downwards to her hips, her conflagration of red hair was shocking. If she had angers to go with it, or more terrible still, if she had sexual desires to go with it, there was nothing in Christianity and nothing in the religion of megalithic standing stones that could help me.

In her presence I thought ...

In her presence, I'm ashamed of Newgrange.

In her presence, I'm ashamed of what we get up to at Imbolc.
At Imbolc, Bealtaine, Lughnasa and Samhain.
In her presence, Skellig Rock and its clochan and cross are a vanity.
Instantly, in awful alarm, I knew I had gone too far.
No! I burst out. No! There is no goddess or god in whose presence Skellig is a vanity.
Anger at myself released itself into anger at her.
Revenge on myself released itself into revenge on her.
Looking at her, desperately seeking to expiate the sacrilege, I repeated what I'd said. No! I said. No! However red her hair, there is no goddess in whose presence Skellig cross is a vanity.
Whether she levelled her gaze at me or whether I only imagined that she levelled it at me I do not know. I only know that I didn't survive it. I swooned.

Now again I was walking through the gap.
Now again I looked up and saw what I thought was a thorn in bloom.
It wasn't.
This time, inwardly keeping a kind of reverent distance, I crossed the threshold.
I crossed it, yes. But I didn't, in crossing it, make the mistake of thinking she isn't dangerous.
On this I needed no warning. She was dangerous.
And what was worse, there was a strange allure in the danger.
Having neither want nor need in it, the allure didn't lure.
It didn't condescend to anything so common as enticement. There was terrible, as though distant, dignity in it.
Why have you come here? she asked.
I often come here. I come to think. I come here to imagine Ireland.
And how do you imagine Ireland?
As Owen Roe imagined it. As Aodhagán imagined it. As a brightness within everyday brightness. As a brightness neither darkened nor done to death by everyday brightness.
And by everyday brightness you mean?
Two and two make four.
And?
That's it. In everyday brightness two and two make four. In everyday brightness the rivers of Ireland don't have their source in Connla's Otherworld well. In everyday brightness Fintan Mac Bóchra will not be believed when, coming back after centuries, he tells us that he has been a hawk in Achill.

Or a salmon in Lough Derg?

Yes. The flowers he smelled in May he ate as haws in October, but it wasn't in our world he was between the flowering and the fruit. He was younger eating the fruit than he was when he smelled the flower.

She looked at me.

I held my nerve.

Ask me, she said. Ask me the question that's on your mind.

How do you imagine Ireland? I asked.

I've never set foot on it, she said.

But you are standing on it, aren't you?

I'm standing in Fódhla.

But isn't Fódhla just another name for Ireland?

Ireland is what the Irish have done to themselves in Fódhla. Ireland is what the Irish have done to themselves and done to the land in Fódhla. Ireland is what the Irish have settled for in Fódhla. Ireland is what shelters the Irish from the eachtras and immrams of Fódhla. Ireland is what shelters the Irish from a vision of Étain undoing her hair at the well in Brí Leith.

Darkening, or fading, I couldn't say which—

Fading, she looked at me and said,

> Ireland is what shelters the Irish from Fódhla.

It is what Banbha thinks.

It is what Eire thinks.

It is what Fódhla thinks.

Tell them what we think.

> Ireland is what shelters the Irish from Fódhla.

Coming to myself, I got up and turned towards home.

Walking through the gap, I walked back into Ireland.

Years later, at Samhain, she walked into my dream.

The sacrilege was yours, she said.

And yours is the fault if Fódhla has sheltered you from

> Skellig Rock

MÓRDHÁIL UISNIG

'Let us think of a culture that has no fixed and sacred primordial site.'
Nietzsche, *Birth of Tragedy*

In a medieval Irish manuscript called Lebor Gabála Erenn we read of The Peoples who, coming in ships or coming in clouds, came to Ireland and occupied it, some evanescently, some permanently. First to come was a group of Antediluvians. They were led by a woman called Cessair. Among them was a sage called Fintan Mac Bóchra. Taking refuge deep inside a hill, he survived the Flood and as salmon, as eagle, as hawk, as human being, he lived on into many ages, all of them ages of Ireland's Dreamtime. Into that Dreamtime, dreaming and being dreamed themselves, Partholon came, Nemed came, Firbolgs and Fomorians came, and, coming in a cloud, bringing great treasures with them, one of them a cauldron, the Tuatha De Danann came.

It being Dreamtime then, the land was appropriated more effectively with myths than it was with weapons. Without myths going before them weapons were useless.

It being Dreamtime then, the land and everything in it was dreaming. Well might a person in those days say, there is a Dream that dreams us.

It being Dreamtime then, a dreaming rock on a dreaming hill became the sacred centre. The hill was called Uisnech. The rock was called Carraig Choitrigi, or, Aill na Mireann.

Thinking of this sacred centre, it is perhaps inevitable that a poem by Yeats will come to mind:

> *Turning and turning in the widening gyre*
> *The falcon cannot hear the falconer;*
> *Things fall apart; the centre cannot hold;*
> *Mere anarchy is loosed upon the world.*
> *The blood-dimmed tide is loosed, and everywhere*
> *The ceremony of innocence is drowned;*
> *The best lack all conviction, while the worst*
> *Are full of passionate intensity.*

Yeats is talking here about our modern condition, our condition at the anarchic end of the Christian Aion. Europa and Ragnarok are connubial now. Consubstantially now, Europa and Ragnarok are one Ragnaropa.

Time was, however, when, if Fintan Mac Bóchra can be believed, there was a centre and, come hell or high water, it held, holding all things, even things going away from it, in a sacred assembly about it.

However widely he ranged in Ireland in those days, the falcon could hear the falconer.

I don't know if, or to what extent, this sacred centre was already established and accepted when, coming next after the Tuatha De Danann, Gaelic-speaking Celts came. In ships they came and their shaman-poet, Amhairghin Glungheal, was first ashore. Setting his right foot on the soil of Ireland he declared:

> *I am Wind on Sea,*
> *I am Ocean-wave,*
> *I am Roar of Sea,*
> *I am Bull of Seven fights,*
> *I am Vulture on Cliff,*
> *I am Dewdrop,*
> *I am Fairest of Flowers,*
> *I am Boar for Boldness,*
> *I am Salmon in Pool,*
> *I am Lake on Plain,*
> *I am Word of Skill,*
> *I am the Point of a Weapon that pours forth Combat.*
> *I am God who fashions fire for a head.*
> *Who smoothes the ruggedness of a mountain?*
> *Who is He who announces the ages of the Moon?*
> *And who the place where fails the sunset?*
> *Who calls the cattle from the House of Tetra?*
> *On whom do the cattle of Tetra smile?*
> *Who is the troop, who the God who fashions edges?*
> *Enchantments about a spear, enchantments of wind?*

It is likely that anyone who has co-operated successfully with a modern European education, anyone whose mind has been marinated in modern common sense, in the modern consensus or conspiracy about reality, will find these first words spoken in Irish in Ireland unacceptable and will dismiss them. What else but delusions of grandeur, what else but the rantings of a madman can these thirteen Amhairghin I ams be? Like the Seven who came against Thebes, these thirteen I ams must be fought, else our strong city, our city on a hill, will be quaked in its Aristotelian foundations, quaked in its clear and distinct Cartesian watch-towers.

But like them or not, they are the first words spoken in Irish in Ireland:

> *I am Wind on Sea,*
> *I am Ocean-wave.*

And orthodox European philosophy is a Hadrian's Wall between us and them. A wall within. A psychic Hadrian's Wall.

> Partholon came
> Nemed came
> Aristotle came
> Descartes came.

And now, the cattle of Tetra, and Tetra himself, they don't smile on us. But who is Tetra? Is he Pasupati, the Horned Lord of Animals? Is he Cernunnos? He doesn't smile on us.

A Third Battle of Magh Tuired might be inevitable, might indeed be already upon us. A battle this time against ourselves, against our closed consensus about reality

It is likely that Amhairghin Glungheal was a shaman. If this be so he will surely have undergone great prostrations and initiations. Of these he has left no record. There are, however, shamans who have. And it might be a good thing now to listen to some of them. We might think of them as openings in Hadrian's Wall, opening into Ireland's Dreamtime. We might think of them as reopening the way to Uisnech, the sacred centre.

My name is Yegor Mikhaylovich Kyzlasov. I live at the mouth of the river Yes, in the village of Kyzlan ... I had been sick and I had been dreaming. In my dreams I had been taken to the Ancestor and cut into pieces on a black table. They chopped me up and threw me into the kettle and I was boiled. There were some men there: two black and two fair ones. Their chieftain was there too. He issued the orders concerning me. I saw all this. While the pieces of my body were boiled, they found a bone around the ribs, which had a hole in the middle. This was the excess-bone. This brought about my becoming a shaman. Because only those men can become shamans in whose body such a bone can be found. One looks across the hole of this bone and begins to see all, to know all, that is when one becomes a shaman ... When I came to from this scare I woke up. This meant that my soul had returned. Then the shamans declared: 'You are the sort of man who may become a shaman. You should become a shaman, you must begin to shamanize' ...

When the shaman goes to the chief-shaman, that is to the family ancestor, he has to cross the Ham Saraschan Harazi Mountain along the way. On the top of that mountain there is a pine tree, its trunk resembles a six-sided log. The shamans carve their symbols into it, between the edges. Whoever places his marking upon it, he then becomes a real shaman. It happens sometimes that a certain marking falls down, it disappears from rhe tree. Then its owner dies. After resting at the foot of this tree, the journey is continued. Then the shaman arrives at a crossing where an invisible shaman is sitting. He guards the crossroads. This is the place where all paths begin: the path of all the animals offered to the spirits, the road of the spirit rabies, the path of the spirits of all other sicknesses, this is where all the wild animals of the forest enter upon their trails. When this crossroads is reached by one who became a shaman, through the spirit of sickness, he must pray to the invisible shaman and offer him wheat-brandy. The right path is shown to him only after the offering has taken place. Then he may continue the journey along the appointed path. In the course of the journey the shaman arrives at a narrow plankbridge across a very fast river and must cross it. After having crossed the river he is not very far away from the Ancestral Shaman but there is still one more obstacle he must conquer. There are two cliffs there. Sometimes they close and then again they withdraw from each other. They keep moving day and night. After they clash they then start to move away from each other again, this is when the shaman may slip across between them. But he who is lazy and does not run perishes there. In such cases the shaman becomes ill and dies. But if he succeeds he is already treading upon the grounds of the Ancestral Shaman, covered with black rocks. So this is where the Ancestor lives. The shaman cannot see him, he merely senses his presence ... When I was asleep because of my sickness my brother came to visit me and told me that I had already crossed the mountain. He also told me that I was ill because of the mountain but that soon I would be healthy again. But I did not get any better for a long time to come. I wandered about in the mountains in my dreams. Then I went further and further, and my brother stayed behind. I even left the mountains behind me. I arrived in another land. There were some people there too. They were all writing something. Their tables were built of black earth and there were drums hung on the sides. There were some tables on the opposite side too, there were drums hanging on the sides of these too but with their bottoms up. Here also all the tables were upside down. The shaman's garments were also turned inside out. I have heard before: these are the drums of those shamans who do not live long. He that chooses from these would die soon. At least the people said so ... So I picked up a white drum and a garment from the other side. That is how I became a shaman.

Following is the account of his initiations by the Inuit shaman, Autdaruta:

When my father died I often went out for long rambles among the hills because I felt that I had been left alone. It was the season when stonecrop springs up, and I gathered it, to preserve in blubber for the winter.

One day, up among the rocks, I heard someone begin to sing. I looked but could see no one. 'Now why should I have heard this song?' I thought to myself and went home.

The next morning, towards daybreak, I went up again to the hills, and then I heard the same thing again, it was someone beginning to sing. 'Now why is this happening to me,' thought I. Just then I saw two men coming towards me. They were inland-dwellers.

'We are sorry for you, because you were an orphan, so we have come to help you,' they said, and so they became my first helping spirits. Then I began to be a magician, but did not speak to anyone about it. The year afterwards we moved south, that was in the season when the small birds come, and we settled down in company with an old and much venerated magician. He could not stand upright, and could only walk by propping up his thighs with his arms. He could not carry his kayak up and down himself, and so it came that I used to help him.

One day he came and said to me, 'Travel east with me and I will teach you something you may need to help you, my poor fatherless boy.'

So we travelled together and he told me on the way that he was going to make a great magician of me. We went ashore up a fjord, close to a cave, and the old man took off his clothes and crept inside. And he told me to watch carefully what happened next. I lay hidden a little way off and waited. It was not long before I saw a great bear come swimming along, crawl ashore, and approach the magician. It flung itself upon him, crunched him up, limb by limb, and ate him. Then it vomited him out again and swam away.

When I went up to the cave the old man lay groaning. He was very much exhausted, but was able to row home himself. On the way back he told me that every time he allowed himself to be devoured alive by the bear he acquired greater power over his helping spirits.

Some time afterwards he took me on a journey again, and this time it was so that I myself might be eaten by the bear. This was necessary if I wished to attain to any good. We rowed off and came to the cave; the old man told me to take my clothes off, and I do not deny that I was somewhat uncomfortable at the thought of being devoured alive.

I had not been lying there long before I heard the bear coming. It attacked me and crunched me up, limb by limb, joint by joint, but strangely enough it did not hurt at all, it was only when it bit me in the heart that it hurt frightfully.

From that day forth I felt I ruled my helping spirits. After that I acquired many new helping spirits and no danger could any longer threaten me, as I was always protected.

The great Kwakiutl shaman whose name was Fool had this to say:

I am a hunter of all kinds of animals, always paddling about for seals, which are what I want most; for to try out the oil from the blubber and sell it to my tribe for gravy. I have always killed lots of hair seals and so have never been poor. I used to be the principal doubter of shamans: what they said about curing the sick and seeing people's souls. I would tell them out loud they were lying. I would be sitting with those beating time for their curing ceremonies and those shamans really hated me.

Well, I was out paddling for seals one fine day with a brave fellow named Leelamiedenole who always served as my helmsman. Nothing ever frightened him, neither gales nor vicious animals, dangerous fish, or the sea monsters that we frequently see when fishing at night. This is why we have to have courageous fellows for our steersmen. I was paddling along at Axolis, when I saw a wolf sitting on a rock, scratching with both paws the two sides of his mouth. He whined as we approached and was not afraid of us, not even when I got out of my small travelling canoe and went to where he sat. He whined and I noticed his mouth was bleeding. I looked in and saw a deer bone stuck crosswise between his teeth on both sides, very firmly. He was evidently expecting me to do something: either to kill him or to help him out of his trouble. So I said to him: 'Friend, you are in trouble and I am going to cure you, like a great shaman— for which I expect you to reward me with the power to get easily anything I want, the way you do. Now you just sit here while I fix up something to help me get rid of that bone.' I went inland and picked up some twigs from a cedar tree which I twisted into a string, and when I returned the wolf was still sitting there on the rock with his mouth open. I took hold of the back of his head and put the string, thin end, into his mouth, tied it to the middle of the bone and pulled. Out came the bone. The wolf only sat staring at me. 'Friend,' I said, your trouble is ended. Now don't forget to reward me for what I have just done for you.'

When I had said that the wolf turned around to the right and trotted off—not fast. And he had gone only a little way when he stopped, turned his muzzle to me and howled—just once. He howled and went into the woods. I stepped into my small canoe and paddled away with my steersman. Neither of us spoke of the wolf. We paddled and anchored in a cave where no wind ever blows, called Foam-Receptacle; lay down in our small canoe, and our eyes immediately closed in sleep; for we had risen before daybreak and were very tired. And I dreamed, that night, of a man who came and spoke to me saying, 'Why did you stop here? Friend, this island is full of seals. I am Harpooner-Body, on whom you took pity today, and I am rewarding you for your kindness, friend. From now on there will be nothing you want that you will not obtain. But for the next four years you must not sleep with your wife.'

I woke and called my steersman. He rose and pulled up the anchor. We went ashore where I washed in the sea and stepped back into the canoe eager to see whether, as Harpooner-Body had said in my dream, there were actually a lot of seals on the rocks of the island. For I did not believe in dreams, or in shamans, or in any of the beliefs of my people; but only in my own mind. We paddled out before dawn and approached the rocky, treeless shore, which I beheld covered with seals, all tight asleep. I cook my yew-wood seal club, stepped ashore, and clubbed four big ones, while the rest tumbled off into the water. I put the four aboard and we travelled home. So there was now at least one thing in which I believed, namely the truth of the Harpooner-Body's words, delivered to me in dream.

And from that time on it was easy for me, when out hunting, to get seals and every other kind of game.

Two years later, in the summer of 1871, I went to Victoria with my wife, my three nephews, and their wives and children. Returning home in our large travelling canoe we came to Rock Bay, on the north side of Seymour Narrows and went ashore there. Stepping out of the canoe, my eldest nephew saw four nice boxes on the beach, full of very nice clothing, two bags of flour, and all kinds of food. We could see no one around who might own these things and so we carried them aboard and moved on. When we came to Beaver Cove, a north-east wind sprang up and we stayed there for six days. It was then ten days after we had found the box, and my whole company was now sick. In the morning we set off. It was calm. And when we arrived at Axolis we unloaded our cargo—all of us sick with the great smallpox, which had been contracted when we picked up the boxes. We all lay in bed in our tent. I saw that our bodies had swelled and were dark red. I did not realize that all the others were dead, but presently, I thought that I was dead. I was sleeping; but then awoke because of all the wolves that were coming, whining and howling. Two were licking my body, vomiting up foam, trying hard to put it all over me; and they were rough when they turned me over. I could feel myself getting stronger, both in body and in mind. The two kept licking, and after they had licked off all that they had vomited, they vomited again and when, again, they had licked this off, I saw that they had taken off all the scabs and sores. And it was only then that I realized that I was lying there among the dead.

Evening fell and the two wolves rested. I must have become afraid, being the only one alive there; for I crawled away to the shelter of a thick spruce where I lay all night. With no bedding and only the shirt I had on, I was cold. The two wolves approached and lay down on each side of me and when morning came they got up and again licked me all over, vomiting up white foam and licking it off. I was getting stronger and when strong enough to stand I realized that one of those two wolves was the one from whose mouth I had taken the bone. All the others had remained in attendance too. And now I was, in fact, quite well. I lay down and there came to me the figure that in my dream, in the place called Foam-Receptacle, had told me that his name was Harpooner-Body. He sat down seaward of me and nudged me with his nose until I responded by lying on my back, whereupon he vomited foam and pressed his nose against the lower end of my sternum. He was vomiting magic power into me and when he had finished he sat back. I became sleepy and dreamed of the wolf that was still sitting at my side. In the dream he became a man who laughed and said, 'Now, Friend, take care of this shaman power that has gone into you. From now on you will cure the sick, you will catch the souls of the sick, and you will be able to throw sickness into anyone in your tribe, who you wish should die. They will all now be afraid of you.' That is what he said to me in my dream.

I woke and was trembling and my mind since then has been different. All the wolves had left me and I was now a shaman. I walked the way to Fern Point where I remained alone for a long time in one of the seven abandoned houses there. On the way I met a. man whom I told of the deaths of my whole crew and he left me in fear and hurried home. I was not depressed, but just kept singing my sacred songs, evening after evening, the four songs of the wolf. For I was like someone drunk, completely happy, all the time. And I stayed there, at Fern Point, for more than the period of one moon.

A passing canoe-man heard my song and spoke of it to the people of Teeguxter, who immediately decided to invite me, the new shaman, whose song had been heard, to come and cure their sick Chief whose name was Causing-To-Be-Well.

Black Elk speaks:

It was summer when I was nine years old and our people were moving slowly towards the Rocky Mountains. We camped one evening in a valley beside a little creek just before it ran into Greasy Grass and there was a man by the name of Man Hip who liked me and asked me to eat with him in his Tepee. While I was eating a voice came and said: 'It is time, now they are calling you.' The voice was so loud and clear that I believed it and I thought I would just go where it wanted me to go. So I got right up and started. As I came out of the Tepee both my thighs began to hurt me and suddenly it was like waking from a dream and there wasn't any voice. So I went back into the Tepee, but I didn't want to eat. Man Hip looked at me in a strange way and asked me what was wrong. I told him that my thighs were hurting me. The next morning the camp moved again and I was riding with some boys. We stopped to get a drink from a creek and when I got off my horse my legs crumpled under me and I couldn't walk. So the boys helped me up and put me on my horse and when we camped again that evening I was sick. The next day the camp moved on to where the different bands of people were coming together and I rode in a pony drag for I was very sick. My legs and my arms were swollen badly and my face was all puffed up. When we had camped again I was lying in our Tepee and my mother and my father were sitting beside me. I could see out through the opening and there two men were coming from the clouds head first, like arrows, slanting down, and I knew they were the same I had seen before. Each now carried a long spear and from the points of these a jagged lightning flashed. They came clear down to the ground this time and stood a little way off and looked at me and said:

'Hurry! Come! Your Grandfathers are calling you!'

Then they turned and left the ground like arrows slanting upward from the bow. When I got up to follow my legs did not hurt anymore and I was very light. I went outside the Tepee and yonder where the men with flaming spears were going a little cloud was coming very fast. It came and stopped and took me and turned back to where it came from, flying fast. And when I looked down I could see my mother and my father and I was sore to be leaving them. Then there was nothing but the air and the swiftness of the little cloud that bore me and those two men still leading up to where white clouds were piled like mountains on a wild blue plain and in them thunder beings lived and leaped and flashed.

Now suddenly there was nothing but a world of cloud and we three were there alone in the middle of a great white plain with snowy hills and mountains staring at us, and it was very still, but there were whispers.

I looked and saw a bay horse standing there and he began to speak: 'Behold me,' he said. 'My life history you shall see.' Then he wheeled about to where the sun goes down and said: 'Behold them! Their history you shall know.'

I looked and there were twelve black horses all abreast with necklaces of bison hooves and they were beautiful, but I was frightened, because their manes were lightning and there was thunder in their nostrils.

Then the bay horse wheeled to where, in the north. The Great White Giant lives and said: 'Behold.' And yonder there were twelve white horses all abreast. Their manes were flowing like a blizzard wind and from their noses came a roaring and all about them white geese soared and circled.

Then the bay horse wheeled round to the east where the sun shines continually and bade me look, and there twelve sorrel horses, with necklaces of elk's teeth, stood abreast with eyes that glimmered like the daybreak star and manes of morning light.

Then the bay horse wheeled once again to look towards the south and yonder stood twelve buckskins all abreast with horns upon their heads and manes that lived and grew like trees and grasses and when I had seen all these the bay horse said: 'Your Grandfathers are having a Council. These horses shall take you so have courage.'

Then all the horses went into formation, four abreast, the blacks, the whites, the sorrels and the buckskins and they stood behind the bay who turned now to the west and neighed and, yonder, suddenly, the sky was terrible with a storm of plunging horses in all colours that shook the world with thunder, neighing back. Now turning to the north the bay horse whinnied and yonder, all the sky roared with a mighty wind of running horses in all colours, neighing back.

And when he whinnied to the east, there too the sky was filled with glowing clouds of manes and tails of horses in all colours singing back.

Then to the south he called and it was crowded with many coloured, happy horses, nickering.

Then the bay horse spoke to me and said: 'See how your horses all come dancing.' I looked and there were horses, horses everywhere, a whole skyful of horses dancing around me.

'Make haste', the bay horse said, and we walked together side by side, while the blacks, the whites, the sorrels and the buckskins followed, marching four by four. I looked about me once again and suddenly the dancing horses without number changed into animals of every kind and into all the fowls that are and these fled back to the four quarters of the world from whence the horses came and vanished.

Then as we walked there was a heaped-up cloud ahead that changed into a Tepee and the open door of it was a rainbow and through it I saw six old men sitting in a row.

The two men with the spears now stood beside me, one on either hand and the horses took their places in their quarters, looking inward, four by four. And the oldest of the Grandfathers spoke with a kind voice and said: 'Come right in and do not fear.' And as he spoke all the horses of the four quarters neighed to cheer me. So I went in and stood before the six, and they looked older than men can ever be, old like hills, like stars.

The oldest spoke again: 'Your Grandfathers all over the world are having a council and they have called you here to teach you.' His voice was very kind, but I shook all over with fear now, for I knew that these were not old men but the Powers of the World. And the first was the Power of the West; the second, of the North, the third of the East;

the fourth of the South; the fifth of the Sky; the sixth of the Earth. I knew this and I was afraid until the first Grandfather spoke again: 'Behold them yonder where the sun goes down, the Thunder Beings! You shall see and have from them my power and they shall take you to the high and lonely centre of the earth that you may see, even to the place where the sun continually shines, they shall take you there to understand.'

And as he spoke of understanding I looked up and saw the rainbow leap with flames of many colours over me.

Now there was a wooden cup in his hand and it was full of water and in the water was the sky. 'Take this,' he said. "It is the power to make live and it is yours.'

Now he had a bow in his hands. 'Take this,' he said. 'It is the power to destroy and it is yours.'

Then he pointed to himself and said: 'Look close at him who is your spirit now, for you are his body and his name is Eagle Wing Stretches.'

And saying this he got up very tall and started running toward where the sun goes down, and suddenly he was a black horse that stopped and turned and looked at me and the horse was very poor and sick and his ribs stood out.

Then the second Grandfather, he of the North, arose with a herb of power in his hand and said: 'Take this and hurry.' I took it and held it toward the black horse yonder. He fattened and was happy and came prancing to his place again and was the first Grandfather sitting there.

The second Grandfather, he of the North, spoke again: 'Take courage, younger brother,' he said, 'on earth a nation you shall make live, for yours shall be the power of the white Giant's Wing, the cleansing wing.' Then he got up very tall and started running toward me, it was a white goose wheeling. I looked about me now and the horses in the west were thunders and the horses in the North were geese. And the second Grandfather sang two songs that were like this:

> They are appearing, may you behold!
> They are appearing, may you behold!
> The Thunder nation is appearing, behold!
> They are appearing, may you behold!
> They are appearing, may you behold!
> The white geese nation is appearing, behold!

And now it was the third Grandfather who spoke, he of where the sun shines continually. 'Take courage, younger brother,' he said, 'for across the earth they shall take you.' Then he pointed to where the daybreak star was shining and beneath the star two men were flying. 'From them you shall have power,' he said, 'from them who have wakened all the beings of the earth with roots and legs and wings'. And as he said this, he held in his hand a peace pipe which had a spotted eagle outstretched upon the seem, and this eagle seemed alive, for it was poised there, fluttering, and its eyes were looking at me. 'With this pipe,' the Grandfather said, 'you shall walk upon the earth and whatever sickens there you shall make well.' Then he pointed to a man who was bright red all over, the colour of good and of plenty, and as he pointed, the red man lay down and rolled and changed into a bison that got up and galloped toward the sorrel horses of the east and they too turned to bison, far and many.

And now the fourth Grandfather spoke, he of the South, the place you are always facing, the place whence comes the power to grow: 'Younger brother,' he said, 'with the powers of the four quarters you shall walk, a relative. Behold, the living centre of a nation I shall give you and with it many you shall save.' And I saw that he was holding in his hand a bright red stick that was alive and as I looked it sprouted at the top and sent forth branches and on the branches many leaves came out and murmured and in the leaves the birds began to sing. And then for just a little while I thought I saw beneath it, in the shade, the circled villages of people and every living thing with roots or legs or wings and all were happy. 'It shall stand in the centre of the nation's circle,' said the Grandfather, 'A cane to walk with and a peoples' heart, and by your powers you shall make it blossom.'

Then when he had been still a little while to hear the birds sing, he spoke again: 'Behold the earth.' So I looked down and saw it lying yonder like a hoop of peoples and in the centre bloomed the holy stick that was a tree and where it stood there crossed two roads, a red one and a black. 'From where the Giant lives (the north) to where you always face (the south) the red road goes, the road of good', the Grandfather said, 'and on it shall your nation walk. The black road goes from where the thunder beings live (the west) to where the sun continually shines (the east), a fearful road, a road of troubles and of war. On this also you shall walk and from it you shall have the power to destroy a people's foes. In four ascents you shall walk the earth with power.' Then he rose very tall and starred running toward the south and was an elk and as he stood among the buckskins yonder, they too were elks.

Now the fifth Grandfather spoke, the oldest of them all, the spirit of the Sky. 'My boy,' he said, 'I have sent for you and you have come. My power you shall see!' He stretched his arms and turned into a spotted eagle hovering. 'Behold' he said, 'all the wings of the air shall come to you, and they and the winds and the stars shall be like relatives. You shall go across the earth with my power.' Then the eagle soared above my head and fluttered there and suddenly the sky was full of friendly wings all coming towards me.

Now I knew the sixth Grandfather was about to speak. He who was the spirit of the earth, and I saw that he was very old. His hair was long and white, he face was all in wrinkles and his eyes were deep and dim. I stared at him for it seemed I knew him somehow. As I stared, he slowly changed, for he was growing backwards into youth, and when he had become a boy, I knew that he was myself with all the years that would be mine at last. When he was old again he said: 'My boy, have courage, for my power shall be yours, and you shall need it, for your nation on earth shall have Great troubles. Come.'

He rose and tottered out through the rainbow door and as I followed I was riding on the bay horse who had talked to me at first and led me to that place.

Then the bay horse stopped and faced the black horse of the West and a voice said:

'They have given you the cup of water to make live the greening day, and also the bow and arrow to destroy.'

The bay horse neighed and the twelve black horses came and stood behind me, four abreast.

The bay horse faced the sorrels of the East and I saw that they had morning stars upon their foreheads and they were very bright. And the voice said: 'They have given you the sacred pipe, and the power that is peace, and the Good Rest Day.' The bay horse neighed and the twelve sorrels stood behind me, four abreast. Then I knew that there were riders on all the horses there behind me, and a voice said: 'now you shall walk the black road with these and as you walk all the nations, that have roots or legs or wings shall fear you.'

Then I started riding toward the east down the fearful road and behind me came horses and riders four abreast, the blacks, the whites, the sorrels and the buckskins, and faraway above the fearful road the daybreak scar was rising very dim.

I looked below me where the earth was silent in a sick green light and saw the hills look up afraid and the grasses on the hills and all the animals and everywhere about me were the cries of frightened birds and sounds of fleeing wings. I was the chief of all the heavens riding there and when I looked behind me the twelve black horses reared and plunged and thundered and their tails and manes were whirling hail and their nostrils snorted lightning. And when I looked below again I saw the slant hail failing, and the long, sharp rain, and where we passed, the trees bowed low and all the hills were dim.

Now the earth was bright again as we rode. I could see the hills and valleys and the creeks and rivers passing under. We came above a place where three streams make a big one, a source of mighty waters, and something terrible was there. Flames were rising from the waters and in the flames a blue man lived. The dust was floating all above him in the air, the grass was short and withered, the trees were wilting, two-legged and four-legged beings lay thin and panting and wings too weak to fly. Then the black horse riders shouted: 'Hoka Hey!' and charged down upon the blue man, but they were driven back. And the white troop shouted charging and was beaten; then the red troop and the yellow.

And when each had failed, they all cried together: 'Eagle Wing Stretches, hurry!' And all the world was filled with voices of all kinds that cheered me, so I charged, I had the cup of water in one hand and in the other was the bow that turned into a spear as the bay horse and I swooped down and the spear's head was sharp lightning. I stabbed the blue man's heart and as it stuck I could hear the thunder rolling and many voices that cried: 'Un-hee!' meaning I had killed. The flames died. The trees and grasses were not withered any more and murmured happily together and every living being cried in gladness with whatever voice it had. Then the four troops of horsemen charged down and struck the dead body of the blue man, counting coup; and suddenly it was only a harmless turtle.

You see I had been riding with the stormclouds and had come to earth as rain and it was drought that I had killed with the power that the six Grandfathers gave me. So we were riding on the earth now down along the river flowing full from the source of waters, and soon I saw ahead the circled village of a people in the valley. And a voice said: 'Behold a nation, it is yours. Make haste, Eagle Wing Stretches.'

I entered the village, riding, with the four horse troops behind me, the blacks, the whites, the sorrels and the buckskins, and the place was filled with moaning and mourning for the dead. The wind was blowing from the south like fever and when I looked around I saw that in nearly every tepee the women and the children and the men lay dying with the dead.

So I rode around the circle of the village looking in upon the sick and the dead and I felt like crying as I rode. But when I looked behind me all the women and the children and the men were getting up and coming forth with happy faces.

And a voice said: 'Behold, they have given you the centre of the nation's hoop to make it live.'

So I rode to the centre of the village, with the horse-troops in their quarters round about me and there the people gathered. And the voice said: 'Give them now the flowering stick that they may flourish, and the sacred pipe that they may know the power that is peace and the wing of the white giant that they may have endurance and face all winds with courage.'

So I took the bright red stick and at the centre of the nation's hoop, I thrust it into the earth. As it touched the earth it leaped mightily in my hand and was a waga chun, the rustling tree, very tall and full of leafy branches and of all birds singing and beneath it all, the animals were mingling with the people like relatives and making happy cries.

The women raised their tremolo of joy and the men shouted all together: 'Here we shall raise our children and be as little chickens under the mother sheo's wing.'

Then I heard the white wind blowing gently through the tree and singing there, and from the east the sacred pipe came flying on its eagle wings and stopped before me there beneath the tree spreading deep peace around it.

Then the daybreak star was rising ...

Kyzlasov, Autdaruta, Fool, Black Elk and, whether or not he belongs to their company, our own Amhairghin Glungheal.

Did the awful road of initiations swallow Amhairghin? Maybe it did.

Maybe, being initiated, Amhairghin, like Kyzlasov, was cut in pieces on a black table and boiled in a great iron kettle.

Murderously dangerous and lawless in an earlier incarnation maybe, like Autdaruta, he consented at last to be devoured by the Angakok Bear.

Maybe wolves foamed him, licked him, healed him, slept either side of him, keeping him warm. Maybe a wolf he had once helped muzzled shaman power into him.

Maybe, leaving his body on a tepee floor, he ascended and walked through a flaming rainbow doorway.

Could it be that much that we now have no capacity for lies behind the first words spoken in Irish in Ireland? Could it be that the awful road of shamanic initiations lies behind them?

Four shamans.

Four shaman initiations.

Four openings in our Hadrian's Wall, in our modern consensus about, against, reality.

Four openings for Ireland's four provinces into Ireland's Dreamtime.

Four openings for Ireland's four provinces into Iath n-Anann.

Four openings for Ireland's four provinces into commonage consciousness.

Four openings for Ireland's four provinces into a humble holy hearing, a Hindu hearing, of Amhairghin's Gita.

The breached wall. The breached consensus. In our psyches breached. In our built world breached.

> By initiating shamans breached,
> By bear breached,
> By wolves breached,
> By bay horse breached.

And now, if we wish, we can walk through, walking the road of initiations to Uisnech, the sacred centre.

Could it be that a great revelation is at hand?

Could it be that in imbas forosnai we will see as we walk that Carraig Choitrigi has become Carraig Om?

Could it be that in imbas forasnai we will see as we walk that Carraig Om or Aill Om is Aill na Mireann, is Aill na Mandukya Mireann, its mireann being vaisvanara, taijasa, susupta and turiya?

> Spores came,
> Seeds came,
> Animals came,
> People came.

And could it be that, walking in commonage consciousness, we will see, as we walk, that Mórdháil Uisnig has become a Mandukya Mórdháil, a Mórdháil that chants the Mandukya Om all night four nights a year, at Samhain, at Imbolc, at Bealtaine, at Lughnasa?

> Mórdháil Uisnig.

The Mandukya Mórdháil, around Aill Om, of all that is.
We have a centre that will hold.

EUROPE'S YEAR ONE REED

> 'There is one thing stronger than all the armies in the world;
> and that is an idea whose time has come.'
> *(Nation,* 15 April 1843)

In the region of the East Alligator River in North Australia there is a pool called Red Lily Billabong. Improbably, a rock rises in solitary assertion out of the water. A protuberance of it resembles a human head.

To Aborigines, this rock is Indjuwanidjuwa. Or rather, it is the form he settled into after his Dreamtime dreamings and wanderings, for, like Kunapipi, Karora and others, Indjuwanidjuwa is one of the Altjeringa Mitjina, one of the Eternal Ones of the Dream.

Its more or less lush surroundings notwithstanding, I think of this billabong as an oasis in Ulro. I think of it as a Bethesda for Ulropeans.

In chapter five of his gospel, St John cells us about Bethesda:

Now there is at Jerusalem by the sheep market a pool, which is called in the Hebrew tongue Bethesda, having five porches. In these lay a great multitude of impotent folk, of blind, halt, withered, waiting for the moving of the water. For an angel went down at a certain season into the pool, and troubled the water; whosoever then first after the troubling of the water stepped in was made whole of whatever disease he had.

Bethesda and Red Lily Billabong. The billabong in which we are healed of all that ails us, of all that cripples us and withers us, philosophically and culturally. The billabong in which we are healed of the Gorgonizing forms of our European sensibility, the Gorgonizing categories of our European understanding.

And the rock that rises out of the water, Rockman, I think of him as a living statue of living liberty, nature's statute of nature's liberty.

His cultural counterpart in New York harbour, that mighty woman with a torch in her hand, she who lights the way of people to freedom—she calls out across all oceans to all old worlds:

> Give me your tired, your poor,
> Your huddled masses yearning
> To breathe free.

Aboriginal Rockman doesn't call out. A Dreamtime dreamer dreaming the dreams that rocks dream, he stands for kinds of liberty, for profundities of liberty, our European enlightenment never imagined.

> Liberty for all things.

Liberty and blessed release for all things from the ancient philosophic regime in our European eyes.

> In Europe, even now, Gorgon is Bourbon
> In Europe, even now, everyone is Bourbon, is Gorgon,
> To star and stone.

As Rockman hears it, it is Medusa's Marseillaise we sing:

> Hot and cold are appearance, sweet and bitter
> are appearance, colour is appearance; in reality
> there are the atoms and the void.

Coming, in biblical times, to Bethesda, there were many who left their crutches behind.

Coming in Gorgon times to Red Lily Billabong, coming to it from his inanimate cold world, maybe Coleridge will leave his dejection behind.

Coming to it from the grating roar of *res extensa* pebbles on Dover Beach, maybe Arnold will leave his despairing recoil from the outside world behind.

Maybe Europa will come.

Maybe Ecclesia will come.

Maybe that mighty enlightened lady who, torch in hand, lights our way to religious, political and economic freedom will come.

Yes.
One day it will be Europe's turn.
It will be Year One Reed for Europe.
Unless we change, it will be Year One Reed for the living earth.
So let us imagine it:

>A new *Mayflower* setting sail for a new Plymouth Rock.

Will the dove we send out bring news of Ulru? Will the raven we send out bring news of Rockman walking before us, leading us to Red Lily Billabong where, released, the universe has left our cosmologies behind.

That's him:

>Rockman in his billabong.

That's him:

>Never once raising a hand against us
>Never coming over the ocean to conquer us
>He might nonetheless be
>Europe's Conquistador

Looking at him, in this our Year One Reed, we know that the forms of our European sensibility and the categories of our European understanding are a Bastille we have yet to storm.

Looking at him, healed of our Medusa mindset, we can imagine it: Michelangelo's captives, liberated at last, walking the songlines of a new European Dreamtime.

And there she is, Medusa herself. Medusa attempting to walk and to sing.

>And sing she will
>And walk she will
>And dream with the dreaming Earth she will.

Yes!
Our defeat in Year One Reed will be a good day for the evolving Dream.

>A good day for the evolving Earth.

And who knows! A time might come when, even here is Europe, Medusa's Marseillaise will at last give way to Blake's Marseillaise:

>*Mock on, mock on, Voltaire, Rousseau:*
>*Mock on, Mock on: 'Tis all in vain!*
>*You throw the sand against the wind.*
>*And the wind blows it back again.*

> *And every sand becomes a gem*
> *Reflected in the beams divine;*
> *Blown back they blind the mocking eye,*
> *But still in Israel's paths they shine.*
>
> *The atoms of Democritus,*
> *And Newton's particles of light*
> *Are sands upon the Red Sea shore*
> *Where Israel's tents do shine so bright.*

Miriam's Marseillaise.
Marseillaise Michelangelo's captives might sing.
Marseillaise Democritus and Newton might sing,
Marseillaise Voltaire and Rousseau might sing.
Marseillaise we all might sing.
The Marseillaise of our Exodus, following Rockman, from Ulro to Uluru:

> The atoms of Democritus,
> And Newton's particles of light
> Are gems upon Uluru's plains
> Where Europe's tents do shine so bright.

ULROPEANS

In the Academia in Florence there are four unfinished sculptures by Michelangelo, or at any rate from his workshop. They are commonly called The Captives. Names assigned to them individually aren't invariable, but they will often be referred to, in series, as, The Youthful Giant, Atlas or The Blockhead, The Bearded Giant, The Awakening Giant.

As we would expect, given their provenance, it isn't always easy, even in their reproduced presence, to remain aesthetically distant and uninvolved. Looking at them isn't, as Schopenhauer might have hoped, to experience a Sabbath day of the will.

Aesthetic responses to them aren't what interests me here, however. My purpose in calling them to mind is philosophical. Given the history of European thinking in the last three centuries, they lend themselves, I believe, to retrospective reinterpreration as portents.

They are images of what we would become.

They are images of us in Cartesian captivity.

They are images of us in hard bondage to Gorgocogito. Let me explain. Let Blake be our guide.

Central to William Blake's understanding of our human condition is the Christian doctrine of the Fall. Open as he was, though, to Platonic, Hermetic and Gnostic influences, Blake didn't understand the doctrine as most Christians do. In his vision of it, our Fall wasn't a homogeneous sinking through homogeneous space into nether or near-nether depths. We declined or sank or wandered desirously downwards through qualitatively distinct states. These he calls

>Eden,
>Beulah,
>Generation,
>Ulro.

It is important that we should think of these as states of mind not as states of independently existing objective reality.

Esse est percipi aut percipere.

In our Ulro starte of mind we perceive the objective world to be an echoing, hard rockiness. We perceive it to exist independently of our perceptions of it.

As desert rock walls would, it echoes our theories and creeds about it back to us.

Like letters undelivered and unopened, our cosmologies come home to us.

In Ulro, any theology we send out should have on it the name and address of the sender.

We receive but what we send out. What we send out comes back to us through slits in our limits of contraction and opacity.

René Descartes was the Moses who led us into this desert of Zin. In it our souls are dried away.

But when in that desert René, like Moses, strikes a *res extensa* rock, only a mocking mirage of water issues from it. Looking into that mirage, we see reflections of ourselves as Michelangelo's captives.

In the image and likeness of The Blockhead are we.

Our heads are blocked into Gorgocogito.

We are bedrocked rockily in the Medusa mindset.

Gorgo was Descartes' God. In the name of Gorgo and her cogito he led us thither.

Gorgo sum, ergo Gorgocogito, ergo Ulro.

What do you think, Bishop of Cloyne? Will you chisel us free? Will you lead us out? Will you be our Perseus? Our philosophical Perseus? Our epistemological Perseus?

Will you sing the songs of Beulah in Ulro? In Ulro-Europa? In Ulropa? Will you sing your Philosopher-King's song?

It is indeed an opinion strangely prevailing amongst men that houses, mountains, rivers, and in a word all sensible objects, have an existence, natural or real, distinct from their being perceived by the understanding. But, with how great an assurance and acquiescence soever this principle may be entertained in the world, yet whoever shall find in his heart to call it in question may, if I mistake not, perceive it to involve a manifest contradiction. For, what are the forementioned objects but the things we perceive by sense? and what do we perceive besides our own ideas or sensations? and is it not plainly repugnant that any one of these, or any combination of them, should exist unperceived?

Will you sing that song to Ulropeans? To Coleridge sitting in dejection, to Arnold on Dover Beach, to Wallace Stevens at Key West?

To whom does the future belong, Bishop? To the captive called The Blockhead? Or to the captive called The Awakening Giant?

Will you help him? Will you give him a hand? Will you give The Awakening Giant an epistemological hand?

Come back, Michelangelo. Come back and chisel us free of the Medusa mindset that has made blockheads of us all.

MONA, OUR MOSES

Asked to make a statement about the universe at large, a modern scientist would probably say, $E=mc^2$. Were I to be asked, I would almost certainly say, Early Spring.

'Early Spring' is the title of a painting by Kuo Hsi, a painter of the Northern Sung Dynasty in China. I will not attempt a verbal equivalent or even a description of the painting. Suffice it to say that in it, given its provenance, is much that you would expect to find: mountains, high shoulders of mountains, summits of mountains, near neighbours of heaven. Mountains that could be apparitions of mountains. Mountains that could be the Void's memory of mountains or the Void's dream of mountains. We cannot say till the mist clears. But the mist of course will never clear. And the Void could wake up or could sink into dreamless sleep and then they'd be gone and we who perceived them, we too would be gone, no apparition or memory of us remaining. But that would be no loss to us or to the Void because the Void is as full when it is empty as it is when innumerable universes have sprouted in it. And the universe we live in, the universe these mountains belong in, that universe isn't only vast in big things, it is vast, universally vast, in littlest things, in starved little things, in things that are desperate attempts to be things, in that fierce wizened will to be a pine growing from a rockwall. And that little wisp crossing a causeway—don't ignore him. Surrendered to the great universal way, working with the great universal way, letting the great universal way have its willess way with them, little wisps such as he is have built that monastery, geomantically perfect, in its high valley.

> The Valley Spirit never dies
> It is named the Mysterious Female.
> And the Doorway of the Mysterious Female
> Is the base from which Heaven and Earth spring.
> It is there within us all the while.
> Draw upon it as you will, it never runs dry.

It hasn't run dry for the monks and sometimes at evening maybe the Mysterious Female comes and meditates with them. Predisposing them to sink into womb-breathing, predisposing them to an effortless return from yu wei to wu yei, the cantor sings:

> Learning consists in adding to one's stock day by day;
> The practice of Tao consists in subtracting day by day,
> Subtracting and yet again subtracting
> Till one has reached inactivity.
> But by this very inactivity
> Everything can be activated.

Afterwards, lying down to sleep for the night, an old monk says, now I'll let the pines do my thinking for me. He paints them, these pines. Lost to himself after hours looking at them, he paints them not as he sees them but as they see themselves. His work done, he closes his eyes and lets Tao speak:

> Heaven is eternal and Earth everlasting.
> How come they be so? It is because they do not foster their own lives;
> That is why they live so long.
> Therefore the Sage
> Puts himself in the background, but is always to the fore,
> Remains outside, but is always there.
> Is it not just because he does not strive for any personal end
> That all his personal ends are fulfilled?

And the dark gorge below the Monastery—it's as if, the mist momentarily dispersed, the Earth was showing us the doorway of the Mysterious

Female, the womb from which, eternally, heaven and earth spring.

Looking up into that gorge the man crossing the causeway will surely remember the Way and its Power:

> He who knows the male yet cleaves to what is female
> Becomes like a ravine, receiving all things under heaven.
> And being such a ravine.
> He knows all the time a power that he never calls upon in vain,
> This is returning to the state of infancy.
> He who knows the white yet cleaves to the black
> Becomes the standard by which all things are tested,
> And being such a standard
> He has all the time a power that never errs,
> He returns to the Limitless.
> He who knows glory, yet cleaves to ignominy,
> Becomes like the Valley that receives into it all things under heaven.
> And being such a valley
> He has all the time a power that suffices;
> He returns to the state of the uncarved block.

It is early spring in the mountains behind you, Mona. You've been blocking the view for a long time, Mona. It is time to come down from your high, humanist chair, Mona. It is time to make contact with the mountains you have turned your back to, Mona, for

> In Tao the only motion is returning.

It is time to return, Mona.
That little man on the causeway, that's Lao Tze.
Singing his song with him, you can cross with him into

Early Spring

Singing his song with him, you can cross with him into

Tao

Great Tao is like a boat that drifts;
It can go this way; It can go that.
The ten thousand creatures owe their existence to it and it does not disown them.
Yet having produced them, it does not take possession of them.
Tao though it covers the ten thousand things like a garment
Makes no claim to be master over them.
Therefore it may be called Lowly.

The ten thousand creatures obey it,
Though they know not that they have a master;
Therefore it is called the Great.
So too the Sage just because he never at any time makes
A show of greatness in fact achieves greatness.

> We will miss you, Mona.
> We will miss you, Spirit of the Valley.
> We will miss you, Mysterious Female.
> Out of the exile into which we conjured you,
> We will follow you.
> Out of the exile into which we conjured you,
> We will follow you
> into
> Early Spring

RAGNAROK AND GINNUNGAGAP

We say of ourselves that we live in a world. But it would perhaps be truer to say that we live in a tale told.

> A tale told by Aztecs,
> A tale told by Maoris,
> A talc told by Hapiru,
> A tale told by persons who call themselves scientists.

The tale told that Vikings lived in had, as all such tales have, a beginning, a middle and an end.

The end as they imagined it was stupendous. They called it Ragnarok. To announce it three cocks crow:

> A cock called Fjalar crows in the birdwood,
> A cock called Goldcomb crows within hearing of Valhalla,
> A cock called Rustred crows at the bars of Hel.

And it begins:

> And now it is
> Axe-time and sword-time,
> Wind-time and wolf-time

It is time when, weary of restraining him in its depths, the Earth yawns, releasing Loki and his hordes into their hunger and thirst and lust for universal destruction.

It is time when, bursting the chains that bind him, and running free, Fenriswolf opens his mouth and with it, foaming already, he takes the measure of earth and sky. And he howls, and he howls, and he howls, and the third time he howls he has it, the third time he howls he knows he has it, he has their measure.

Everywhere now there is war. To exist now, to be now, is to be a war. There is war in all, and between all, the nine worlds that are in Yggdrasil, the World Tree. There is war between cosmos and chaos.

In the end there is nothing, neither cosmos nor chaos. There is only Ginnungagap, the Great Yawn, the Great Emptiness.

> It is a mysterious Emptiness, though,
> It is an Emptiness that somehow seeds itself,
> In time it will be a pregnant Emptiness,
> In time a new Universe will be born from it.

A tale told. A tale that sheltered Vikings on the high wild seas between the Faroe Islands and Iceland, sheltered them and housed them on the no man's nowhere of icebergs and fogs between Iceland and Newfoundland. And who knows! Echoes of it might yet haunt the Viking foundations of Dublin.

We don't, therefore, need to import such words as Ragnarok and Ginnungagap into Ireland. They, and their cognates, were spoken and heard beside the Black Pool long before the Germanic dialects of the Angles and Saxons had evolved into English. They are old Dublin words. And the sibyl, the spakona, whom the Vikings set up and enthroned in Clonmacnoise, she too might have spoken them, speaking them there at the monastic heart of the country. They are Irish words. It is time, maybe, that we reclaimed them.

I do not know whether or not the universe undergoes a Ragnarok. And if it does I do not know whether it undergoes it the way that Nordic spakonas and volvas say that it does.

Certain it is, though, that there are persons who undergo an inner Ragnarok, a psychic Ragnarok. In the course of undergoing it, shaken now at their foundations, they come to see that, conscious and unconscious, psyche in them is an eclipse. An eclipse asleep. An eclipse awake. An eclipse of thinking, imagining, hearing, seeing, touch, taste and smell.

It's a seeing, it's a realization, that shatters us, deeply, in our deepest, self-conscious foundations.

It is now a time of great woe.

It is I-am-sore-amazed time.
It is I-am-sore-broken-in-the-place-of-dragons time.
It is I-am-a-brother-to-dragons-and-a-companion-to-owls time.
It is wide-breaking-in-of-waters time.
It is dark-night-of-the-soul-time.
It is passive-dark-night-of-the-spirit time.

It is time to listen to St John of the Cross. He can speak to us, he can comfort us, he has been through it, he has left logbooks, the best there are.

No rock of faith presenting itself, it is time for the abyss of faith.

It is time for total surrender to Divine Good shepherding.

I cannot find you, God. And the reason I cannot find you is simple: it is with that in me that eclipses you that I seek you.

> I can't sense you or know you or name you, God.
> I can't find you inside me or in the world outside,
> but I still want to be your servant. God.

Our faith is abyssal now. Our praying is abyssal: may I be as out of your way awake God as I am in dreamless sleep.

Our final homecoming isn't our doing. It is God's doing.

Ragnarok and Ginnungagap are words that have meaning on our way home.

They are words we might speak again in Clonmacnoise. Born as they are out of our initial Job and Jonah terror they aren't, in the end, appropriate words. The good words are

> Dark Night of the Soul
> and
> Divine Ungrund.

So ask not for whom Fjalar crows. Ask not for whom Goldcomb crows. Ask not for whom Rustred crows.

> They crow for you.

They crow to remind you of the glorious homecoming that awaits you.

THE THERANTHROPIC

Time was when to voyage in the Mediterranean was to voyage in the folk imaginations of many peoples. Sometimes, therefore, in spite of the best efforts of the best master mariners, a voyage would become an odyssey. It isn't only subjectively that we cross from one to another state, from the state of waking say to the state of dreaming. Unobserved by us until it has happened, the sea we are sailing in can lapse or cross into some other state too. If it is on land we are, and we are on horseback, the horse will know. Coming to a standstill, refusing, the horse will give warning.

Time was when Epitherses, a man in good standing with everyone who knew him, boarded a boat carrying passengers and freight to Italy. 'It was already evening', we are told,

when, near the Echinades Islands, the wind dropped, and the ship drifted near Paxi. Almost everybody was awake, and a good many had not finished their after-dinner wine. Suddenly from the island of Paxi was heard the voice of someone loudly calling Thamus, so that all were amazed. Thamus was an Egyptian pilot, not known by name even to many on board. Twice he was called and made no reply, but the third time he answered; and the caller, raising his voice, said, 'When you come opposite to Palodes, announce that Great Pan is dead.' On hearing this, all, said Epitherses, were astonished and reasoned among themselves whether it was better to carry out the order or to refuse to meddle and let the matter go. Under the circumstances, Thamus made up his mind that if there should be a breeze he would sail past and keep quiet, but no wind and a smooth sea about the place, he would announce what he had heard. So, when he came opposite Palodes, and there was neither wind nor wave, Thamus, from the stern, looking toward the land, said the words as he had heard them: 'Great Pan is dead.' Even before he had finished, there was a great cry of lamentation, not of one person, but of many, mingled with exclamations of amazement.

It brings another annunciation to mind, the annunciation which Christians celebrate ringing their church bells, eighteen times each time, three times a day:

And in the sixth month the angel Gabriel was sent from God unto a city of Galilee, named Nazareth, to a virgin espoused to a man whose name was Joseph, of the house of David; and the virgin's name was Mary. And the angel came in unto her and said, Hail, thou that art highly favoured, the Lord is with thee: Blessed art thou among women. And when she saw him, she was troubled at his saying, and cast in her mind what manner of salutation this should be. And the angel said unto her, Fear not Mary: for thou hast found favour with God. And, behold, thou shalt conceive in thy womb, and bring forth a son and shalt call his name Jesus. He shall be great, and shall be called the son of the Highest: and the Lord God shall give unto him the throne of his father David; and he shall reign over the house of Jacob forever: and of his kingdom there shall be no end. Then said Mary unto the angel, how shall this be, seeing that I know not a man? And the angel answered and said unto her, the Holy Ghost shall come upon thee, and the power of the Highest shall overshadow thee, therefore also that holy thing which shall be born of thee shall be called the Son of God. And, behold, thy cousin Elizabeth, she hath also conceived a son in her old age, and this is the sixth month with her, who was called barren. For with God nothing shall be impossible. And Mary said, behold the handmaid of the Lord: be it unto me according to thy word. And the angel departed from her.

Thamus, an Egyptian pilot, announcing the death of a God. Gabriel, an angel, announcing the birth of a God.

The Death, and the Birth, each in its uniquely awful way, is awful trouble. Hearing a lion roar behind me, how can I not be instantly in a paralysis of terror?

How can I, hearing the sermon on the mount, not be earthquaked, mindquaked, lifequaked—hearing it, how can I not be quaked in depths below life and mind I had hitherto no inklings of?

> The Birth troubles me,
> The Death troubles me.

Looking back across the Christian centuries, we can now see, without polemical intent, that the death of Pan was, in effect, the death of the theranthropic. More precisely, but also more perniciously perhaps, it was the death of all religiously benign perceptions of the theranthropic. It was only in demonized form, it was only as devil, that the theranthropic survived our conversion to Christian cultus and creed.

This was, was it not, a calamity?

However anatomically improbable or odd it might be, the theranthropic, benignly conceived, is, I think, a necessary reality.

Given the rootedness of phylogenetic aliveness and life in us, it is psychologically and religiously necessary.

The theranthropic doesn't have to exist actually in order to exist psychologically.

Religiously and psychologically, it is desirable that the theranthropic should exist, therefore it exists.

Cow-horned, Hathor is.
Falcon-headed, Horus is.
Athena is. She is owl-eyed.
Anatomically horse-haunted, Demeter is.
Goat-groined, goat-legged, smelling of goat, Pan is.

> *The Roman empire stood appalled,*
> *It dropped the reins of peace and war*
> *When that Fierce Virgin and her Star*
> *Out of the fabulous darkness called.*

The coming of Christianity meant other things too.

It meant the going away, into hellish, if temporary exile, of the theranthropic. Hathor, Horus, Athena, Epona, Cernunnos, Demeter, Pan: divinities all, all of them theranthropic, all of them like the Children of Israel, gone away, gone down into songless, into mirthless, captivity in the Christian underworld:

> By the rivers of the Christian underworld, there we set down, yea, we wept, when we remembered Egypt, Greece and Gaul. We hanged our harps and our Pan pipes upon the willows in the midst thereof. For there they that carried us away required of us a song: And they that wasted us required of us mirth, saying, sing us one of your country's songs. But how, we asked, how can we sing our songs in a strange land?

A land that isn't hospitable to the theranthropic is a strange land.

Was Crete a strange land? Pasiphae, its queen, having mated with a bull from the sea, gave birth to a bull-shouldered, bull-headed child. She suppressed it, suppressing the phylogenetic in herself, exiling it to an underworld labyrinth from which it couldn't emerge.

Parvati, Goddess wife of the God Shiva, didn't seek to suppress her elephant-headed child. She welcomed him, she mothered him, she called him Ganesha. And now, among Hindus, he is a lovely God, he is a good God. having an elephant's intelligence and strength, he removes obstacles, inner and outer. Obstacles to enlightenment and release from samsara, them he will also sometimes remove.

Crete, it would seem, wasn't hospitable to the theranthropic. For psyche and society, the consequences were woeful. Now and henceforward, it wasn't only geologically that Crete was an earthquake zone.

Crete and Christendom.

In Christendom, there is a psalm we recite. It isn't, however, as dazed and bewildered Cretan survivors that we recite it. Vesperly, in the plenteous serenity of Gregorian Chant, we speak:

> *O God, thou hast cast us off,*
> *Thou hast scattered us,*
> *Thou hast been displeased:*
> *O turn thyself to us again.*
>
> *Thou hast made the earth to tremble,*
> *Thou hast broken it:*
> *Heal the breaches thereof,*
> *For it shaketh.*
>
> *Thou hast shewed thy people hard things:*
> *Thou hast made us to drink*
> *the wine of astonishment.*

Suppressed, the phylogenetic in us will sometimes build and gather and grow to such an intensity that, release, when it comes, is seismic, to psyche and society.

Coping with nature in us isn't easy. Coping with all Africa and its prodigies, in us as impulse and energy, isn't easy.

I sometimes imagine that it is easier for a Hindu than it is for a Christian.

Hinduism, I imagine, is religiously more hospitable to more of what I am than Christianity is. It is more hospitable to more of what we are phylogenetically, chakrally and abyssally.

Hinduism is religiously hospitable to the awful, to the terrible, in its Goddesses and Gods.

Religiously hospitable to the bhairavic in its Goddesses and Gods, would it not also, I wonder, be religiously hospitable to the bhairavic in me?

Hospitable to Ganesha, would it not also be hospitable to the theranthropic in me?

The abhaya mudra of Shiva Nataraja—how deeply into me does it reach? Will it be there before me, comforting me, in every deep and depth I come into going inward into Divine Ground? When, like Job, I awaken to the phylogenetic in me, will it be there?

When, like Jonah, I awaken to the abyssal in me, will it be there, comforting me, telling me to fear nor, telling me Tehom is Turiya?

Job was in trouble.

Daniel was in trouble.

Having crossed the Kedron into Gethsemane, Jesus was in trouble. He was sore amazed.

When all that was phylogenetically archaic in them was bhairavically awake in them, Job and Jesus were in trouble. Something more awful than Hell, maybe, was naked before them. Something more awful than Destruction had no covering.

Can Christianity watch with Job?

Not speaking biblical platitudes at him, as his comforters did, can it watch with him?

Can anyone who hasn't lived the theranthropic, can anyone who hasn't, in himself or in herself, suffered it, watch with him?

Can a religion which isn't hospitable to the theranthropic watch with him? Can a religion which has excluded it, demonized it, damned it, watch with him?

Crossing the Kedron with Him, can Christianity watch with Jesus? Can the religion he founded watch with him? Or will He, coming to it there in Gethsemane, find it asleep?

Crossing the Kedron, Christianity grows.

It is by crossing the Kedron with its Founder, it is by watching with Him in Gethsemane, it is by watching with Him on Golgotha, that Christianity grows.

In its willingness to cross the Kedron and watch with its Founder, in its willingness to move, while watching, from Evangel to Evangelanta. There are many religions, including itself in its mystical tradition, that can help Christianity.

Could it be that, even now, the Eagle, the Ox, the Lion and the Man are Magi journeying cowards an Evangelantic understanding of the Triduum Sacrum?

And it wouldn't be impious, would it, to assume that our biblical understanding of things crossed the Kedron with Jesus? It wouldn't be impious, would it, to imagine that it underwent an immense purification and dereliction? And we can, can't we, allow ourselves to hope that waiting somewhere to be found and recognized there is a Risen Bible?

Crossing the Kedron, Christianity grows.

So, when you come opposite a coast of it

announce, calling out into Christendom, that Christianity lives,

announce, calling out, that
Christianity is hospitable,
announce, calling out, that
Christianity will watch,
announce, calling out, that
watching with its Founder in Gethsemane and on Golgotha
Christianity
will grow
will grow
will grow
will grow.

And when you come opposite Palodes, when there is no wind and the sea is smooth,

announce, calling out, that Pan lives,

announce, calling out, that like Hanuman
Pan has a beautiful bright shrine
to
Urddhva Vahini
in
His shaggy, now shining, theranthropic chest.

KATHODOS

In a funerary papyrus of the Ptolemaic period, there is a vignette of Horemheb adoring the Gods of the Caverns. As we would expect, some of the Gods are theranthropic. Having human bodies, they nonetheless have animal heads.

When did we last go down into these caverns? And when, standing before them as Horemheb does, did we last give homage to these Gods?

And is it time now again that someone going down will be our Horemheb, offering them, hands raised in homage, our pious remembrance of them?

Theranthropic ourselves in so many of our instincts and energies and impulses, don't we, therefore, still need theranthropic Gods?

Did the Children of Israel leave Egypt too soon?

And did we, northern Europeans, did we walk away from Cernunnos, the Horned God, too soon?

> Mary isn't ever Bhairavi,
> Jesus isn't ever Bhairava,
> Our God isn't ever Pashupati.

A consequence of this, I think, is a sense, unconscious perhaps, of psychological exclusion and destitution. My animal impulses, energies and instincts aren't affirmed for me in any Imago Dei, they aren't mirrored affirmatively back to me from Iconostasis, Alchemists' Window or Belle Verrière. This is unfortunate, sometimes hugely so, for all those instincts in me which are excluded from the White Mass might begin to imagine and participate in a Black Mass, and this, were it to happen, would be a most dreadful, a most perilous, response. Like the sorcerer's apprentice, we might be able, having found the formula, to summon the spirits, but we mightn't, having entertained them, be able to send them away.

Have we need in Christendom for a Lingaraja Temple?

Have we spiritual, psychological need in Judaism, Islam and Christendom for a Bhuvaneshvar, a Kandariya Mahadeo?

Did we leave the Land of Goshen too soon?

Did we enter the fierce austerities, the fierce Zin deserts of Cartesian cogito too soon?

Then came the children of Israel, even the whole congregation, into the desert of Zin in the first month, and Miriam died there, and was buried there. And there was no water for the congregation: and they gathered themselves together against Moses and against Aaron. And the people chode with Moses, and spake, saying. Would God that we had died where our brethren died before the Lord! And why have ye brought up the congregation of the Lord into this wilderness, that we and our cattle should die there? And wherefore have ye made us to come up out of Egypt to bring us in unto this evil place? it is no place of seed, or of figs, or of vines, or of pomegranates: neither is there any water to drink.

Moses struck the rock and water flowed forth.

But while Moses was on the summit, talking to a totally transcendent God, the people below, standing afar off, gave their jewellery to Aaron, he melted it down, and out of the furnace came an old Egyptian God, theriomorphic, but golden.

And the people remembered the fish which they did eat in Egypt freely. They remembered the cucumbers, and the melons, and the leeks.

Then Moses came down from the Mountain. The commandment was shadowless: 'Thou shalt nor make unto thee any graven image, or any likeness of anything that is in heaven above, or that is in the earth beneath, or that is in the water under the earth.'

I imagine an Aaron who, shaking dust and ashes on his head, climbs to the Bright Summit and pleads with Our God, argues with Our God, about this.

How dreadful are these heights! How dreadful it is on these heights to speak to our God, to plead with Him here and to argue with Him. Is it a good commandment, God? Given who we are and what we are, is it a wise commandment, God? Are we able for it, God?

In Judaism, Islam and Christendom the commandment has been welcomed, it has prevailed. In Judaism, Islam and Christendom we have, as a consequence, no Book of Underworld Caverns, no Book of Underworld Gates. We believe we don't need them.

On the night of Good Friday Hell was harrowed once and for all, Christians believe, and we therefore have no need of an Amduat, a Book of What Is in the Underworld, a Book whose words of power would speak themselves for us in the Underworld, a Book that would open underworld gates for us, a Book whose words would appease and mollify the theriomorphic and theranthropic Numina of the Underworld, a Book whose words of power would walk with us, would see us through.

The unregenerate depths of our psyches have been harrowed, we believe. We have need of no such books. To die is to sleep in Christ, in his victory over sin and death. On the last day we will rise in Christ. Put ye on Christ, is the Christian answer.

Egyptians put on Osiris. Having died, a person put Him on, put on his exact image and likeness. So perfect and complete was the likeness that the dead person was referred to as the Osiris.

A long and perilous journey awaited the Osiris, Egyptians believed. A journey through Underworld Caverns, through Underworld Gates, the first Gate called the All-Devouring.

In the vignette of him, which we referred to earlier, Horemheb is in the Caverns worshipping Gods we have long since ignored, Gods our jealous God forbids us to acknowledge, or homage.

But if Hell was harrowed, if on the night of Good Friday a voice called out in the Underworld saying: Lift up your heads, O ye gates; and be ye lift up, ye everlasting doors; and the King of glory shall come in—if Hell was harrowed, if the unregenerate depths of our psyches were harrowed, why then are we still so frightened of them, why are we so troubled by them, why are so many of us unable to integrate them, why are so many of us fugitives from our own natures, refugees who take refuge from awareness of self in the self forgetfulness of objective preoccupation?

'There is all Africa and her prodigies in us.'

'In us is all whatsoever the Sun shines upon, in us are Heaven and Hell, and also all the deeps.'

'O the mind, mind has mountains, cliffs of fall frightful, sheer, no-man-fathomed: hold them cheap may who ne'er hung there.'

Anodos too soon.

Exodus too soon.

Not all of what I am emerged, in my anodos, into ego consciousness. Not all of what I inwardly am walked dryshod with me through the sea of my psyche into the desert clarities of my European, Cartesian cogito.

Maybe a kathodos is called for.

And maybe it wasn't because there was no room in the inn that Mary gave birth to her child in a stable. And maybe it wasn't because of Herod's published intentions that Mary took her infant down into Egypt with her.

Maybe Mary knew that every great going forward involves a return.

Maybe a kathodos is called for.

And maybe setting out we should sing: 'O the mind, mind has mountains, cliffs of fall frightful, sheer, no-man-fathomed: hold them cheap may who ne'er hung there.'

The mind has mountains. And maybe the Ancient Egyptians knew two of them: west of them on the horizon, Manu, the red-desert mountain into which, serenely, the Sun descends every evening; and east of them, on the horizon, Bakhu, the beautiful fervent mountain out of which, every rooming, the Sun reappears.

Between Manu in the west and Bakhu in the east there is, Egyptians believed, an immense, immensely perilous. Underworld journey.

'Let not the pit shut her mouth upon me,' says the Sun that goes down, serenely, into it.

'Fearfulness and trembling are come upon me, and horror hath overwhelmed me.'

'Hell is naked before me and destruction hath no covering.' I am come before 'the king of terrors'.

I am 'sore amazed'. I am 'sore broken in the place of dragons'. Or am I? Have I only dreamed it?

In the morning, beautiful and victorious, the Sun reappears. Its name now, its morning name, is Horakhty, Horus of the Horizon.

And maybe a morning will come when Horakhty won't rise alone. Maybe all the Astonishments and Terrors and Wonders of the Underworld will rise with Him. Maybe Ammit and Apep and Sobk and Mafdet and Wepwawet will rise with Horus. Maybe all our instincts, all our repressions, will rise.

Maybe all that we are in our Underworlds will rise.

It is Easter Morning in our natures now.

> Risen with Horus are we,
> Of the eastern horizon are we,
> Glorious are we.
> And all is well,
> And all is well,
> And all manner of Underworld thing is well.

A SONGLINE OF THE GREEK DREAMTIME

Feeding the sacred Snake in a room below ground in his house Sophocles was when he heard a knocking on his door.

Hearing it also, the Snake coiled rearing his head, his tongue a child of lightning.

Must be Socrates, Sophocles thought, drawing back the bolt.

Strangely, the door opened in a way it had never opened before. It had opened, he feared, into a dangerous depth of himself and his world.

Come in, he said, greatly surprised to see who was there. It wasn't from his everyday self he said it.

It's for the Snake, she said, opening a bag and showing him three live frogs.

It's the door directly opposite, he said, pointing to a steep descent of stone steps.

Five steps down, she was underground.

Not an ordinary votary, Sophocles thought.

No. Not an ordinary human being either.

In her nature somewhere, somewhere out of view in it, she is injured, hugely.

And there it was again, the seeing he couldn't get used to, but had to submit to, momentarily losing his everyday sense of himself.

Like the Pythia of Apollo at Delphi, Sophocles had recently been favoured with a terrible gift, the gift of seeing what eyes cannot see, of knowing what mind cannot know.

Having no choice in the matter, he was Pythia not to Apollo but to Asclepius, the God who, in his form as a black Snake, resided underground in his house.

To begin with, his being an age of reason, he resisted. But, like it or not, the ancient dark way of ages more ancient than Athens had claimed him.

She has been injured, yes. That anyone can see. But there is something more. She is God-injured.

God-injured like Leda.

God-injured like Io.

Could be lines in a new choric ode, he thought.

> God-injured like Leda
> God-injured like Io

Such lines in normal times might well be the initial inspiration for a new play.

But not now.

Now was no time for writing.

A play about God-injured Io might well have something to say to a fate-injured, plague-injured people.

Aeschylus, who fought at Marathon, he brought the Erinyes to transformation at Areopagus Rock.

But to what transforming Rock or Grove could I bring Plague?

And wouldn't it be a sin against the ancient way of the world to attempt to do so?

And what else but what they did could the people have done? Going to Epidaurus, they came home, coming in solemn procession, with Asclepius, the healing God.

And what else but what I did could I have done? There being no temple, not yet, for the God, I offered him my house.

No, he thought, I'm not Aeschylus. I cannot bring the ancient way of the world to Areopagus Rock.

No, I didn't fight at Marathon.

Judged at sixteen to be the most beautiful boy in Athens, I was chosen to lead the victory procession.

An old man now, I feed the ancient Snake. Sometimes underground in my house I am Pythia to the ancient Snake. And that to the bright young men in the agora who have taken their stand with reason and logic, that to them is a relapse into ancient error. Proud that their fathers had fought for civilization in a Battle of Marathon outside the walls, they are determined to fight for it in an even more critical Battle of Marathon within the walls. In their eyes I am the autochthonous Xerxes. And that indeed is a strange fate for the beautiful boy who, almost sixty years ago, led the victory procession.

Xerxes within the walls—if that, as they see me, is who I am, then so be it. It is an anagnorisis Oedipus, if he could hear of it, would smile at.

How many times, he wondered, would he have to defend himself against the accusation that he hadn't in his plays released humanity, as Aeschylus had released Orestes, from the delusions and dooms of the archaic imagination, from the delusions and dooms of the old bad dream?

But no. He couldn't do it. He couldn't or wouldn't cross over from the fierce pharmacy of the theatre to the pleasantries and ironies of the agora. A syllogism, he once said to Socrates, is no bulwark against the Bull from the sea. And to Aeschylus he said, a Bull from the sea that walks to Areopagus Rock in a play won't necessarily walk to Areopagus Rock in reality.

He remembered the morning he sat alone in the theatre of Dionysus under the Acropolis. He had no particular reason for going there but, finding himself there, he fell to thinking of what he had seen there, fifty suppliant women, each of them hiding a bridal knife; Iphigenia, the daughter of Agamemnon and Clytemnestra, sacrificed to Artemis on the shore at Aulis; Agamemnon murdered by his wife Clytemnestra; Clytemnestra murdered by her son Orestes; Oedipus killing Laius, his father; Oedipus marrying Jocasta, his mother; Oedipus gouging his eyes out; two sons of Oedipus, sons who were also his brothers, both of them lying dead. The one outside and the other inside the seventh gate of Thebes.

Sitting there, trying to remember some lines from a satyr play, it surprised him and half-horrified him to see a snake emerging at the dead centre of the orchestra. It was a black snake. Raising himself up, he sipped the air in a lordly way and as though finding human history as bloody as he expected it to be, he turned again to his hole, slipped back down and was gone, leaving Sophocles with a sense of awful election.

And now, nineteen years later, Plague was having a kind of victory procession in the city, and Plague being utterly democratic, a person didn't have to be beautiful and a boy to be chosen to walk at the head of it. And Plague had a face. And Sophocles had seen it, on a corpse stretched out on the side of the sacred road to Eleusis. Sunbaked, it simmered at open eye and open mouth. It was like no mask he had ever imagined, or seen at the theatre. And if, in the interests of reality, someone were to sacrilegiously set up this corpse on stage, then all other masks, whatever the play, would be masks of shame, masks ashamed of their own helplessness, masks ashamed of their own theatricality, masks ashamed of their own masquerade.

Daring to do no more by way of obsequies than shake dust on the corpse, Sophocles went his way to Eleusis but like it or not, he had to recognize that a play was already writing itself in his mind.

Drawing near a place so holy, he wished he could suffocate it, but he couldn't and so, allowing it life, he turned off the road and sat on a rock.

It was a simple idea. Melpomene, the tragic Muse, is walking the road to Eleusis. Seeing the corpse, she sees how utterly beyond the aesthetic and redemptive reach of metaphor it is, how utterly beyond the aesthetic and redemptive reach of myth it is, and now she is the doomed heroine of her own doomed art. In a horrifying access of prophetic vision, she sees the theatre at Athens returning to nature, she sees goats grazing its sides. Standing in that hollow, grassy place, standing where Clytemnestra stood, where Oedipus stood, where Agave stood, she hears the sound of a pissing goat, but no sound at all, no whisper or echo, of the old goat-song.

And that's where Sophocles had second thoughts.
Was having them still.

He must write plays. But why there, at the dead heart of the orchestra? Why was it there that the God of healing rose and sipped the air? Air smelling of the pollutions and murders of the House of Atreus. Air smelling of the pollutions and murders of the House of Laius. Air smelling of the pollutions and murders of Mycenaean times. But since, in the theatre, history cedes ground to myth, Sophocles knew that the pollutions and murders of Mycenaean times are the pollutions and murders of modern times, of our times, of all times.

He must sing the goat-song.
But how or where?
Was Aeschylus right, after all?
Are there cracks in Areopagus Rock?
Are there cracks in reality? Cracks into which we can sow our yearnings? Can the roots of our yearnings become the roots of reality? Is the real responsive to religion? If we sing it well, will the mountains sing our song? Is reality with us in ways we haven't allowed for? Is it with us in depths of

ourselves we haven't often come into? Of only one thing he was sure: it was there, where every year we enact our most awful dooms, that the God of healing rose. And how, having that God in his house, how, being Pythia to that God, could he ever again write a play like Oedipus Tyrannus.

At every turn in his arguments with himself, Sophocles encountered Aeschylus.

Aeschylus didn't only fight for a new humanity outside the walls. He fought for it inside the walls. Coming home from Marathon, he led humanity in an anodos from an order of doom to an order of freedom. He led us from an order in which reality doomed us to an order in which reality wished us well.

Sitting there, waiting for the woman to come up from below ground in his house, Sophocles imagined the successful anodos of Persephone, he imagined the failed anodos of Eurydice.

Aeschylus, he could see, was the Orpheus of our day. Going back and down, he sang his goat-song at the roots of human history, at the roots of the human mind.

Finding them to be red roots, he didn't despair.

Even if, at the end of it, we only arrive at ground occupied at the beginning, we must forever have the courage to set out on a new anodos. And how great a blessing it is that someone once imagined that he could lead us as far as Areopagus Rock.

Sophocles wondered.

Could this anodos, called the Oresteia, be anything more than a pious wish?

Aeschylus had certainly led us from one to another state of mind. But whether reality would re-form itself so as to correspond to this new state of mind, that remained to be seen.

Could it be that reality, internal and external, are a single state of mind? And if this were so, wouldn't it then follow that anything happening anywhere in it is happening in all of it?

Could it be that we can ascend into hope? Into the hope that, in our deepest yearnings, we will not be eternally contradicted by an eternally contradicting order of things.

One thing Sophocles had to concede: it wasn't in a mood of impious, Promethean rebellion that Aeschylus led us out. This time, walking ahead of us, he walked piously, pouring libations. Thinking of this, Sophocles concluded that there is freedom from and freedom with. There is the freedom that would put all things under our feet and the freedom that is willing to accord to reality the deciding vote, the final say.

Sophocles had argued his way to an act of faith. And even though he knew that to do so would show it to have scant regard for the facts of our situation, he was nonetheless willing to formulate it: there is a way of living in and with reality that enables it to work with us.

He would join the anodos into a new way of being in the world. Pouring a libation at the beginning, at the mild-point, and at the end, he would write a sequel to the play in which he had doomed Oedipus. That more than fifty years later, would be his Battle of Marathon within the walls. It would be his Battle of Marathon within his own mind. Within him, in the shape of inherited, ancient attitudes, was the native Xerxes he must fight.

If Aeschylus could lead the old, doomed humanity to Areopagus Rock so, in a final capitulation to hope, would he lead the old, doomed humanity to Colonus.

It would be a kind of expiation. Where, more than fifty years ago, the victory procession was led by a beautiful boy, it would now be led by Oedipus, the old blind King, club-footed and bad in the walk, who, within himself, was carrying the pollutions of the ages.

Having grown up beside it, Sophocles knew the Grove at Colonus. To look at, it was as ordinary a wood as you would ever hope to seek fire-faggots in, and yet you only had to come close to it and it gave you the shivers. Its very ordinariness gave you the shivers. Indeed, there were old men who claimed that it gave itself the shivers. Why else, when there was no breeze, would an oak tree tremble in every leaf?

Here, if you are wise, his father cold Sophocles, you will go beyond everything in yourself that you have every relied on and you will pour a libation. Here, he said, your willingness to call will become your willingness to hear the God who calls. A willingness to hear must precede your ability to hear.

In his new play about him, Sophocles would travel with Oedipus into that willingness.

There he said to himself, speaking audibly now:

> There Hercules lets fall his club.
> There Orpheus lets fall his lyre.
> There Socrates lets fall his confidence in dialectics.
> There, at this great threshold, our goat-song falls silent.
> There, at this great threshold, anodos becomes exaltation.

Living in his house with a god was simplifying Sophocles. In one way it was simplifying him, in another way it was threatening to sunder him, to schism him. The challenge was, could he stand in the presence of the god and not fall into a higher and lower nature? Could he stand in the presence of the god and, more than ever, be a unity of nature? He knew what Socrates thought. He knew what Plato thought. And he himself sometimes thought that he was, in this, giving himself a reason to hold on, for a little while yet, to his Pan-pipes.

It was a night of almost mortuary silence in the city. But to come to know how deceptive a silence that was, he would only have to go out and walk under the open windows of his own or any other street, and then he would hear how troubled was the sleep of a people who, even now, believed themselves gifted beyond all others.

Three nights earlier, five doors down from him, Sophocles had closed the eyes of a sculptor who, on the day that Plague beckoned to him, was putting the finishing touches to his section of the Panathenaic Procession.

The procession he joined was Panathenaic too, but the maiden who walked at the head of it had no mantle to bring down the dark road to Hades, had no peplos to bring down the dark road to Persephone.

> In Athens
> Plague and Parthenon
>
> In the wood in
> Erinyes whining and nightingales singing.

Will things ever be otherwise for humanity? At one level of our being, and that the level we mostly live from, is that our lot?

> Plague pulling us down
> The Parthenon drawing us up.

And Heraclitus telling us that the way up and the way down are one way.

Listening to himself, Sophocles realized that he was sinking back into the old rut. But that didn't surprise him, or disappoint him. He had long ago accepted that altered ideas didn't always mean an altered mind or an altered heart. Even when he was still a young man, he only had to sit down to write and instantly he was old, in the way that our oldest instincts are old, in the way even that the hills are old. If the hills didn't have a say in what he said, he'd be saying what the young men in the stoa were everyday saying. If the hills didn't have a say in what he wrote, he wouldn't have written at all.

Isn't it time, he thought, that the Maidens of Athens made a peplos for Persephone?

Isn't it time that we sculpted a Panathenaic Procession on the pediment of the Parthenon, a procession that at one point turns from the light of day and goes underground?

As he saw it, a procession going down with a peplos for Persephone is a procession going down with a peplos for those depths of ourselves which, independently of our minds, our myths remember and make safe.

Sophocles was well aware that myths are hospitable to our depths in a way very often that our minds are not, and that's why he continued to be so opposed to so much that was happening in the stoa and also of late in the theatre.

Bringing an argument he one day had with Euripides to an end, he said it is in myths more than in houses that we are housed. It is in myths that our instinctive depths are housed, and if they aren't so housed, you can be sure that somewhere along the road we are walking, and it doesn't matter whether it is an ascending or descending road, somewhere along it they are waiting in ambush for us. And that's why on the way to heaven and to hell, the flattest road is precipitous.

And that's why also the nine stone steps in his house were, for Sophocles, a necessary reverence between him and his underworld. And by underworld he initially meant all that was archaic in himself. The Snake was archaic. A woman, and she a priestess, feeding three live frogs to him was archaic. But Sophocles had long ago accepted, from deep within himself he had accepted, that the Snake is as contemporary as the most recent Socratic syllogism.

The syllogism and the Snake

It was the old difficulty.

In the age of the syllogism Sophocles had opened his house to the Snake. And the nine stone seeps didn't exist as a distance between him and his depths. They existed as an act of reverence and humility, as an outward sign that he would never go down seeking to dominate, to plunder or to aggrandize. They existed as a sign that it is prayerfully, pouring a libation, that he would go down.

Going down, Sophocles would be a choephoros.

Of this he was sure: as much as they needed a strong city wall, Athenians needed a ritual that would be their communal correlative of his nine stone steps. And to enact it in his honour would he hoped be an acceptable offering of appeasement and atonement to the Snake who rose sipping the air at the heart of the orchestra.

An act of appeasement and atonement for having gone, sword in hand, into the primeval world.

An act of appeasement and atonement for having gone, sword in hand, into the labyrinth.

An act of appeasement and atonement for having gone, sword in hand, into the underworld.

Thinking he had come to terms with what had emerged, Sophocles went to his door and with altogether more ease and with altogether more hope than he had ever done so before, he looked up at the Parthenon.

And that's how his next play might end, he thought.

Invoking the help of the healing God in his house as he wrote it, it might end with humanity looking up.

Coming back to his chair, he knew he had no choice but to sit it out.

When he awoke she was sitting opposite him.

'How long have I slept?' he asked.

'It only matters that you slept like a man who has come into his peace,' she replied.

'I was beginning to think—before I fell asleep, that is, I was beginning to think that I'd have to call upon Orpheus to go down and bring you back'. The suggestion of savagery in his voice was a way of telling her that, in his case, any talk about a final entry into final peace was premature.

'You are God-injured, aren't you,' he said. 'You are God-injured like Io, God-injured like Leda. Or worse. You are God-injured like Hippolytus, God-injured like Actaeon. Looking at you I can almost see the rearing horses. Looking at you I can almost hear the howling hounds.'

'You mustn't aggrandize me into your goat-song or into any of the archetypes dramatists are so blinded by,' she said, a little savagely, returning the compliment.

'Yet you are injured,' he said.

'Injured, yes. But not God-injured. I am Height-injured. But even that's not it. The Heights didn't rape me, didn't even so much as lay a hand on me, didn't in any way impede me, or oppose me, didn't, as though I were Actaeon, look at me with that killing Artemis look that would have turned my own instincts upon me, and yet I was injured, hugely.'

'But if not by the Heights, then by what?'

'By my own unreadiness for them. It was to my own unreadiness for the Heights that I was Io, that I was Leda, that I was Hippolytus, that I was Actaeon. And now I am doing what I warned you not to do, I am assimilating myself, rather grandly, to mythic archetypes. But I am Diotima from Mantinea, and its very simple: the Heights we aren't yet able for are our Hell'.

'Do you mean that the Heights become their own opposite.'

'No. The Heights are eternally what they are. Entering them prematurely, I was illuminated in the ancient, archaic depths of my being and, not being ready to see what I saw, I became my own Hell, and the Hell I became—it was hurtful, it was hideous, and it was vast. And there was a kind of vast malice in it. It would see you go down into perdition and remaining imperturbable and unimpressed, it wouldn't lift a hand to help you.'

'And Socrates knows nothing of this?'

'I talked to Socrates when I didn't yet know what Heraclitus knew. I talked to Socrates when I didn't yet know that the way up and the way down are one way. It is like setting up a ladder against a rock wall by a lake. The lake mirrors your ascent as a descent. And so, thinking that I was ready for the Heights when I wasn't simultaneously ready for the depths, that was my catastrophe, that was the avalanche I set off, looking ever upwards, on the Mount of Perfection. It carried me down into a Deep below all depths. Of how it was with me in the years that followed I will say nothing. You must rest content with what you sensed in me, looking at me, yesterday morning in your door. Although I didn't at first know it, or know it for a long time, the Deep was the Divine Deep. What that Divine Deep is, in and for itself, I do not know. I only know, and it is from a reverent, worshipping distance that I know—I can hardly tell you because I can hardly tell myself what I know—I only know that when, by its grace, it makes us ready, then, eternally in an eternal moment, it is our blessedness and our bliss.'

'So why, knowing what you know, did you come here?'

'I came here to do what I've done. I came here to go down, praying as I did so, into my underworld. A healing God being there before me, I felt that now at last I was ready, that now at last I was safe. And I came here because, for a long time now, this city has needed what has happened between us. For a long time now, this city has needed this Second Symposium.'

'You have work to do,' she said, walking through the door he opened for her into the morning.

'Yes,' he said, seeing himself offering the play he would write to the Pit, seeing himself offering the play he would write to the Avalanche.

The Avalanche and the Pit

Now he could see: with every new god who comes there will come an alarmed awareness of both. And if in his presence, if in the very rumour of him, no such awareness is evoked, then we can safely conclude that the god who has come isn't a great god, isn't a god who can lead us out of our House of Laius, isn't a god who can lead us out of our House of Atreus, isn't a god with whom we can walk into a new way of being in the world.

Avalanche and Pit

Between them, inwardly more than outwardly, he stood.

Something else there was though that he could see: relying only on his own great intellect, Oedipus had opened an outer road. With the help of the god who had emerged, he himself had opened an inner road. He himself was the Sphinx he had defeated.

Walking back to his desk was like walking to Colonus.

A SONGLINE OF THE HEBREW DREAMTIME

There is a moment in the Old Testament when, quite out of the blue, we find that the Bible is enacting an exodus not from Egypt but from itself. It occurs where one of his comforters says to Job:

> For thou shall be in league with the stones of the field, and the beasts of the field shall be at peace with thee.

To see how startling this is we only need to keep it in mind as we read what God said to Noah and his sons after the flood:

> And God blessed Noah and his sons, and said unto them, be fruitful and multiply, and replenish the earth. And the fear of you and the dread of you shall be upon every beast of the earth, and upon every fowl of the air, upon all that moveth upon the earth, and upon all the fishes of the sea; into your hand are they delivered. Every moving thing that liveth shall be meat for you; even as the green Herb have I given you all things.

Never was such hurt done to the earth as was done to it in this address. It set us on the road to ecological havoc. And we must come off that road. In the way that Job came off it, we must come off it.

In the words of the book he gave his name to, Job endured a wide breaking in of waters. He in other words endured a second Flood, a second Exodus. He endured them biblically on our behalf. He emerged, and in him we emerged, from our biblical will to domination.

In Job we now know that we cannot rule over and subdue our own human inwardness:

> When I say my bed shall comfort me, my couch shall ease my complaint, then thou scares! me with dreams and terrifiest me through visions, so that my soul chooseth strangling and death rather than my life.

In Job we now know that we cannot rule over and subdue outwardness:

> Canst thou draw out Leviathan with an hook? Or his tongue with a cord which thou lettest down? Canst thou put an hook into his nose? Or bore his jaws through with a thorn? Will he make many supplications unto thee? Will he make a covenant with thee? Wilt thou take him for a servant forever? Wilt thou play with him as with a bird? Or wilt thou bind him for thy maidens? Shall the companions make a banquet of him?

Shall they part him among the merchants? Canst thou fill his skin with barbed irons? Or his head with fish spears? Lay thine hand upon him, remember the battle, do no more. Behold, the hope of him is in vain ...

In Job our biblical will to domination became ecological dust and ashes in our hands. Job sprinkled his head with them. And, there being no shortage of them, so should we.

But the Book of Job isn't an ecological manifesto. Given the richness of its metaphors, how could it be? It is a passion play and, as such, it would be doing it great violence to reduce it to doctrine or dogma. 'Woe to you lawyers,' Jesus said. And there are not a few who would agree with Arnold when he said that 'The strongest part of our religion today is its unconscious poetry.' For all that however, I think we can say that Job's agony was veil-rending. In him the veil of traditional assumptions was rent. And that's why his comforters couldn't comfort him, they being the guardians of the veil, they being the guardians of a way of seeing and understanding things which, in calamity after calamity, Job was being broken out of:

Now a thing was secretly brought to me, and mine ear received a little thereof. In thoughts from the visions of the night when deep sleep falleth on men, fear came upon me, and trembling, which made all my bones to shake. Then a spirit passed before my face; the hair of my flesh stood up ...

For the arrows of the Almighty are within me, the poison whereof drinketh up my spirit: the terrors of God do set themselves in array against me.

So am I made to possess months of vanity, and wearisome nights are appointed to me.

For He breaketh me with a tempest, and multiplieth my wounds without cause.

Thou huntest me as a fierce lion, and again Thou showest thyself marvellous upon me.

I was at ease, but He hath broken me asunder:

He hath also taken me by the neck, and shaken me to pieces, and set me up for his mark.

My days are past, my purposes are broken off, even the thoughts of my heart.

I have said to corruption thou art my father; to the worm, thou art my mother and my sister.

Hell is naked before me, and destruction hath no covering.

I am a brother to dragons, and a companion to owls.

That is Job's via dolorosa, his and ours, to an ecological Ash Wednesday. That is Job's exodus, his and ours, from an old to a new way of being in the world.

That is Job's desert wandering, his and ours, to an ecological Easter morning when, greeting each other, we will say.

Like Job, you can be in league with the stones of the field.

As it was with Job, so can it be with you, the beasts of savannah and sea can be at peace with you.

The sacred, great and dangerous earth regained might yet turn out to be

Paradise Regained.

Paradise in this case isn't a walled garden. Nor is it the earth of Messianic expectations:

The wolf also shall dwell with the lamb, and the leopard shall lie down with the kid; and the calf and the young lion and the fading together; and a little child shall lead them. And the cow and the bear shall feed, their young ones shall lie down together; and the lion shall eat straw like the ox. And the suckling child shall play on the hole of the asp, and the weaned child shall put his hand on the cockatrice's den. They shall not hurt nor destroy in all my holy mountain.

The earth that Job walked out into is the earth the Yoruba. know. The leopard they know will not lie down with the kid:

> Gentle hunter
> his tail plays on the ground
> while he crushes the skull
>
> Beautiful death
> who puts on a spotted robe
> when he goes to his victim
> Playful killer
> whose loving embrace
> splits the antelope's heart.

The earth that Job walked out into is the earth the Navajo know. The bear they know will not feed with the cow, nor will their young ones lie down together:

> My moccasins are black obsidian,
> leggings are black obsidian,
> My shirt is black obsidian.
> I am girded with a black arrowsnake.
> Black snakes go up from my head.
> With zigzag lightning darting from the ends of my feet I step.
> With zigzag lightning streaming from my knees I step.
> With zigzag lightning streaming from the tip of my tongue I speak.
>
> Now a disk of pollen rests on the crown of my head.
> Grey arrowsnakes and rattlesnakes eat it.
> Black obsidian and zigzag lightning stream out of me in four ways.
> Where they strike the earth, bad things, bad talk does not like it.
> It causes the arrows to spread out.

> Long life, something frightful I am
> Now I am.
>
> There is danger where I move my feet.
> I am whirlwind.
> There is danger where I move my feet.
> I am a black bear.
>
> When I walk, where I step, lightning flies from me.
> Where I walk, one to be feared I am.
> Where I walk, long life.
> One to be feared I am.
> There is danger where I walk.

Yes indeed, it wouldn't be safe to walk between a black bear and her cubs. But, contrary to our biblical view, the hope of bear is not in vain, the hope of leopard is not in vain, the hope of Leviathan is not in vain. Notwithstanding that they menace us, or murder us, we can be in league with them. In the way that our Palaeolithic ancestors understood and experienced these things, we can be bear dreamers, leopard dreamers, Leviathan dreamers. On any night, not just on those nights when we are on a vision quest, bear can walk into our dreams and leave us her bear songs, her bear medicines.

There is a Native American story of origins which, in different versions, is shared by many tribes. In it the creator or maker of all things calls himself Old Man. Before he retires from view, he gives us a last instruction:

> Now, if you are overcome, you may go to sleep and get power. Something will come to you in your dream, and that will help you. Whatever those animals who appear to you in your sleep tell you to do, you must obey them. Be guided by them. If you want help, are alone and travelling, and cry aloud for aid, your prayer will be answered—perhaps by the eagles, or by the buffalo, or by the bears. Whatever animal answers your prayer, you must listen.

Think now of two things. Think of what Yahweh said to a new humanity after the Flood. And think of what Old Man said to humanity after creation.

Between them lies Job's passion.

Job's passion is Job's exodus from the one way of being in the world to the other way of being in the world.

Job's passion is Job's exodus from our biblical will to dominate the earth to our aboriginal desire to be in league with the earth.

Where else but from here, taking nothing but our staff and our sandals with us, can we set our for the sacred, great and dangerous earth we were born into?

ANCIENT SLEEP

Time was when the moods of the sea were the moods of Poseidon's psyche. Dream moods of ancient sleep, of older than ancient sleep, they mostly were.

Our of ancient sleep the Minotaur was born. He was bull from the heart up. Rejected and suppressed, he turned carnivorous. In a labyrinth under city and psyche he ate adolescence.

Safe from foreign conquest an ancient city might be, safe by virtue of strong walls and hoplite resistance, but, as Thebes so well reminds us, it wasn't always inwardly safe, not safe at all, neither by day nor by night, from its own irruptive underworld. As Freud might have it, where the civilized, civic ego was, the Minotauric id might, at any moment, be.

A people might win the day at Marathon and win it again at Salamis,
but, although seeming to have won, they might, most terribly,
lose it that night in the labyrinth.
Dawn was a red onslaught.
Inwardly in our dreams, our Salamis sails haemorrhaged.

Theseus didn't succeed. Hilt-deep in him, a hero's sword gives life to the Minotaur. His earth-muffled, hurt bellowing interrupted the funeral eulogy of the dead at Marathon and at Salamis.

Regarding suppressed life, life in the labyrinth, we are heirs to ancient failure. During all the Christian centuries we have been heirs to it.

So what can we do?

There is, thankfully, not altogether much that we need to do because now at last there is evidence, in five etchings by Picasso, that something stupendous is happening: led by a little girl who has flowers in her arm or a dove in her arms, the Minotaur, hugely blind, hugely at large, is coming back into our culture.

Looking at these etchings, it isn't amiss to imagine that in them art is anticipating history. It isn't amiss to imagine that what is happening in them is happening in life: his pathetically vast bull's head looking blindly skyward, the Minotaur is walking among us.

Our sleep sometimes is phylogenetically ancient.

Out of ancient sleep, out of sleep older than ancient, in Greeks then, in us now, the Minotaur is born.

Christians welcome Mary and her haloed child.

Hindus welcome Parvati and her elephant-headed child.

And it might be that a day will come, a silent night will come, when Europeans will welcome Pasiphae and her bull-headed baby.

Faint as a Leonardo cartoon, a pattern of stains on the back wall of a lantern-lit stable shows Pasiphae, Parvati, and Mary watching their babies playing on the straw.

Announce it. Angel. Announce this new Good News. Announce it in Guernica.

RIFT MAN

The Great Rift Valley extends south-south-eastwards out of Africa into the Indian Ocean. Out of Africa northwards it extends into Palestine. In this northern extension of it, below sea level in it, are the Dead Sea, the Jordan and the Sea of Galilee.

> Rift Valley seas,
> A Rift Valley river.
> Seas below sea-level,
> Below sea-level a religious river.

Below sea-level here, according to Mark, a religious immensity had its origins:

The beginning of the gospel of Jesus Christ, the Son of God; As it is written in the prophets. Behold, I send my messenger before thy face, which shall prepare thy way before thee. The voice of one crying in the wilderness, Prepare ye the way of the Lord, make his path straight. John did baptize in the wilderness, and preach the baptism of repentance for the remission of sins. And there went out unto him all the land of Judaea, and they of Jerusalem, and were all baptized of him in the river of Jordan, confessing their sins. And John was clothed with camel's hair, and with a girdle of a skin about his loins; and he did eat locusts and wild honey; and preached, saying, There cometh one mightier than I after me, the latchet of whose shoes I am not worthy to stoop down and unloose. I indeed have baptized you with water: but he shall baptize you with the Holy Ghost. And it came to pass in those days that Jesus came from Nazareth in Galilee, and was baptized of John in Jordan. And straightway coming up out of the water, he saw the heavens opened and the Spirit like a dove descending upon him: And there came a voice from heaven, saying, Thou art my beloved Son in whom I am well pleased. And immediately the Spirit driveth him into the wilderness. And he was there in the wilderness forty days, tempted of Satan; and was with the wild beasts; and the angels ministered unto him.

> Rift in the Earth below,
> Rift in the Heavens above.

The pool, when it stilled, mirrored both rifts making them one wide opening, inwards into his own immensities, outwards into the World's immensities.

>   Rift Man,
>   Gorge Man.

Gorge-deep as, deeper than, Cherubim and Seraphim bliss above. Gorge-deep as, deeper than, the first fossil footprint below.

How can a person look upon the God of Mount Sinai and live?

How can a person looking in, look upon his own immensities and live?

Is mind in us able for psyche in us?

Is psyche in us able for itself? Can it become what it is, all that it is, and at the end of the day not a hair of another person's head will have been harmed?

Imagine a doorway. Its threshold says:

> O the mind, mind has mountains, cliffs of fall frightful, sheer,
> no-man-fathomed: hold them cheap may who ne'er hung there.

Its lintel says:

> In us is all whatsoever the sun shines upon. And in us also is
> all whatsoever the sun doesn't shine upon. In us are
> all the Heavens, all the Hells and all the Deeps.

Its left jamb says:

> I am fearfully and wonderfully made.

Its right jamb says:

> There is all Africa and her prodigies in us.

There is no such door but could it be that Jesus walked through it, spent forty days walking through it.

In it, walking through it, he was

>   Rift Man,
>   Gorge Man,
>   Man walking through.

He was with beasts. He was with beastly energies which are in us. Energies from within, from a Mesozoic within, from a Palaeozoic within, they came flush with him, flush with foot, with femur, with face.

Angels ministered to him.

Tigers and eagles and snakes ministered to

>   Rift Man,
>   Gorge Man,
>   Olduvai Man.

Transfigured Man walking through a door whose lintel and threshold and jambs are Beatitudes.

>   Blessed is he.
>   Blessed are we.
>   Blessed, and of the Horizon like Horus, is he.
>   Blessed, and of the Horizon like Horus, are we.
>
>   Blessed is all that in us is.

CROSSING THE KEDRON

Dry tonight, it is nonetheless Grand-Canyon loud. Dry tonight, it is nonetheless Colorado-river deep in the world's karma.

And Jesus must go down, must ford and be forded by the stream Greek tragedy didn't come to, didn't cross.
   Little wonder that Peter, James and John fell asleep.
   Aeschylus, Sophocles and Euripides—had he chosen these great Greeks to watch with him, they also would have slept, unable, awake, to exist in the vicinity of such passionate immensities.
   In the vicinity of such passionate immensities, even the rocks were metamorphosed. And stars that were close to the earth that night burned sapphire blue.
   Dear Jesus!
   Dear, dear, dear Jesus!
   In its most ancient roots and lobes and depths the human psyche came to the boil in you that night, Jesus.
   Karmically, it came to the boil.
   Putting your hand to your brow you felt the whole phylum. Emerging from within, the whole phylum was flush with your face. In the image and likeness of Coatlicue you were. You were the karmic pleroma. You were sore amazed.
   Dear Jesus!

Dear, dear, dear Jesus!
The Passion Matthew didn't script. Bach didn't score.
Living it, it living him, Jesus became script.
Living it, it living him, Jesus became score.
He became the first sound

OM

The sound that isn't the sound of any two things striking together.
The sound of which the universe is a blossoming.

Going out into it tonight, that first vibration out of the Divine Silence recreates the ageing universe, sublimes it.

WATCHING WITH JESUS

I

In St Matthew's Gospel it is written,

Then cometh Jesus with them unto a place called Gethsemane, and saith unto his disciples, Sit ye here, while I go and pray yonder. And he took with him Peter and the sons of Zebedee, and began to be sorrowful, and very heavy. Then saith he unto them, My soul is exceeding sorrowful, even unto death: tarry ye here and watch with me.

Continuing to read, we learn that these, his three chosen companions, didn't watch with Jesus. Leaving him in an extremity of red anguish, they fell asleep. But we shouldn't perhaps judge them harshly on this account, it being possible that for them sleep was a kind of fainting, a stratagem for shutting out the immensities that had engulfed them.

> *O God, thou hast cast us off,*
> *Thou hast scattered us,*
> *Thou hast been displeased;*
> *O turn thyself to us again.*
>
> *Thou hast made the earth to tremble;*
> *Thou hast broken it:*
> *Heal the breaches thereof; for it shaketh.*
>
> *Thou hast shewed thy people hard things:*
> *Thou hast made us to drink the wine of astonishment.*

Breached earth. Breached psyche.

Earthquake and psyquake. The psyche's sutures opened. And in the cloud no rainbow that anyone could see. Little wonder they fell asleep. Little wonder that Jesus began to be sore amazed.

And he went forward a little, and fell on the ground, and prayed that, if it were possible, the hour might pass from him. And he said, Abba, Father, all things are possible unto thee; take away this cup from me: nevertheless not what I will, but what thou wilt.

And still they slept. And we shouldn't blame them. Rather should we have compassion for them, because to watch with Jesus isn't only to look on, it isn't only to be a spectator, it is to undergo, in a separate red solitude, what he is undergoing.

Having crossed the Kedron, Jesus is now Grand-Canyon deep in the earth's karma. Earthly bad blood boiling over in him. Palaeozoic, Mesozoic, Kainozoic bad blood, overboiling, transformed fin and femur in him. Forehead in him. Self-consciousness in him.

Jesus, our friend, is in trouble.

Inwardly he has come before the Karmic King of Terrors. He's a brother to dragons and a companion to owls.

He's in trouble.

Phylogeny is coming flush with ontogeny in him and anyone who watches with him, then or now, will know

> That there is all Africa and her prodigies in us.
> That in us also is all whatsoever the Sun shines upon.
> In us are all the Heavens, all the Hells and all the Deeps.

That mind has mountains, cliffs of fall frightful, sheer, no man-fathomed.

Karmically now he is Vishvarupa.

In Gethsemane now, on the deepest Grand-Canyon floor of it, he is Coatlicue. Anatomically, like her, he is mostly Mesozoic.

And he cometh unto the disciples, and findeth them asleep, and saith unto Peter, What, could ye not watch with me one hour? Watch and pray, that ye enter not into temptation: the spirit indeed is willing, but the flesh is weak. He went away again the second time ...

But how far away did he go? As far away as the Devonian? As far away, downwards and backwards, as the Cambrian?

'Watch and pray.'

But, remembering that now tonight we are in Gethsemane, remembering that now tonight we are walking karmically under a karmic overhang of Silurian sea floors, remembering where we are, we ask, now, tonight, is it enough to watch with Kainozoic eyes? Is it enough to watch with Jewish eyes? With Greek eyes? With eyes that watched The Arreidae on stage? With eyes that watched The Labdacidae on stage? With eyes that watched Oedipus blinding his eyes?

Is it enough to watch from the heart of the Minotaur myth? Enough to watch from the heart of the Andromeda myth?

Are all myths, including the Minotaur myth, too modest in Gethsemane? Too modest, too myopic, and, when all is said and done, too trivial.

Knowing where it is we are, knowing how Grand-Canyon deep we are in the world's karma, can Judaism teach us how to watch, how to pray? Can Hinduism reach us? Under these overhangs here, here in this place of igneous anguish, here we ask, can a fully evolved Christianity teach us how to watch, how to pray?

The spirit is willing, but the biological is weak.

Palaeozoic, Mesozoic or Kainozoic, whatever its stage of evolution, the biological is weak. Too weak for Gethsemane. Too weak to watch there, to pray there.

> He went away again the second time and prayed, saying, O my Father, if this cup may not pass away from me, except I drink it, thy will be done. And he came and found them asleep again: for their eyes were heavy. And he left them and went away again, and prayed the third time, saying the same words. Then cometh he to his disciples, and saith unto them, Sleep on now, and take your rest: behold, the hour is at hand ...

Jesus, our friend, friend to trilobite, friend to stegosaurus, friend to Neanderthal, friend to us, friend to every stage and phase of evolution in us, He, Jesus, he had taken the cup: incarnating each phase of evolution in its turn, he had prayed palaeozoically in the Palaeozoic, he had prayed mesozoically in the Mesozoic, he had prayed kainozoically in the Kainozoic.

He had prayed with and from the Silurian lobes or nodes of the universal mind. He had prayed with and from the medulla of stegosaurus. He had prayed in and from the commonage consciousness of the Pleistocene.

He climbed. And behold him now. Behold the man. Orient his name.

But Jesus is Orient with a difference, he is Horus with a difference: all the unredeemed, dark impulses and energies of the Duat have come over the horizon in him, with him.

How delighted by sun-rise, by Horus-rise, were the green baboons of The Egyptian Book of the Dead.

How de-lighted this morning by Christ-rise are they.

How de-lighted are we.

II

The Great Ecumene is a religious ecumene, is the ecumene of all that is.

Parousia, Christians, by extension, might call it.

Parousia. Pleroma. Great Ecumene.

The Great Ecumene includes the Divine Mirum, Plenum, out of which it has emanated.

All emanation is emanation within the Divine. The Divine within which emanations emanate remains transcendent, immanently transcendent.

There is no outside. No outer darkness. Nothing is eternally lost. Nothing is eternally shut out.

No matter how far downwards, into the limits of opacity and contraction, a thing might descend or sink, it isn't on that account excluded. It isn't on that account excommunicated, execumened.

All limits of opacity, contraction and forgetfulness are limits within the Divine Mirum.

It is within the Divine Plenum that emanation and return take place.

That the Divine is transcendent yet inapprehensibly immanent is Good News.

'Sleep on now,' he said to his disciples, 'Sleep on now and take your rest: behold, the hour is at hand ... '

At hand the hour when Jesus, our friend, walked into Good Friday.

Fifteen hours later, on the cross, exhausted, his head fell forward onto his chest and he looked down into Adam's empty skull, into his own and Adam's complete kenosis, into his own and Adam's *De Profundis,* into his own and Adam's abyssal praying: I can't sense you, or know you, or name you, God. Eclipsing you with the eclipse I empirically am, I can't find you inside me, or in the world outside, but I still want to be your servant, God. The skull at the foot of the cross.

There are Hindus who would call it the Koshaless skull.

And, looking down into it with Jesus, we might, with the Chandogya Upanishad, say:

> Yatra na anyat pasyati, na anyat srinori, na anyad vijanati, sa bhuma.

Upon the emptiness of the empty skull the Divine Plenum supervenes. Upon the emptiness of the empty skull the Divine Mirum, not moving, moves.

!O Dichosa Ventura

III

There is an Easter which is an awakening to ordinariness.

Ordinariness, for those who have a capacity for it, is tremendous.

Every river is a medicine river.

Every bush is a burning bush, burning with green fire, burning with red fire, burning with jewel-blue fire, burning with fire auroral but ordinary, but burning with fire we haven't senses or faculties for.

Every stone is a yearning. If it wasn't, there would be no Venus de Milo. Every stone has a capacity for Gothic ecstasy. If it hadn't, there would be no cathedrals. Every stone is an a-stone-ishment turned inwards into its own rose-window wonders.

To stand on the floor of the Grand Canyon is to stand on a blessed, a delighted, symbiosis of samadhi and magma. To stand on the floor of the Grand Canyon is to stand on a blessed, delighted identity of samadhi and magma. To stand on the floor of the Grand Canyon is to stand on blessed, delighted sa-magma-madhi.

On Easter morning it isn't only Horus-Christ who is of the horizon. Apophis also, and all the theriomorphs of the Duat, are of the horizon.

On Easter morning all ordinary things are of the horizon.

> Shouldn't we therefore rejoice,
> Shouldn't we be exceedingly glad,
> Shouldn't we dance with the green baboons?

On the spot where the Buddha won enlightenment there is a temple called Budh Gaya.

On Easter morning, Horus-Christ coming over the horizon, can't we, looking east, look forward to a time when the whole earth will be Budh Gaia?

> Shouldn't we rejoice?
> Shouldn't we be exceedingly glad?
> Shouldn't we dance with the green baboons?

THE NEW HEROISM

Recently in London, I decided I would spend a morning in Westminster Abbey. Westminster Abbey isn't Chartres, nor is it Hagia Sophia. But this morning I didn't need it to be anything other than what it was, a vast architectural Te Deum that I could sit in and walk around in. In particular, I wanted, in this the century of Auschwitz, to make contact with medieval optimism. Sitting under the stone embower of The Lady Chapel, I wanted if possible to experience a kind of crypt confidence in the deepest, unconsciously motivating lobes of the human mind.

Emerging from the London underground, I crossed the street, aware, by reason of need, that there is an ancient holy well in the crypt of Chartres cathedral. Less phylogenetically esoteric or occult than we are, maybe Cernunnos drank from it. Looking like the sorcerer of Les Trois Frères, maybe a Pleistocene shaman drank from it.

Having crossed into it, I was only yet getting used to the gaunt vastness of the abbey when, on the intercom system, there was an announcement saying that, shortly, there would be a communion rite in St George's Chapel which, the announcer informed us, was located to the right inside the main entrance.

Not, to begin with, without some misgivings, I retraced my steps.

Facing us from behind the altar in this dragon-slayer's chapel, the minister called out:

The Lord be with you.

And with you, we, the congregation of six persons, replied.

Almighty God, we prayed,

> Almighty God,
> To whom all hearts are open,
> All desires known
> And from whom no secrets are hidden:
> Cleanse the thoughts of our hearts
> By the inspiration of your Holy Spirit,
> That we may perfectly love you
> And worthily magnify your holy name:
> Through Christ our Lord. Amen.

Inviting us to confess our sins the minister said:

God so loved the world that he gave His only Son, Jesus Christ, to save us from our sins, to be our advocate in Heaven and to bring us to eternal life. Let us confess our sins, in penitence and faith, firmly resolved to keep God's Commandments and to live in love and peace with all men.

We all prayed:

> Almighty God, our heavenly Father,

> We have sinned against you and against
> Our fellow men
> In thought and word and deed,
> Through negligence, through weakness,
> Through our own deliberate fault.
> We are truly sorry,
> And repent of all our sins.
> For the sake of your Son Jesus Christ,
> Who died for us,
> Forgive us all that is past,
> And grant that we may serve you in
> Newness of life
> To the glory of your name.
> Amen.

The minister prayed that God would pardon us:

> Almighty God
> Who forgives all who truly repent,
> Have mercy upon you,
> Pardon and deliver you from all your sins,
> Confirm and strengthen you in all goodness,
> And keep you in life eternal,
> Through Jesus Christ our Lord.
> Amen.
>
> Lord have mercy,
> Lord have mercy.
>
> Christ have mercy,
> Christ have mercy.
>
> Lord have mercy,
> Lord have mercy.

Then we recited the Gloria:

> Glory to God in the highest and peace to his people on earth.
> Lord God, heavenly King, Almighty God and Father,
> We worship you, we give you thanks, we praise you for your glory.
> Lord Jesus Christ, only son of the Father, Lord God, Lamb of God,
> Have mercy on us;
> You take away the sin of the world: Have mercy on us;
> You are seated at the right hand of the Father; Receive our prayer.

> For you alone are the Holy One
> You alone are the Lord
> You alone are the Most High,
> Jesus Christ
> With the Holy Spirit
> In the glory of God the Father.
> Amen.

Then there was the Ministry of the Word, the Creed, the Intercession.

Crossing solemnly into the Ministry of the Sacrament, there was the Peace, the Preparation of the Gifts, the Eucharistic Prayer.

Here now, in this dragon-slayer's chapel, was Stevens' 'The holy hush of ancient sacrifice'.

While the gifts of bread and wine were being prepared I imagined, briefly but shudderingly, that Demeter and Dionysus were sitting either side of me. How astonished they were. And how destitute. 'Twas as if their own myths, their own cults, had walked out on them. But not everything was lost. Sacramentally enabled thereto, they were watching with Jesus.

Watching with him into and through the awful Gethsemane process of integration and growing in which phylogeny in us comes flush with ontogeny in us.

Watching with him into and through an immense epistemological crisis.

Watching with him into and through that final dying, looking down into the Golgotha Skull.

This was a small chapel. From where I knelt I could hear the sound of water poured, of water dripping, dropping, into the wine in the chalice. Also, more awfully, I could hear the sound of the bread breaking.

These, I realized listening to them, are among the most serious sounds in Christendom.

Were I a Gnostic I might have imagined that the sound of the bread breaking was the sound of the Heimarmene breaking.

Were I a Buddhist I might have imagined that now at last I had heard the sound of the Suf sea of samsara opening.

But I was a Christian and for me these were the sounds of the universe being redeemed. They were the sounds of the universe turning back, as upon a hinge, towards its divine source. Christ was the hinge, the living hinge, and for him the turning was agony.

We received, saying, as the bread and wine were being passed among us:

> Lamb of God, you take away the sins of the world:
> Have mercy on us.
>
> Lamb of God, you take away the sins of the world:

> Have mercy on us.
> Lamb of God, you take away the sins of the world:
> Grant us peace.

After communion the minister prayed:

> Father of all, we give you thanks and Praise,
> That when we were still far off
> You met us in your Son, and brought us Home.
> Dying and living, he declared your Love, gave us grace,
> And opened the gate of glory.
> May we who share Christ's body live his risen life:
> We who drink his cup bring life to others:
> We whom the Spirit lights, give light to the world.
> Keep us firm in the hope you have set before us,
> So we and all your children shall be free,
> And the whole earth live to praise your
> Name: through Christ our Lord,
> Amen.

We all prayed:

> Almighty God,
> We thank you for feeding us
> With body and blood of your Son
> Jesus Christ.
> Through him we offer you our souls and bodies
> To be a living sacrifice.
> Send us out
> In the power of your Spirit
> To live and work
> To your praise and glory.
> Amen.

Then there was the blessing, the minister making the sign of the cross towards us, saying:

> The peace of God, which passes all
> Understanding, keep your hearts and
> Minds in the knowledge and love of God,
> And of his Son Jesus Christ our Lord:
> And the blessing of God almighty, the
> Father, the Son and the Holy Spirit
> Be among you, and remain with you
> Always.

Amen.

Then there was the Dismissal: Go in peace to love, and serve the Lord, the minister said.

In the name of Christ, Amen, we said.

The Eucharist, blessed be it, is difficult for me. What an anthropologist, looking at it from the outside, might call its carnivorous, cannibalistic core, its totemic core, that troubles me. But I often remind myself that there is maybe no good reason why I should feel superior or standoffish. I am all too aware that a carnivore's dentition beats the beatitudes to a place in my head. So, whenever it comes my way, whatever my initial misgivings, I take the Eucharist. I sometimes imagine it to be a kind of initiatic test, an initiatic overcoming of strong aversion. And, if nothing else, taking it is of course an encounter with something I unsentimentally am. Receiving the blessed blood, I ask it to mingle with my own palaeozoically old, karmically old, blood, and, as it mingles with it, I ask it to heal it alchemically. I ask the Christ who is in the host to go down into my inner hells and harrow them. The difficulty remains, as it did that day in St George's Chapel.

Continuing to sit there late into the afternoon, I found myself sometimes feeling sorry for myself. Feeling sorry also, almost, for Christianity.

I sometimes ache for Christianity. I ache for it and yearn for it, that it would continue to be a great religion sheltering us in our abyssal and phylogenetic depths, sheltering us in our precipitous heights.

Ignoring, for the moment, the great Christological claims that Christians make for Him, Jesus is, to say the least, a new kind of hero. A hero in whose presence St George, for all his Christian splendour, is, I think, atavistic.

According to one version of his legend, St George was born in Cappadocia. He was already a young, self-consciously Christian man, handsome and brave, at a time when, far off in Libya, a terrible fire-breathing dragon had laid a city and its surrounding countryside under hard carnivorous bondage. To appease him, the people, to begin with, gave him two sheep a day. When their stock of sheep was running low they altered their offering, giving him now a human being and a sheep every day. At last the king's daughter, bridally arrayed, was exposed. And that's when St George, armed with spear and sword and shield, rode to the rescue. Byzantine icons of this event show St George spearing the pest, but the Golden Legend has it that, merely by making the sign of the cross towards him, St George overpowered him. Unmolested and released, the king's daughter led him, meek and docile now, into the city and there, in front of all the people, St George beheaded him. So impressed by what they had seen were the people that they converted, there and then, all of them, to Christianity. And, how delightful a task to them it was to build a shrine to their heroic deliverer.

In icons of St George, he is himself handsome, his horse is handsome, his sword is handsome. Even the hooves of his horse are virtues. And the phallus of his horse is virtuously vital. Nonetheless, here in his chapel in Westminster Abbey, I couldn't help but feel that he was, even in his glory, atavistic. In him, as hero and as saint, there was, I felt, a regression to pre-Christian myopia.

A killed dragon isn't a dead dragon.

A killed dragon is still a dangerous dragon.

A dragon dead is more dangerous maybe than a dragon alive.

We don't, by killing him, get rid of a dragon. Rather do we, by killing him, sow him, as we would soil, with pestilence.

There is, I think, a better way than the way of the hero who, with his sore and great and strong sword, would lobotomize the earth, would lobotomize the human mind, his and ours.

It mightn't, in our century, be amiss to conclude that this very ancient way doesn't work.

But we aren't destitute. There is a way, the way that Jesus took when, crossing the Kedron, he went down Grand-Canyon deep into the earth's karma, when, standing there on the deepest of all Gethsemane floors, he consciously inherited all that we humanly are even though this, at one stage, might have meant that phylogeny was as out of doors in him as it is in Coatlicue, as it is in Cernunnos, as it is in Pashupati.

Jesus is he among us who is most incarnate.

Jesus is our hero of integration.

As a consequence of what was accomplished in Gethsemane, there is now no depth of nature, inside or outside, that isn't potentially a blessing, a medicine. As a native of North America might say, there is now muladhara medicine, eagle medicine, elk medicine, bear medicine, otter and owl medicine, dragon medicine, Grendel medicine. Hydra medicine, Python medicine, Leviathan medicine. The earth itself is big medicine.

As Buddhists bring flowers to Mucalinda Buddha, so now can we bring flowers to:

> Hydra Herakles,
> Pytho Apollo,
> Apophis Horus,
> Tiamat Marduk,
> Draco George,
> Fafnir Sigurd,

>   Kundalini Mary.
>
> Flowers to statues of these carved from
>
> >   Gethsemane rock,
> >   Calvary rock,
> >   Golgotha rock.
>
> Let us bring in summer, let us bring flowers to statues of these carved from
>
> >   every stratum of Grand Canyon rock.
>
> Let us bring in summer, let us bring crinoids to a statue of Jesus the Christ carved from
>
> >   a stone egg of stegosaurus.
>
> Jesus the Christ is he among us who is most incarnate.
> He is our hero of integration.
> He has enabled us, now again, to drink from the well of commonage consciousness in the crypt, a well a Pleistocene shaman might have drunk from, a well Cernunnos might have drunk from.
> Grand-Canyon deep in the earth's karma, Jesus has enabled us to be incarnate. He has enabled us who, hitherto, were only on the earth, to be of the earth.
> Being of the earth isn't of course the whole truth about us.
> Let us bring in summer, let us bring in flowers to a statue of Jesus the Christ carved in
>
> >   Altjeringa rock,
> >   Uluru rock.
>
> Let us bring in summer, let us bring flowers to statues of Jesus the Christ carved in
>
> >   Manu rock,
> >   Duar rock,
> >   Bakhu rock.
>
> >   All rock is mind in hibernation.
>
> Let us bring in summer, let us bring flowers to statues of Jesus the Christ carved in
>
> >   the stone wish-bone, the stone wing-bone, of archaeornis.
>
> Being of the earth, as we've imagined the earth, isn't the whole truth about ourselves. Jesus walked onwards and forwards from Gethsemane. But

from it came the raven that Noah sent out saying,

> Tehom is Turiya.

Back from it came the Paraclete saying,

> The end of the journey is blessedness, is bliss.

Maybe, coming again, Raven and Paraclete will bring new liturgies, new ways of enacting newness of life.

PASSOVER

> 'At stroke of midnight soul cannot endure
> A bodily or mental furniture.'
> W.B. Yeats

These are shocking lines. Rooted, as most of us are, in our empirical identities, they might even be devastating lines. They de-vast-state us, as, in the person of Jesus, humanity was de-vast-stated on Golgotha.

Plato, a teacher of commanding stature in these matters, he didn't state us so vastly. He did, however, give currency to the idea that body entombs the soul. It didn't, it seems, occur to him that mind entombs it also. As we might conclude from Yeats's lines: even when mind is at its best, unrestrained and free, exercising its highest, noblest and most visionary powers, even then it entombs the soul, even then it palls and appalls it.

The senses and faculties with which we seek Reality eclipse Reality.

> Vision veils.
> In or out of the body, vision veils.
> Supercelestial vision veils.

The Triduum Sacrum didn't engulf Plato. The Triduum Sacrum didn't earthquake, eyequake, psyquake Plato.

> It eyequaked, mindquaked, psyquaked Christ.

Christ came to Golgotha. He came to

> The hill of the skull
> The hill of the empty skull

The hill of the Koshaless Skull.

Good Friday is serious. Democratic as Death, Good Friday is a universal opportunity.

On Good Friday, in the person of Jesus, European philosophy moved house. It moved, it passed over, from metaphysic to metanoesis.

The new house European philosophy moved into is a new song:

Yatra na anyat pasyati, na anyat srinoti, na anyad vijanati, sa bhuma.

> Christ's song,
> Miriam's song. Her song now.
>
> Our song,
> Our Passover song.
>
> Song we sing in the Desert of Zin,
> Song we sing in the Garden of the Sepulchre,
> Song two angels sing in the tomb.

Yatra na anyat pasyati, na anyat srinoti, na anyad vijanati, sa bhuma.

REDEEMING OUR HEROES IN THE LIGHT OF THE TRIDUUM SACRUM

I
FAUST

> Look again at your feet Faust,
> Your house smells like a stable.
> The seagreen horse
> And the high halfhoof of stars
> You saw must be conjured
> Tonight from your table.
>
> But the demons we dream of
> No longer desire us
> And the stakes we embraced
> At our birth burn out.
> In the books she is Venus,
> In the flesh she's the virus
> That holds every cell

> Like a bit in its mouth.
> And neighing for the beast
> You must migrate through,
> You dream in the shade
> Of the carnal tree:
> Aquarius walks in the desert
> Towards you;
> And archangels
> Grow wild at the edge of the sea.

Typically, in our culture, the hero is someone who performs a great task. He slays a dragon fulsome to overflowing in poisonous malignancies. He rids a region of its autochthonous monsters, opening it up to human incursion and settlement. Wielding it against the Demons of Earthquake and Eclipse, his sword is lair to most awful devourings. Sailing through fire and flood, he brings home the great and necessary boon. He establishes a new order.

As Racine understands him, Theseus is exemplary:

> *Les monstres étouffés et les brigands punis,*
> *Procruste, Cercyon, et Sciron, et Sinnis,*
> *Et les os dispersés du géant d'Epidaure,*
> *Et la Crête fumant du sang du Minotaure.*

But such an order founded in such a way is fragile. Think of Thebes. Westward out of Asia following a cow Cadmus came. Wherever the cow would lie down, that's where he would build his city.

The cow lay down in dragon country. Wielding his ravenous sword, a sword that hungered and thirsted for horrible hearthurt, Cadmus fought and fought and fought the many-splendoured, and many-horrored, many-carbuncled dragon.

The dragon died.

Not knowing that a dead dragon isn't dead, not knowing that a dragon is more virulent, more potent posthumously than it is while it is alive, not knowing, Cadmus built his city, strong, he supposed, against all comers in its walls, strong against anything that might come against it in its seven gates.

From the beginning it was a troubled city, sphinx-haunted, womb-plundered, an odour in it of decaying thunder.

Strong against siege and assault from outside, it was troubled from within by bad dreams. And the many-splendoured dreams were as awful as those that were many-horrored.

Dragon dreams. Dreams that emerged through sword wounds, dragon wounds, in the psyche.

Waking at night, even the King would sometimes think that his room was a dragon's den. And the den was underground.

Are there Underworlds Hades hasn't heard of, isn't Lord in? he asked; Teiresias didn't know.

The liver omens of cow and owl were bad.

The King was his mother's husband. He was brother to his daughters.

Dreaming, the King saw dragon wounds. In the morning his eyes were wounded with the wounds he saw.

In the lion gate going away, he didn't look back. Blind, but accompanied by his daughter who was his sister, he walked into exile.

In the dream of someone buried alive he came, northwards and westwards out of Asia, following a cow, and the cow gave birth to seven lean lowings in the seven gates and the prophet, his voice a lean lowing, lowed:

> But the cormorant and the bittern shall possess it, the owl also and the raven shall dwell in it; and he shall screech out upon it the line of confusion, and the stones of emptiness. They shall call the nobles thereof to the kingdom, but none shall be there, and all her princes shall be nothing. And thorns shall come up in her palaces, nettles and brambles in the fortresses thereof: and it shall be an habitation for dragons and a court for owls. The wild beasts of the desert shall also meet the wild beasts of the island and the satyr shall cry to his fellow; the screech owl also shall rest there, and find for herself a place of rest. There shall the great owl make her nest, and lay, and hatch, and gather under her shadow: there shall the vultures also be gathered, everyone with her mate.

That's the fable.

The point I would like to make is that it isn't good to slay the Dragon. It isn't good to rid the earth of its autochthonous monsters. It isn't good, hoping for peace in our city, for peace in our minds, to lobotomize the psyche, to lobotomize the earth.

Faust, in this understanding of him, doesn't slay dragons. He doesn't suppress his animal or chakral nature. And yet, as the poem imagines him, he is a hero. A hero of inclusion not of exclusion.

A hero of integration, smelling of stables, seeing angels, he stands psychically unlobotomized on the unlobotomized earth.

Maybe one day, following a cow, Cadmus will come into the many splendoured city Faust has built.

Can you see them, Cadmus and Faust, sitting down to talk in the East Pagoda Hall of a Green Dragon Temple?

II
CON CÉAD CHATHACH

And sometimes seen
Through our bronze-green eyes
The king, it seemed
And his hall had aged
But when war was the mask,
The measure of all things,
Our loves were,
Like our wars, well waged.

No need to tell
The peasant then
Of the green girls
He had never known:
He was bent above
A richer earth
And an Eve still slept
In every bone.

But then I swore
I would not rest;
Had I not seen
The king's corpse lowered.
I swore that night
I would mirror the West
And the afterlife mirror
On the edge of my sword.

Their fists had let
Their lifelines free;
The dead were blind
To the promised glamour;
The eye I dug up
Was unable to see,
The dead ear
Was an anvil and hammer.

Their bronze-green eyes
Are blind, and now
In the tombs of Celtic kings
Long years have taught

> Their fingers how
> The earth is the true
> Sixth sense of things.

The hall is a kind of earthly Celtic Valhalla. Sometimes there are intimations of mortality in its warriors and walls. Evanescently, everyone and everything has aged. It is twilight all day sometimes. Yet no one takes particular notice. There are wars to be waged and loves to be waged, and after every war and before every love there is torch-bright, boisterous feasting.

War is waged. Love is waged. Food is wagered, and waged.

Truculently, afraid of no gainsaying, everyone praises his own bravery.

But the Doomsday Roosters are crowing.

Perched on the crossbeam of a gibbet behind the hall, Fjalar is crowing. In the birdwood, unseen, Goldencomb is crowing. At the bars of Hel, his wings wide, Rustred is crowing.

The King dies.

The frightful, boar-headed, boar-bristled Warrior Lord of Sorca has abducted him.

This is insult. This is provocation.

Con Céad Chathach takes down his sword and goes out. He will bring the King back.

Con of the Hundred Battles, all of them rich in awful blows, all of them won. And now again, his sword drawn, mirroring whatever comes against him, on the uninhibited, savage edge of it, he crosses into Sorca.

This, his last battle, he loses. There is no one to fight.

Hearing here is a hammer and anvil fallen forever asunder. He returns but not to the Hall, not to his warrior ways. He falls in with the peasant, seeding red earth.

> No need to tell
> This peasant now
> Of the green girls
> He has never known:
> He is bent above
> A richer earth
> And an Eve
> Still sleeps in every bone.

Can you see them, the three ragnarok cocks on your gibbet, all three of them crowing?

> On the gibbet crowing,
> In the birdwood crowing,

Crowing before the bars of Hel.

Announcing ragnarok. Ragnarok in eye and mind. Ragnarok during which all cosmologies which are bad for the world, which harm the stars and the earth, ragnarok during which all bad cosmologies will be washed away, out of our hearts, out of our hands.

We have no need, not now, not ever, for a new heaven and a new earth. We only need eyes to see that every bush is a burning bush, burning with green fire, with red fire, with jewel-blue fire, with fire we haven't senses or chakras for.

A ragnarok which puts off the old shoe of old habits of feeling from off our hearts.

Morning now. There is evening and morning a first day, and people and leopards are abroad walking the earth with barefoot hearts and barefoot minds.

And above us at night Ursa is a transverberation of stars.

If it happened to Teresa it can happen to Ursa, and to Leo, and to Draco. in every atom and star of it the universe we live in is transverberated.

A Transverberated Universe.

And, at the end of all seeking, physical and spiritual, what will the subatomic physicist find? Sown into the lining of every particle, sown into the lining of every intuition of existence, a Pascalian memorial of

A Night of Fire
Depuis environ dix heures et demie du soir jusques environ minuit et demi,
Feu.
Oubli du monde et de tout, hormis Dieu
Joie, joie, joie, pleurs de joie.

Their bronze-green eyes
Are blind, and now
In the tombs of Celtic kings
Long years have taught
Their fingers how
The earth is the true
Sixth sense of things.

HEALING THE CITY
(It 'had missed its chance with one of the Lords of life'.)

Erichthonios, so says tradition, was the first Athenian. And he, quite literally, was autochthonous, sprung from the earth itself, the earth having been impregnated by Hephaestus's desire for Athena.

Cecrops, the tradition further informs us, was the first king of Athens. He it was who first sought to civilize his people and their place. And it was he who presided over a contest between Poseidon and Athena as to which of them should be divine patron of the city. Poseidon's gift was the horse, Athena's the olive tree. Concluding that her gift would be more useful, Cecrops chose Athena, and named his city for her.

A great and glorious city it became, its citizens insisted. And, still its heirs, we agree.

Citizens of this city claimed that they were the teachers of Hellas. And had they been able to see into the future they would, almost surely, have also claimed that they were the teachers of Europe as far west as the Atlantic, as far north as the Arctic.

Old and venerable Athenian conversations were heard and were listened to in our northern foggy forests, as for instance:

Socrates: Where have you come from, my dear Phaedrus, and where are you going?

Phaedrus: I have been with Lysias, the son of Cephalus, Socrates, and I am going for a walk outside the walls after a long session with him that has lasted since early morning. Our common friend, Acumenus, says that a country walk is more refreshing than a stroll in the city squares; that is why I am going in this direction.

Socrates: Acumenus is quite right my friend. So Lysias was in the city, was he?

Phaedrus: Yes, he was visiting Epicrates, in the house you see there near the temple of Olympian Zeus, the house that used to belong to Morychus.

Socrates: What were you doing there? Lysias was entertaining you with his eloquence I suppose.

Phaedrus: You shall hear if you can spare the time to go with me.

Socrates: Spare the time! Don't you realize that to me an account of what passed between you and Lysias is, to use Pindar's phrase, a matter that takes precedence even over business.

Phaedrus: Come along then.

Socrates did go along. And, more eager to listen to Socrates than to Phaedrus, there have been, down the ages, many Europeans who have also gone along.

There have been many, in many lands, who have walked with Socrates into his vision of Time and Eternity. Many there are who, with him, have looked upwards into the heights, where, incorruptibly, he claimed, the Good, the True and the Beautiful are. And, yearning for something like it, there have been not a few who, peripatetic with him, have walked into and through and around and about his ideal city.

An ideal city. Not necessarily the city Socrates designed. Or Plato designed. The city which, for all its glories, Athens didn't become.

In the fifth century there were some Athenians and some who came to their city who, given a chance, would have happily and confidently inaugurated an age of enlightenment. It didn't happen, partly, perhaps, because a war broke out between Athens and Sparta and, with increasing awful toll, physically and mentally, it went on and on and on. And that wasn't all: plague broke out. Who could have imagined it? Plague in this city of marble altars, panathenaic processions, Pheidian draperies and divine caryatids. A city of light. A city so close to the healing light of Colonus, to the healing, liberating light of Eleusis. Wasn't it to Eleusis, here in Attica, that a Divine Mother of Sorrows came? And wasn't it to Colonus, also in Attica, that an old and blind and polluted King, now an outcast, came? Athens was a great city. Athenians were proud of it. Athenians were the teachers of Hellas. Athenians could inherit and deal with the pursuing and plaguing consequences of Mycenae's conjugal axe, of its matricidal sword. Only recently, at Areopagus rock here in their city, Erinyes had, by literary fiat, become Eumenides.

That's what Athens was, what it imagined itself to be.

Teacher of Hellas. Healer of Hellas.

City of literary, of philosophic pharmacy.

City of dramaturgic therapy.

And hither they came, the burdened ones.

But maybe the Erinyes weren't mocked. Not mocked by literary nor philosophic fiat.

The plague and the long war took an awful toll. Inwardly and outwardly the caryatids, literary, philosophic and scientific, which had hitherto supported civilization, began to give way.

Superstitions, long dead, lived again.

Old remedies, old medicines, old magical consolations, none of them rationally vindicated, were resorted to.

And then one day, his sacred snake going before him, Asclepius, God of healing, was solemnly inducted and welcomed into Athens.

To many among the intellectual elite, this must have seemed like a capitulation to unreason.

Aeschylus, he who had always been on the side of reformation and reason, always on the side of evolution not atavism, Aeschylus, he who had fought Asians, he had written a play called *Seven Against Thebes*.

Seven against Thebes.

One, a black one, and he a reptile, had come against Athens.

But no. The reptile of unreason hadn't come as The Seven had come. He had been brought. He had been welcomed.

How strange! Coming from afar, from Epidaurus, a healing snake had come to heal the healer of Hellas.

And wonderful to relate! There being as yet no official sanctuary for the God, it was in the house of Sophocles, poet of old Mycenaean, old Theban trouble, it was here, in a room in this pharmakon's house, that the snake was given temporary residence.

Seven against Thebes.

One, who was seven, against Athens.

One, who was seven, against civilization:

> The irrational against reason.
> Illusion against reality.
> Self deception against gnothi seauton.
> Sleep and sitting in seance against the second stasimon,
> Incubation, divination and dreams against wide-awake, watchful diagnosis.
> Python against Apollo.
> Hydra against Herakles.

Phylogeneric, old lobes had begun to cake over. Centuries of civilized living hadn't lobotomized them. But rationalists didn't despair. They didn't go to their Acropolis wailing wall, to their Areopagus wailing wall. What was happening was but a temporary regression in troubled times. Come what would, the real was rational and only the rational was real. And this great truth by which they lived would continue to command and, one day, would be given universal allegiance.

And now a fancy:

As if the sacred snake allowed us to ignore historical fact, I imagine that it was already late that evening when Phaedrus and Socrates came back within the city wall. And it was where they had met this morning, hard by the temple of Olympian Zeus, that they now parted. Socrates had walked but a little way down a side street when, suddenly erupting, the voice of his daimon warned him not to go home. As he was, at that moment, passing by Sophocles's door, he turned and went in.

What a coincidence, the old man exclaimed, rising arthritically from his chair. What a coincidence! I've just been thinking about you.

In what connection? Socrates asked, surprised by the sudden attention.

In connection with horses. I was thinking of the horse Poseidon would have given to us had Cecrops chosen him to be patron of our city. That's the horse the horses you talk about put *me* in mind of, Poseidon's horse. Horse from Poseidon's stables. Horse from his meadows under the sea. Horse never handled. Horse never bridled. Horse never harnessed. Horse never heard until now in our city. In the nights now I hear him. His neighings, near at hand, awaken me, and I lie there thinking, thinking, wondering what it would be like had Poseidon won. Our city, had he won, would be called Poseidonia not Athenai. And I'm sure of it Socrates. I am sure that citizens in a city called Poseidonia would understand and experience themselves very differently from ourselves, who are citizens in a city called Athenai. All day, Socrates, all day long, sitting here, I've been imagining something. Imagining it or seeing it. Seeing it I think. Since the neighings last night I've been seeing two processions, long and glorious, a panathenaic procession coming from the land, and coming from the sea a panposeidoniac procession. Reaching the foot of the Acropolis both processions interwove themselves into a caduceus, surrounding it, singing marvellously. Disengaged, they climbed the Acropolis separately, from opposite directions, and then on the summit they wove the caduceus again, first about Athena's olive tree, then about Poseidon's horse and then about them both, Poseidon standing by the olive tree, Athena standing by the horse.

We are sick, Socrates.

And I know why.

In dreams sent by the snake I have seen why. We are sick because we rejected the horse. We closed our seven gates to the centaur in us.

And tomorrow you will go with me, won't you, you will go with me to Pericles and to Pheidias and we will persuade them to institute what I have seen, what the snake in me has seen, seeing what it dreamed. We will persuade them to institute what has instituted itself.

I'm sore, Sophocles said, sitting down.

I'm sore in my bones. Sore. And sometimes I think, these nights I think, it was walking through me that the horse we rejected walked back into Athens.

Have you ever felt like that, Socrates? Sore like that?

No, Socrates said, sitting down. No. I have never felt trampled like that in my head. No. I've never felt hurt, never been broken, giving benign birth to my own or people's repressions.

Standing in his door that night the old arthritic caryatid of culture called down the street after Socrates: tell Diotima when you see her that the horse we rejected is back. Tell her that now at last that we are ready to listen.

And his house didn't smell of Mycenae tonight, Socrates thought, going in his own door. His house didn't smell of Mycenae or Thebes. Maybe Thebes and Mycenae have been healed in him too.

In a dream that night Socrates saw the old caryatid. He was pointing downwards from an acropolis to a great caduceus of Triton and Python, carved by Pheidias. The foundation it was for the wall of a sacred city.

You've been in a trance all morning, Xantippe said. What were you looking at?

At a shining caryatid on an acropolis. I've a funeral to go to today.

In the night he heard the caryatid singing:

> εὐίππου, ξένε, τᾶσδε χώρας
> ἵκου τὰ κράτιστα γᾶς ἔπαυλα,
> τὸν ἀργῆτα Κολωνόν, ἔνθ'
> ἁ λίγεια μινύρεται
> θαμίζουσα μάλιστ' ἀηδὼν
> χλωραῖς ὑπὸ βάσσαις,
> τὸν οἰνωπὸν ἔχουσα κισσὸν
> καὶ τὰν ἄβατον θεοῦ
> φυλλάδα μυριόκαρπον ἀνήλιον
> ἀνήνεμόν τε πάντων
> χειμώνων· ἵν' ὁ βακχιώτας
> ἀεὶ Διόνυσος ἐμβατεύει
> θεαῖς ἀμφιπολῶν τιθήναις.

Our city come to Colonus.
Our culture come to Colonus.
Europa come to Colonus.

HOLY CITY

In his lair-lit wilderness long before Cadmus, following a cow, came, the Dragon had dreamed of a holy city. Having killed that dream, Cadmus built Big Trouble. Big Trouble has many names: Uruk, Babylon, Thebes, Tula, London:

> *I wander through each chartered street,*
> *Near where the chartered Thames does flow,*

> *And mark in every face I meet*
> *Marks of weakness, marks of woe.*
> *In every cry of every man,*
> *In every infant's cry of fear,*
> *In every voice; in every ban,*
> *The mind-forged manacles I hear.*
>
> *How the chimney-sweeper's cry*
> *Every blackening church appals;*
> *And every hapless soldier's sigh*
> *Runs in blood down palace walls.*
>
> *But most through midnight streets I hear*
> *How the youthful harlot's curse*
> *Blasts the new-born infant's tear*
> *And blights with plagues the marriage hearse.*

> Uruk,
> Thebes,
> Tula.

Gilgamesh built Uruk, first city of Sumer, a city psychically in his image and likeness: unable to integrate the wild man in himself, Gilgamesh corrupted him, and centuries later, in Babylon, Nebuchadnezzar, its king, paid the price; in sudden, awful regression he crawled out of his species and, going about on all fours, he ate grass, like a ruminant, on the steppes.

> King of kings,
> Lord of lords,
> Ruminant.

And Babylon the glory of kingdoms, the beauty of the Chaldees' excellency, shall be as when God overthrew Sodom and Gomorrah. It shall never be inhabited, neither shall it be dwelt in from generation to generation: neither shall the Arabian pitch tent there; neither shall the shepherds make their fold there. But wild beasts of the desert shall lie there; and their houses shall be full of doleful creatures and owls shall dwell there, and satyrs shall dance there. And the wild beasts of the islands shall cry in their desolate houses, and dragons in their pleasant palaces: and her time is near to come, and her days shall not be prolonged.

Isaiah, our greatly corrupted Enkidu, in terrorist mood, in Blitzkrieg mood, in Final Solution mood: a portent, he, calling the very possibility of civilized assembly in doubt. Calling Jerusalem, old and new, heavenly and earthly, in doubt.

> *I wander through each chartered street,*
> *Near where the chartered Thames does flow.*

How charterable is Enkidu? And you Gilgamesh, how charterable are you? And you Nebuchadnezzar?

How charterable, in our depths, are we? In our depths, how Magna Cartable?

Is our birth 'a sleep and a forgetting'?

Are there uncharterable sushumnas and chakras in us?

Are there depths in us, and heights in us, which no city wall or law can contain?

At Colonus, hearing thunder, I ask it.

Out of Asia, following a cow, Cadmus came. Where the cow would lie down, there he would build his city.

Between mountains, unechoing and unchartered, they walked.

Not echoing their lowings, neither hers nor his. Lonely, these two.

Grazing one night, her head udder-deep in its own shadow, the cow lay down in dragon country.

The dragon slain, his teeth sown, Cadmus bigged a city. But here, also, the royal bedroom one night was lair-lit, and, a club-foot writing it, writing appeared on a Sphinx-watched wall.

Iridescent in lair light, the writing was dragon-scaled, red and green.

But the cormorant and the bittern shall possess it; the owl also and the raven shall dwell in it: and he shall stretch out upon it the line of confusion, and the stones of emptiness. They shall call the nobles thereof to the kingdom, but none shall be there, and all her princes shall be nothing. And thorns shall come up in her palaces, nettles and brambles in the fortresses thereof, and it shall be an habitation of dragons, and a court for owls. The wild beasts of the desert shall also meet with the wild beasts of the island, and the satyr shall cry to his fellow; the screech owl also shall rest there, and find for herself a place of rest. There shall the great owl make her nest, and lay, and hatch, and gather under her shadow: there shall the vultures also be gathered, every one with her mate.

Quetzalcoatl, the quetzal-feathered serpent, built a city, calling it Tula. In it he was king, his head-dress an iridescent splay of quetzal feathers. A good king, and wise, teaching his people, honouring the Gods—the Sun God, the Rain God, the Goddess of Earth, the God of Flowers, the Corn God, the War God.

A Good King.
A Chartered People.
Chartered, yet not manacled.
Chartered and happy.

Unable for what he saw one night in a smoking mirror, unable to acknowledge or integrate or live with whatever he saw, he left his city and walked towards the coast. A journey strange and yet more strange it was.

Reaching the coast, he boarded a raft of serpents which, carrying him eastwards into the morning, carried him out of view, out of our world, but not out of Toltec, not out of Aztec, longing.

> Uruk,
> Thebes,
> Tula.

And a tragic chorus of three and three: Gilgamesh, Cadmus and Quetzalcoatl singing the strophe; Aeschylus, Sophocles and Euripides singing the antistrophe.

Wearing the grave masks of the Atreidae, wearing the wounded tunics of the Labdacidae, and taking the gorgeous, grave-fragrant, grave lyres of Sumer, they sing tragically to the wild beasts of the desert and to the wild beasts of the islands, for nowhere among them now is Enkidu, nowhere among them now is Pashupati, we, we believe, being so civilized that we have no need of Him, no need of the bearded, yogic, cephalically and phallically horned Lord of wild places and wild animals.

> For Him their lament is,
> For Him and for us.

For Uruk they sing. For the cormorant who lives there now. And Yeats would have us believe that their ancient eyes, as they sing, are glittering, that their ancient glittering eyes are gay.

Maybe. *Sub specie aeternitatis* there is much that is brutally possible.

Six city builders, building with stones, building with words: walking now where the cormorant and the screech owl and the great owl and the vultures are gathered, walking in lair light, hearing a satyr call to his fellow, they sing, for they are libation bearers now, pouring water, pouring wine, appeasing old hurt to earth and hearth.

Enkidu was corrupted. But Blake, ferociously spiritual, would begin again:

> *Bring me my Bow of burning gold!*
> *Bring me my Arrows of desire!*
> *Bring me my spear: O clouds, unfold!*
> *Bring me my chariot of fire.*
>
> *I will not cease from Mental Fight,*
> *Nor shall my Sword sleep in my hand*
> *Till we have built Jerusalem*
> *In England's green and pleasant land.*

But wait awhile, William. Before we board your chariot of fire there is something we would know. We know how hospitable to Angels and Saints and to Jesus the Imagination, your town, will be. But will it be hospitable also to Tyger? Will it be hospitable to Forests of the Night? And to Pashupati, in them? To Cernunnos in them? Will the Dragon be slain? Or will he be welcome? And honoured? Will there be a Green Dragon Temple in your city?

If not? If not, the cormorant, once again, will have the last word.

But, yes, we understand. We know that what you so fiercely intend, William, isn't a city in the conventional sense. Taking spear, and sword, and bow, taking arrows of desire, you intend a state of mind. You intend that souls that are lapsed from a Divine and Blessed Eternity shall realize and know that they are so lapsed. You intend that we, who are asleep, shall awake.

But there's the rub.

To too suddenly awaken might be dangerous.

You well remember your mentor Jacob Boehme who said:

*In us also is all whatsoever the Sun shines upon. In us are
all the Heavens, all the Hells and all the Deeps.*

And Sir Thomas Browne has claimed that

*There is all Africa and her prodigies
in us.*

And you yourself have said that

*In your own bosom you bear
Your Heaven and Earth and all you behold.*

And Hopkins has said that

*Mind has mountains, cliffs
of fall frightful, sheer,
no-man-fathomed.*

An awful lot to wake up to.

Maybe we would awaken, and wake up to, more than we could handle.

Hearing the Ragnarok rush of your Chariot of Fire, breached by your spear, our heaven-bearing, earth-bearing, hell-bearing bosoms breached, breached by your spear to our innermost, pre-cosmic, pre-psychic Deeps, so breached, so opened, there might, mightn't there, be a wide rushing in of waters, and who knows if the raven we send out or the dove we send out will ever come back bringing us news of a world, of a mind, we can inhabit and live in.

Cool it, William.

There mightn't be an ark for the dove to come back to.

It might be timely to recall your own words:

> *The roaring of lions, the howling of*
> *wolves, the raging of the stormy sea*
> *and the destructive sword are portions*
> *of eternity too great for the eye of man.*

Of more immediate import: aren't there portions of our minds which are too great for our minds?

Are there Hells or pits of Hell which aren't marriageable? Is the Earth we live on marriageable to a reality ontologically higher and more blessed than itself?

It would seem that Zoroastrians, Mandaeans and Gnostics believed that it wasn't.

Our hope is, yes.

Our hope is that there is no Abyss or Pit of Hell which isn't, even now, marriageable to the Highest Heaven, to the Highest Blessedness, to Bliss beyond Heaven and Blessedness.

> Tiamat is marriageable,
> Python is marriageable,
> Leviathan is marriageable,
> All Dragons, red and green, earthly and astral,
> Are marriageable.

That's why we would follow a cow out of Asia.

Where the cow lies down, we will build, to begin with, a Green Dragon Temple.

Where the cow lies down, building it about a Green Dragon's lair, we will build a holy city.

RAGNAROK

> How slow the fall of flesh,
> flowing Dark beneath this tree,
> Ash that's dead.

Beside wet murmurs there the wings flit,
Bird of the far Dark.

Beneath her hoverings, there no shelter,
Dust by the wind disturbed.
There at a trembling crowds crave entrance,
Climb towards branch and bird.
Peeled by the Frost, bone, trunk transforming
Branch into burning tongues,
But dead by the Murmurs
Hands are preserving—
Wind, by the wind disturbed.

In the Nordic world there is talk of Ragnarok; talk, that is, of a periodic release of cataclysmic, destructive energies that reduce all simultaneously existing worlds to chaos. But chaos isn't the end of the story. As we normally understand it, chaos is a vast confusion of energies. And this confusion, more or less malignant, is itself resolved into the stillness and silence of Ginnungagap. Ginnungagap is the Great Void, the Great Emptiness, the Great Indifference, out of which again a system of simultaneously existing worlds will arise.

In the Buddhist world, in contrast to this Nordic view, there is talk of Asraya paravritti; talk, that is, of a revulsion at the root in us of consciousness—of a revulsion that is characterized by an unremitting determination to destroy those inner psychological needs in which worldly experience has its source and continuance. And it is advisedly in this context that we speak, not of world, but of worldly experience. For, as Buddhists understand it, there isn't an anteriorly existing, independently existing, world of which we have, or can have, experience. In this estimation of it, world dissolves into worldly experience which has its source within. It follows that, for a Buddhist, Ragnarok is an inner psychological, not an outer cosmological, sequence of things happening, things done.

How interesting it is, in this regard, to compare or contrast Volva's Voluspa and Gautama's Udana. In the first case it is primarily a world that is thought of as existing independently of our experience of it which is undergoing Ragnarok. In the second case, it is primarily the experiencer who undergoes it.

Continuing to compare and contrast the Nordic and the Buddhist world views: in the Nordic world there is the howling of Fenriswolf; in the Buddhist world there is the roaring of Sugata Lion.

In the Nordic world, announcing Ragnarok, three cocks crow. A cock called Fjalar crows from a gibbet. A cock called Goldcomb crows from a birdwood. A cock called Rustred crows from the bars of Hel. In the Buddhist world Simhanada Avalokreshvara roars the lion-roar with which he would awaken all worlds from their dream of being worlds.

The Nordic and the Buddhist understanding of all things: how different they are! And yet, in this poem, the difference has disappeared: graduating into it, our Nordic understanding has lost its identity in a Buddhist or oriental understanding.

Unheard in the poem, out of view in it, Fjalar, Goldcomb and Rustred have crowed and, having slipped his chains, Fenriswolf has run free, he has howled, but even as he howled he changed, Fenriswolf became Sugatawolf and hearing him, listening to him, Yggdrasil's dream of its own Ragnarok becomes an awakening, a Great Awakening, from its dream experience of itself as the World Tree.

Awakening from its troubled dream of itself as World Tree, Yggdrasil becomes Bodhi Tree.

World Tree, Good Friday Tree, Bodhi Tree. It is Yggdrasil as Good Friday Tree that the poem has a brief vision of as we see it, Yggdrasil is beginning to be derelict. Its dream of itself as World Tree is dissolving.

No matter how strong its boughs might be, no matter how oak-able it might be to support its own dream of itself as World Tree, there is nonetheless a Fall taking place.

It is a time of hoverings and murmurings in the World Tree. Abyss murmurings and bird hoverings.

Fall-Time, Sap-sinking-Time, Twilight All-day-Time. Time again when boughs are bones, when leaves are burning tongues, all of them tongues of Ragnarok fire.

> Coo Coo ric oo
> Coo Coo ric oo
> Coo Coo ric oo

> Fjalar crowing from the gibber.
> Goldcomb crowing from the bone boughs.
> Rustred crowing from the burst bars.

And now their shadows are one bird. Bird whose substance is shadow. Bird of the fur dark. If that's what she is. We can't say what she is. We see only hoverings, we only hear wings. And we sometimes see or hear nothing at all, she being a condensation in momentary birdform of the Advaita Dark that was before multiplicity was.

Seeing her, a Mahayana Buddhist might say: she, almost, is Animitta; she, almost, is Tathata. She is the raven who, in biblical narratives of the Flood, flies to and fro finding no place for the sole of her foot.

And she doesn't come back bringing evidence that dreaming-awareness-of or waking-awareness-of have returned. We have gone beyond awareness-of in all its modes, dreaming, waking and chonyid. Sixteen cubits upwards the Waters prevail.

>There are no waters.
>There is no prevailing.
>Ginnungagap Volva called it.
>Call it the Divine-without-Form-and-Void,
>Call it Turiya.
>Call it World Tree,
>Good Friday Tree,
>Bodhi Tree.

Tree to which, in which, we pray;

>Shelter us, Sheltering Tree.
>Be our inner and our outer Yggdrasil sheltering us.
>Shelter us. Tree of all Worlds inner and outer.
>Shelter us. Beautiful Tree.
>Shelter us, Bodhi Tree.

And how beautiful upon the mountains are the feet of him that bringeth Good News, telling us that

>Fenriswolf is Sugatawolf.

Telling us that, the shadow of three cocks crowing are one Abhaya Mudra, one Fear-not Gesture.

>The Fear-not Gesture of Ragnarok.
>The Fear-not Gesture of Ginnungagap.

>Ragnarok is Pralaya.
>Ginnungagap is Turiya.

The bow in the cloud is the Fear-not Gesture in the cloud.

In the form of the Mandukya Upanishad in the cloud is the Abhaya Mudra in the cloud.

>Tehom is Turiya.
>Split the wood. Brahman is there.
>Wedge the stone, Brahman is there.
>Brahmanirguna is.
>All this is Brahman.

>Shantih Shantih Shantih.

BASTILLE DAY

And like peasants elsewhere, the peasants of Europe didn't wait passively for winter to go and summer to come. They ritually carried out winter and, ritually again, they brought in summer. Making an effigy of it, they carried out Death and, emblematically in a green branch, they brought in Life.

As we would expect, Frazer opens the magic casement, backwards this time, into our own, not so remote rural past:

> In the villages near Eriangen, when the fourth Sunday in Lent came round, the peasant girls used to dress themselves in all their finery with flowers in their hair. Thus attired they repaired to the neighbouring town, carrying puppets which were adorned with leaves and covered with white cloths. These they took from house to house in pairs, stopping at every door where they expected to receive something and singing a few lines in which they announced that it was Mid-Lent and that they were about to throw Death into the water. When they had collected some trifling gratuities they went to the river Reritz and flung the puppets representing Death into the stream. This was done to ensure a fruitful and prosperous year; further, it was considered a safeguard against pestilence and sudden death. At Nuremberg girls of seven to eighteen years of age go through the streets bearing a little open coffin, in which is a doll hidden under a shroud. Others carry a beech branch, with an apple fastened to it for a head, in an open box. They sing 'We carry Death into the water, it is well' or 'We carry Death in to the water, carry him in and out again'. In some parts of Bavaria down to 1780, it was believed that a fatal epidemic would ensue if the custom of 'Carrying out Death' was not observed.
>
> In some villages of Thüringen on the fourth Sunday of Lent, children used to carry a puppet of birch twigs through the village and then throw it into a pool while they sang 'We carry the old Death out behind the headman's old house; we have got Summer and Kroden's power is destroyed.' At Debschwitz or Dobschwitz, near Gera, the ceremony of driving out Death is or was annually observed on the first of March. The young people make up a figure of straw or the like materials, dress it in old clothes, which they have begged from houses in the village, and carry it out and throw it in the river. On returning to the village they break the good news to the people, and receive eggs and other victuals as a reward. The ceremony is or was supposed to purify the village and to protect the inhabitants from sickness and plague. In other villages of Thüringen in which the population was originally Slavonic, the carrying out of the puppet is accompanied with the singing of a song, which begins 'Now we carry Death out of the village and Spring into the village ...'

In Bohemia the children go out with a straw-man, representing Death, to the end of the village, where they burn it singing,

> *Now carry we Death out of the village,*
> *The new summer into the village.*
> *Welcome, dear Summer,*
> *Green little corn.*

At Tabor in Bohemia the figure of Death is carried out of the town and flung from a high rock into the water, while they sing

> *Death swims in the water,*
> *Summer will soon be here,*
> *We carried Death away for you*
> *We brought the summer.*
> *And do thou, O holy Markets,*
> *Give us a good year*
> *For wheat and for rye.*

In other parts of Bohemia they carry Death to the end of the village,

> *We carry Death out of the village,*
> *And the new year into the village.*
> *Dear Spring, we bid you welcome,*
> *Green grass, we bid you welcome.*

Behind the village they erect a pyre on which they burn the straw figure, reviling and scoffing at it the while. Then they return singing,

> *We have carried away Death*
> *And brought Life back.*
> *He has taken up his quarters in the village*
> *Therefore sing joyous songs.*

Thoroughly scientific in our outlook now, we no longer practise such customs. Heirs to what we still imagine to have been a great enlightenment, we take no little pride in having emancipated ourselves from—it is Marx's phrase—the idiocy of rural life.

And yet we aren't as liberated, nor are we as enlightened, as we imagine ourselves to be. We aren't enlightenment beings. We aren't beings whose essence is enlightenment. We aren't Bodhisattvas.

And there is something more lethal than Death that we might carry out.

> It blights us. It blights our world.
> Call it our Medusa mindset.
> Call it Gorgocogito.

Easier altogether to name it than to explain it, this something more lethal than Death, this something our children should throw into the river.

It is Platonic belief that, aboriginally, we were souls in a supercelestial realm; but for reasons which, in the extant writings, aren't always immediately convincing, we have, it is claimed, wandered downwards into incarnate existence in a world of shadows.

This is the doctrine Wordsworth rehearses:

> *Our birth is but a sleep and a forgetting:*
> *The Soul that rises with us, our life's Star,*
> *Hath had elsewhere its setting,*
> *And cometh from afar:*
> *Not in entire forgetfulness,*
> *And not in utter nakedness,*
> *But trailing clouds of glory do we come*
> *From God, who is our home:*
> *Heaven lies about us in our infancy!*
>
> *Shades of the prison-house begin to close*
> *Upon the growing Boy,*
> *But he beholds the light, and whence it flows,*
> *He sees it in his joy;*
> *The Youth, who daily farther from the east*
> *Must travel, still is Nature's priest,*
> *And by the vision splendid*
> *Is on his way attended;*
> *At length the man perceives it die away*
> *And fade into the light of common day.*

As Plotinus has it: 'Life here, with the things of earth, is a sinking, a defeat, a failing of the wing.'

As William Blake understands it, this sinking continued all the way downwards into what he calls the limit of opacity and the limit of contraction.

Imagine a hand contracted into a fist, imagine a life contracted to economic purpose.

> Clenched heart,
> Clenched mind,
> Clenched life.

Looked at through clenched eyes, what else but matter for economic exploitation is the earth, what else but economic opportunities are mountains and oceans, what else but economic man-hours are persons.

It might be no harm, at this point, to quote a poem called 'Paradise Lost':

> *Between nature's*
> *Pink period and blue*
> *We were fauns, we looked on.*

> *Being cold, a priori and few*
> *We turned towards time at will*
> *And we watched the yew*
> *With wide eyes.*
>
> *That it might see us,*
> *Understand,*
> *We solved the earth.*
>
> *That it might see us,*
> *Show its hand,*
> *We blitz the rock*
> *With metaphors,*
>
> *We blitz the land.*

As this little poem imagines it, it was inwardly in our senses and faculties that the Fall occurred. It was to us as perceivers of the world, not to the world we perceive, that it happened. Given his philosophical position, this would be necessarily so for Berkeley. But Blake also is relevant. Blake believed that there are four conditions or states. He called them

> Eden,
> Beulah,
> Generation,
> Ulro.

It is only secondarily that these are objective states. Primarily, they are states of the perceiver.

The poem logs our declension into Ulro. It logs our declension as perceivers into the Medusa mindset, into Gorgocogito. Medusa's head is pure horror. The very sight of it turns anyone who looks at it to stone.

I imagine, by extension, that anything she perceives is, in the perceiving, petra-fied.

As Kant might have said it, the forms of her sensibility and the categories of her understanding are petra-fying forms, petra-fying categories.

As she perceives it, petra-fying it, so is her world. She walks among her petra-factions. She lives in Ulro. And René Descartes is her consort, her accomplice. Among us he is her plenipotentiary.

> The Mind altering, alters all,
> Altering unfavourably it unfavourably alters all it sees.

Then come the children of Israel, even the whole congregation into the desert of Zin, in the first month: and the people abode in Kadesh; and Miriam died there, and was buried there. And there was no water for the congregation: and they gathered themselves together against Moses and against Aaron. And the people chode with Moses, and spoke, saying, Would god that we had died when our brethren died before the Lord! And why have ye brought up the congregation of the Lord into this wilderness, that we and our cattle should die there? And wherefore have ye made us to come up out of Egypt, to bring us into this evil place? It is no place of seed, or of figs, or of vines, or of pomegranates, neither is there any water to drink. And Moses and Aaron went from the presence of the assembly unto the door of the tabernacle of the congregation, and they fell upon their faces: and the glory of the Lord appeared unto them. And the Lord spake unto Moses, saying. Take the rod and gather thou the assembly together, thou, and Aaron, thy brother, and speak ye unto the rock before their eyes, and it shall give forth his water, and thou shalt bring forth to them water out of the rock: so thou shall give the congregation and their Guests drink. And Moses took the rod from before the Lord, as he commanded him. And Moses and Aaron gathered the congregation together before the rock, and he said unto them, Hear now, ye rebels: must we fetch you water out of the rock? And Moses lifted up his hand, and with his rod he smote the rock twice: and the water came out abundantly, and the congregation drank, and the beasts also.

Us also. Led by Medusa's plenipotentiaries we have wandered for three centuries now, in Ulro. Like Michelangelo's captives we are embedded, not physically, but philosophically, in Medusa mindset.

> That it might see us
> Understand
> We solved the earth.

> That it might see us
> Show its hand
> We blitz the rock
> With metaphors,

> We blitz the land.

Ulro rocks don't receive our cosmologies. Like letters undelivered, unopened, they echo them back to us.

> Europe is Ulropa,
> We are Ulropeans.

And our Universe, our Ulroverse, had its origin in a Big Bang. And it will end in a Big Crunch. And

> *An archive now of its own despair*
> *The earth still builds the granite stair*
> *Only those it breaks can comprehend.*
> *Stegosaurus now is a lost dead-end*
> *And man, at best, an obedient bend*
> *Hardens already into his truth:*
> *Already now in his youngest youth*

> *He fails and is petra-fied where*
> *Behind him he hears some appalling brute*
> *Climbing, forgivably, up for his share,*

But maybe we've got it all wrong. Maybe all our statements about the universe are statements out of, and about, our Medusa mindset.

The mind altering, alters all.

So perhaps there is hope. We can perhaps imagine it, Bastille Day for Michelangelo's Captives. Bastille Day for everyone who is embedded in the Medusa mindset. Bastille Day for rocks, rainbows, rivers and stars. Rocks, rainbows, rivers and stars walking free of our petra-fying perceptions of them.

> Quatorze Juillet
> Quatorze Éternité.

And no one smote our Ulro rock. No one smote our Medusa mindset. No one took an insurrectionary axe to its ancient regime.
The mind altering, alters all. And now again

> The corn is orient and immortal wheat.

Now again

> Every bush is a burning bush,
> Every river is a medicine river.
> Every stone is an a-stone-ishment
> turned inwards on its own rose window wonders.

And carrying the last memories of our Medusa mindset out of our culture Berkeley and Blake sing a short song:

> Quatorze Juillet
> Quatorze Éternité.

Returning they sing

> Quatorze Juillet
> Quatorze Éternité.

IMMRAM EVA

'Your soul hath set sail like a returning Odysseus for its native land.'
                                                                Plotinus

There is a poem by Eva Gore-Booth called 'The Mystic':

> *Nay, though green fields are fair*
> *And the fiords are blue,*
> *I need a clearer air, I need a region new,*
> *Out beyond the Northern Lights,*
> *Where the white Polar Day*
> *To herself in silence sings,*
> *Without thought of words or wings,*
> *The secret of a hundred nights.*
>
> *I shall find there I know*
> *The lost city of my birth,*
> *Innocent white wastes of snow,*
> *A new heaven and a new earth.*
> *Neither lamb, nor calf nor kid,*
> *In those lonely meadows play,*
> *All things calm and silent are*
> *Underneath the Polar star,*
> *Where all my dreams are hid.*
>
> *I am sick of wind and tide—*
> *Tired of this rocking boat,*
> *Creaking ever as we glide*
> *Into the white remote;*
> *Out there no sound is heard*
> *Save the iceberg's crash and grind,*
> *No human voice e'er shuddered through*
> *The realms of white, the realms of blue,*
> *Nor cry of a sea-bird.*
>
> *Lying at ease in the dark ship*
> *I watch the last pale night depart,*
> *I dreamt I saw blue shadows slip*
> *O'er the white snowfields of my heart;*
> *And the world has grown so wide*
> *There was room for all mankind—*
> *The icebergs roundabout the Pole*

Crashed in the silence of my soul,
And hemmed me in on every side.

In that crowded world of white
There are many joys unknown,
Without colour there is light,
Loneliness for the alone,
Heedless stars, that blaze and shine,
O'er the world's untrodden edge;
You come with me you who dare,
Leave the cart and the plough-share
For the white horizon line.

Over many seas we sail,
Passing many peopled shores,
Like the Greek in the old tale
Homeward sailing from the wars.
Gentle voices bid us rest
from green isle or barren sedge,
'In our world all things are new,
We have passed away from you,
You must seek another guest.'

Voices of enchanted time
Call us to leave our ships,
Hyacinths of honeyed rhyme
Float from Aphrodite's lips;
We for Circe born unkind,
All the songs the sirens sing
Seem but idly to oppress
Hearts in love with loneliness,
Sails that flutter in the wind.

O'er the wide cold wastes serene
Rise the walls of wandering white,
Circles of strange gods unseen
In the electric arc unite.
Arctic faces flash and glide,
Glimmers many a flaming wing,
Where the aether strains to hold
The hard heart of the Manifold
All the greater gods abide.

This surely is a song of innocence. And given the enormity of the yearning, the heedless, innocent enormity of it, it is our great loss that there isn't a corresponding song of experience. No old logbook comes shorewards towards us on the little waves of Breffny. And even if the twilight is Celtic and you are walking a road into Cloonagh, you won't have to sit and listen, spellbound by a glittering eye, to the tale of an Ancient Mariner:

> *And now there came both mist and snow*
> *And it grew wondrous cold:*
> *And ice, mast-high, came floating by,*
> *As green as emerald.*
>
> *And through the drifts the snowy clifts*
> *Did send a dismal sheen:*
> *Nor shapes of men nor beasts we ken—*
> *The ice was all between.*
>
> *The ice was here, the ice was there,*
> *The ice was all around.*
> *It crackd and growl'd, and roar'd and howl'd,*
> *Like voices in a swound!*

A most awful voyage. A most awful rite of passage:

> *The icebergs round about the Pole*
> *Crashed in the silence of my soul.*

And yet how without undergoing it, or, how without undergoing something like it, can European humanity have a good future?

If a plant is left too long in its grow-bag, its roots reaching the plastic will turn round and round and round, and, finding no outlet into wild, nourishing nature, will, having nowhere else to go, re-enter the exhausted sour soil and, thriving till now, the plane, root and branch, will begin to sicken.

It would be foolish to suggest that Hebrew prophecy, Greek philosophy and science, Roman engineering and law are an exhausted sour soil, but it mightn't be at all foolish to suggest that they lack certain kinds of cultural nourishment that we now need.

It might be time, if we aren't going to sicken further, to break out of our cultural grow-bag. It might be time to make contact with wild nature.

> You come with me you who dare,
> Leave the cart and the plough-share
> For the white horizon line.

Given that I am the kind of person I am, I hesitate, wisely I think. I have read of a voyage to the heart of darkness: it ended horribly, not only for the person that undertook it. How then, Eva, are you so sure that your journey into the heart of white brightness will prosper?

Yeats, your friend, a man not lacking in courage, a man of great yearnings, some of them, like Cleopatra's, immortal yearnings—he didn't sail away from culture. Leaving this island in the Atlantic, he sailed southward and then, sailing a course through the Pillars of Hercules, he charted a course for Byzantium and, his voyage having prospered, he made landfall there, and he prayed:

> O sages standing in God's holy fire
> As in the gold mosaic of a wall,
> Come from the holy fire, perne in a gyre,
> And be the singing-masters of my soul.

Like the Psalmist he might have exulted:

> Blessed be the Lord: for he hath showed me
> his marvellous kindness in a strong city.

He lived in a strong tower. A Norman tower. And the Normans were wont to strengthen the foundations of their towers with bull's blood.

Unlike Bulkington, outward bound again on the *Pequod*, Yeats didn't do business in great waters, he stayed creatively close to his chiselled hearthstone.

In Yeats's vision of it, there it is:

> The light of evening, Lissadell,
> Great windows open to the south,
> Two girls in silk kimonos, both
> Beautiful, one a gazelle.

One of them, Eva, needs clearer air, she needs a religion new.

She needs greater Gods. Gods greater than Aphrodite, Circe and Poseidon. And she will come to them where they abide, where

> No sound is heard
> Save the iceberg's crash and grind.

She will come to them where there is

> Loneliness for the alone.

She will come to them where

> Heedless stars ... blaze and shine
> O'er the world's untrodden edge.

Will your greater Gods house you, Eva? Will they henge you? Stonehenge you? Icehenge you?

Eva Gore-Booth in an icehenge.

> Give Eva land.
> Give her land, lots of land,
> Don't fence her in.

The truth is, of course, that we are fenced in. Within and without there's a Hadrian's Wall that cuts us off from the transnordic north, it cuts us off from land never opened by the ploughshare, it cuts us off from the land of the Ancestral Shaman. Like an immune system, psychological and cultural, this wall. It keeps commonage consciousness at bay.

So could it be, after all, that Eva's instinct is right? Could it be, after all, that her voyage out beyond our culture is as necessary as Yeats's voyage back into it?

How strange that we who for centuries have drawn cultural nourishment from the Mediterranean might need now to draw it from the transnordic north.

In our behaviour now, we are Aids virus to the earth. We are doing to the earth what the Aids virus does to the human body: we are breaking down its immune system. Assumptions and axioms of our classical Christian inheritance enable us to do this. Our classical Christian inheritance is therefore suspect.

Bon voyage, Eva. May you fare more fortunately with the Angakok Bear than a sailor we've heard of fared with the Albatross.

> May you, for our sake, fare more fortunately.
> May Takanakapsaluk and all her sea-beasts favour you.

A song of innocence called The Mystic.

A song of experience called The Ancient Mariner.

We have, maybe, no choice. We must, maybe, hazard our innocence. 'We must start on a new venture towards God.'

SILA ERSINARSINIVDLUGE

In the year 1821 the sarcophagus of Pharaoh Sety I was brought from the Valley of the Kings to England. Hollowed from a block of translucent alabaster, it is inscribed inside and outside with the complete text of The Book of Gates.

Its translucent whiteness yellowing, the blue inlay of its hieroglyphs fallen out, it is housed today in the basement of a small museum in London.

As Shakespeare imagined it, there once was a night so wild, so irruptively awful, that even the Planets, the Divine Governors of the world, kept to their caves. Chaos, it seemed, had come again. Lear, an old King of Britain, and his fool and a friend were out of doors that night, wandering about in a treeless heath, A terrible portentous parody of the Magi they were. And like the Magi, although not following a star, they came to a hovel and in it, lying on straw, they saw not God become Man, but Man become Animal. They saw the thing itself, bare and forked. They saw unaccommodated man.

How accommodated Sety was. On his throne how accommodated. In his sarcophagus how accommodated, religiously, culturally and cosmologically.

And us?

Think of us?

Think of Kepler and Pascal.

Think of Kepler's horror and Pascal's terror.

Think of Kepler's horror when, fearlessly confronting the evidence, he and others concluded our universe has neither centre nor circumference.

And there is a night when, unaccommodated, Pascal isn't imperturbably able for the universe of infinite ages and spaces we live in: 'The eternal silence of those infinite spaces terrifies me,' he cries. And it might be that cry is the birth cry of unaccommodated, modern humanity.

As D.H. Lawrence would have it, we are naked under our clothes.

But ... in his igloo one night an old Eskimo shaman, for the moment concluding, said to Rasmussen,

'Sila Ersinarsinivdiuge'
(Don't be afraid of the universe.)

How come that he wasn't naked under his clothes? How come that, sitting there by the light and fire of his seal-oil lamp, how come that, sitting in his snow house, he wasn't cosmologically cold? How come that, sitting in his snow house, he was at home?

What furs invisible to us was he wearing?

What psychological, cosmological furs, growing like good dreams from within, was he dressed in?

Or is it that, being a shaman, he was long accustomed to living from and in those inner depths where the universe itself does our thinking and dreaming and imagining for us?

Are there, within us all, depths in which the universe is imaginatively able for itself? depths in which it is able for its own dreams? for its own stupendousness? And in what sense and to what extent is the universe objective?

... in your own bosom you bear your Heaven and Earth and all you behold; and though it appear without it is within, in your imagination ...

So says Blake. Blake lived in Beulah. He lived, sometimes maybe, in Eden. But ...

Poor Tom's acold.

Acold his hands. Acold his heart.

And our last ounce of civet or science won't do.

Mount-Palomar big, our eyes haven't blossomed into big seeing, our eyes haven't blossomed into rose windows.

Poor Tom's acold.

Even if we wrapped him in the mainsail of the homeward-bound *Beagle* and gave him Fitzroys' Bible to read, he would still be acold.

Even if, writing it hieroglyphically, we wrote the last paragraph of *The Origin of Species* on his high *Homo habilis* brow and gave him Newton's *Principia* and Einstein's *General Theory* to read, he would be cold.

The Planets stay in their caves tonight.

'Tis a wild night to be out of doors. Indoors tonight we are out of doors.

On a heath, windswept and treeless, a hovel. On a tundra, blizzards crossing it, a snow hut. Will someone go to the snow hut? Will you go Cordelia? Or you, Gloucester, will you go?

Go, and don't be afraid: sitting by his Pleistocene stone lamp, his Pleistocene eyes closed, the medicine man will see you coming. Going in, you will of necessity, bend very low. Like birth it will be. Like being reborn back into the commonage consciousness of Altamira and Lascaux. Greet him. Sit with him and when you are warm tell him Tom is cold.

A healer, he will of course come, bringing commonage consciousness. He will bring it in his clothes, in his masks, in his medicine bundle. In his moods, and in all his states of mind dreaming and waking he will bring it, and be it, singing it. Singing it, singing it, singing it, until, anamnesially, Altamira and Lascaux are our inner earth ears initiating us into horse hearing, into bison-, owl- and auroch-hearing. We hear the lost herds as they hear themselves grazing and dreaming. Singing it, singing it, singing it, until anamnesially, the smell of a woolly rhinoceros in oestrus revives in us and magically one with her, wearing her masks, dancing her dance, we are conceived by her—slowly, over hours, her dance, our dance, conceives us, and again, over hours, slowly, her dance gives us birth.

As Animal she is our Totem. As Dance she is our Mother.

As Dance she is always in oestrus, always ready to reabsorb us, to reconceive us in her image and likeness, to give us birth wearing her horn, our sign upon us of our identity with her, our sign upon us of commonage consciousness.

But will this ounce of shamanic civet save us?

Will commonage consciousness so accommodate us, so shelter us, that we will never at any time be out at elbow or heel?

As Plato, Plotinus, and as Wordsworth in one great ode, understood it, we are souls who have come down or lapsed into the universe.

Imagine a soul descending: it sees a sign saying

ACCOMMODATION
FULL COSMOLOGICAL BED AND BOARD

As it turns out, the accommodation, if that's what it is, is stupendous: stupendously lovely, stupendously frightful. So lovely sometimes we can only just endure it. So frightful sometimes that we turn away unable simultaneously to see and stay sane. We cope. We creosote our brainstems, we creosote cogito consciousness in us, against psychic bad weather. We refuse the Great Life. We refuse to voyage into and through our own Poseidon angers, enmities, wraths. We jump ship, we come ashore, and, throughout all our life thereafter, it is under our own Circe wands we live, regressed and reduced, and acold.

A House called the limit of contraction,
A House called the limit of opacity.

These houses aren't weatherproof. Sometimes, if only in dreams, our limits are breached and the creosoted, safe indoors is the big outdoors and out there somewhere, in a treeless nowhere under a cracked welkin, under a welkin ripped at its lightning seams, out there in a wild somewhere, smelling their way, are the King and his fool and their friend. The hovel they stumble upon doesn't shelter them, for in it, lying on a litter of straw, cracked like the world, cracked like the King, Tom O'Bedlam is portent.

O God, thou hast cast us off, thou hast scattered us, thou hast been displeased; O turn thyself to us again. Thou hast made the earth to tremble: thou hast broken it; heal the breaches thereof: for it shaketh. Thou hast showed thy people hard things; thou hast made us to drink the wine of astonishment.

Shamans drink that wine. Aua drank it and in his snow hut one night, blizzards crossing the ice-cap, he ended his conversation with Rasmussen saying,

'Sila ersinarsinivdiuge.'
(Don't be afraid of the Universe.)

Same thing as saying, don't be afraid of yourself.

Even if all Africa and its prodigies are in you, don't be afraid.

Even if your mind has mountains, even if it has cliffs of fall frightful, even if it has chasms and deeps no-man-fathomed, don't be afraid, for:

> All shall be well,
> And all shall be well,
> And all manner of thing shall be well.
> At the level of Atman Brahman in us
> All is well,
> And all is well,
> And all manner of thing is well.

At the level of Atman Brahman the universe is well. Silam Inua speaks to us in blizzards. It speaks to us in all weathers, universal and local. It speaks to us in cosmic silence, in the eternal silence of those infinite spaces.

Smaller than a snow hut, vaster than our system of universes, Silam Inua, including them, transcending them, is centre and circumference.

The answer to Pascal's night of terror is Pascal's night of fire:

> *L'an de grâce 1654.*
> *Lundi, 23 novembre, jour de Saint Clément, Pape*
> *et martyr, et autres au martyrologe*
> *Veille de Saint Chrysogone, martyr, et autres,*
> *depuis environ dix heures et demie du soir jusques environ minuit et demi*
> *Feu.*

> *Dieu d'Abraham, Dieu d'Isaac, Dieu de Jacob,*
> *Non des philosophes et des savants*
> *Certitude. Certitude. Sentiment. Joie. Paix (...)*
> *Oubli du monde et de tout, hormis Dieu (...)*
> *Joie! Joie! Joie! pleurs de joie.*

> Night of astronomical horror.
> Night of astronomical terror.
> Night of astonishment night
> Prodigious night,
> Night of fall frightful,
> No-man-fathomed night,
> Night of Fire.

Fire everything, in the depths of its being, sits at.

Out of doors on a godless wild night, wet and acold, the outcast King and his fool and his friend sit at it.

Lying on a litter of straw, Poor Tom O'Bedlam sits at it.
In the depth of itself, freezing-point sits at it.
Draco and Leo sit at it. Scorpio, her poisoned tail in her mouth, sucking it, sits at it. Cancer sits at it.
The eternal silence of those infinite spaces sits at it.
Every system of universes, past, present and to come, sits at it.

Sitting at it,
Losing our illusory selfhood,
We become it.

It is only superficially, it is only in our dream of ourselves as ego identities, that we are unaccommodated.
So, sail on Sety.
Dressed in your hieroglyphic stone coat, the gates in contraction and in opacity open.
Lying in your hieroglyphic stone boat you have been given a heart for the Big World. With his words of power, his lustrations, and his adze, the Shem Priest has opened your mouth, so you can say it—sailing among the circumpolar stars, a star at the tiller, stars moving the oars, a star at the lookout, you can, sailing onwards, say it:
Your mouth opened by the Shem Priest's adze not closed by Circe's wand, you can, sailing onwards, say it:

Silam Inua,
Sila ersinarsinivdluge.

SHAMAN

Being awake in the way that modern people are awake isn't something I'm good at. After only a few years in it, therefore, I left the modern world and came back, putting my hand, happily now, to the spade and the shovel I had left down.

Ivy I had planted against the walls had grown thick and strong, blinding two windows. I didn't cut it, preferring an intuitive twilight in the house. It was for the same reason also that I didn't often light the lamp. Even on winter nights I didn't often light it. Itself so full of shadows, there is more understanding in firelight for the kind of man I am.

Bringing water from the well and turf from the shed, these were the last two jobs I would do, darkness closing in, on a winter's evening.

If the weather was hard I'd select hard sods. Cut from the deepest spit of a high bog, they were older, I'd remind myself sometimes, than Ireland's oldest folktale.

What that folktale was I didn't know, but how strange it was, crossing a yard at nightfall with a prehistoric landscape in a bag on my back. For the rest of the night I would sit prehistorically by the fire and life and light of it. That suited me. That was something I was good at. It came naturally to me on winter nights to sink to the sod's level. It came naturally to me, sitting there, to sink into the deepest spit of mind in me. And that was a dreaming spit, dreaming its dream with a hawthorn bush, dreaming their dreams with mountain and star.

One night the chimney wasn't drawing so well. The wind was from the north and when it gusted there would be a downdraught of billowing, blue smoke into the room.

It was hard on my eyes. I closed them, continuing to sit there, inhaling the fragrance.

Soon something was happening. Landscapes I had glimpses of, landscapes Partholon might have walked in, were taking me over. It was like they were fostering me. I was and yet I wasn't myself. I was their dream of me. I was doing their dream of me. I was digging peat. In the deepest spit, between two tree stumps, I uncovered a pair of boars. Of deerhide I thought. But I couldn't be sure, so strangely transparent in places were they. Going up onto the bank, I put off my own boors and I put them on, criss-crossing a tracery of thongs about my shins and collops, knotting them under my knees. To test them, to get the feel of them, I got up and starred walking, going the wind's way.

A lake I came to, following an otter path, was strange. It didn't mirror some things it should mirror. It didn't mirror a red horse on a ridge. It didn't mirror its own islands. It didn't mirror a wood growing along one side of it. And yet, so clear, so deadly calm, so far-sighted a lake I had never seen. It mirrored mountains so far away it must, you would think, be clairvoyant.

Otters, I thought, wouldn't lead me astray, wouldn't lead me to evil, so I kept to the path, going with it, not frightened.

As I entered the wood the horse on the ridge behind me neighed. It was a red neighing.

Farther along I smelled something dead. Something big, I thought, a boar or a deer. And yet, though I searched a long while, I found no carcass. There was no sign of anything carnivorous feeding.

How can this be? I wondered, walking on. How can there be such a strong smell of death where nothing has died?

From a long way off I heard it. It was a birch. Invisible beings wielding invisible axes were felling it. It was frightful. Every axe blow to it was an axe blow to me. All savage damage to it was savage damage to me. I was a limbless trunk. Infinitely felled, infinitely hurt, I was a stump of me.

I was me and I kept going.

The two sides of the path came together. I entered thick darkness and I didn't see the house until, seeing an old man by the fire, I realized I'd already walked into it.

The chair he pointed to was withered. He was withered himself. And the fire was withered.

It was a fire of three last gasps. It gave no heat. But it didn't go out.

The house smelled of stored apples, like apples in March, too shrivelled for use.

Where am I? I asked.

What where could there be when the two sides of your path have come together? What where could there be when both sides of the mirror are blind?

Even his words were withered. Leaving his mouth they were withered. They were born withered.

Only people the lake doesn't mirror come this far, he said.

I kept silent, wondering.

I knew you were coming, he said. I heard the red neighing.

Where are we? I asked.

In a wood, he said.

What wood? Where?

In a wood between worlds. In a wood the lake doesn't mirror.

Does it mirror this house?

No.

Does it mirror the smoke from its chimney?

There is no smoke from its chimney.

Does it mirror you?

He didn't answer.

Does it mirror me?

No, It doesn't mirror you. You heard the red neighing didn't you? And there's something more. It was your own death, all your own deaths, that you smelled coming into the wood.

Who are you? I asked.

I'm the mask of your own state of mind. As you yourself are so do you see me.

You have otter's whiskers.

Have I?

An otter path led to your house.

If it did, then it led to that, he said, pointing to a hag-bed I hadn't seen. I went and lay down.

And now, he said, bending over me, touching my mouth with his stick, now you must ask no more questions. Your words have no meanings now. Like the boughs outside all their meanings have fallen from them. All their mirrorings are quenched.

I felt weak.

So weak I couldn't even be weak.

Consciousness blurred. It brightened. It blurred. Breathing was hard. Every breath was the last breath, the death-rattle breath, of beings I had been. In a seizure of sightless seeing I had unblurred, perfect vision of a doe I had been. All my deaths were dying me. Like the fire, it wasn't for life, it was for death I was gasping. Only all my deaths was life in me, and it death-rattled me, and it death-rattled me, and it death-rattled me, and then, in a moment of clarity consenting to be, consenting not to be, it death-rattled the life I'd been living, modern life, out of me. And now when I thought it was over, it came again death-rattling six spit of history out of me.

Like a dropped fawn, mother-licked, I struggled to my feet. But there was no chair, no fire.

Like a mirror turned away, there was no house.

Self-detached, like placenta, and fallen to the ground, the boots I'd been wearing were being overgrown. Looking at them, I felt sure that in time a high bog would cover them.

The boots I had put off I found, how, I don't know. And I came home, how I don't know. I only know that I was sitting in my own chair by my own fire when I heard a knocking.

The man who opened my door and came in had come, he said, because he had dreamed that I was a healer.

PROTHALAMION

Now again I lived amphibiously. Now again, my head fashioned as much for fantasy as for fact, I had come home, to the lake-mirrored house I had walked out of into adult identity.

A difficult identity it was. Like a shoe a size or two too small, it hurt me, it inhibited me. But, fearing irrational irruption, I kept it laced down.

That one irruption, my neighbours will well remember, that was enough.

It wasn't only in my heart that I was heartbroken. I was heartbroken in my clothes, I was heartbroken in my feet, but I continued walking.

On a road that argued its way into wild mountains I knew, arguing too, that here I would stay.

Maybe the colour that breaks out of furze, maybe the fragrance and colour that break out of heather would break out of me here. Maybe I wasn't a lost cause.

Mistaking me for a man with dogs, the sheep of three mountains cascaded upwards. Up between rocks they poured, up to the safety of shoulders from which, looking down, they kept me in view.

It saddened me that they fled from me. Maybe they sensed something in me. Maybe, seeing into my depths, they saw that I was a man with dogs.

Would I ever be right?

So blue were the shoulders of rock they looked down at me from, so zealously blue, it would be hard, looking at them, not to believe in a world soul.

Do these sheep only graze the hard grass of these wind-rummaged, wild mountains?

Do they graze this blue? Are there in them lungs we don't know about? Are there in them lungs with which they breathe this blue?

I took up where I had left off, looking after a rich man's salmon river.

My house was river-mirrored. That, chiefly, was why I had come back. Also, my work requiring it, I'd be out a lot at night, and that suited the kind of man I was.

A life of little rituals, of little sacraments, suited me. Before going out at night, knowing I'd be out for hours, I would smoor the fire. Using a small shovel, I'd pour ashes onto its vehemence, extinguishing all flames, covering all coals. Inhibited in this way, it would live on, barely breathing. Raking it out, hours later when I had come back, cold and wet maybe, I would find a few coals. Released from near suffocation, they would now become the glowing, then flaming, heart of a new fire. Sacraments such as this saved me I think. They gave shape to a solitude I wasn't always happily able for.

Nights there were when mind in me didn't smoor me. Dreaming didn't smoor me. Waking didn't smoor me. The ashes of ordinary hearing and seeing didn't inhibit a flaming in me.

I would sit in a pantheon of bushes. And on the bog road into the mountains, even if I met an ecstasy coming towards me, I'd pass it by saying good night. Compared to the thronged rock tumults of these mountains, an ecstasy to a sixth or a seventh heaven would be a trivial, if rapturous, regression to bliss.

Vernacular nature, nature vernacular in grouse comb and thunder, that was enough. That was as much as I could sacredly cope with.

Sitting one night by the fire, my house river-mirrored, I sang five love songs.

As I sang each song I asked it, as water might ask a bowl, to give me its shape. I asked it, singing it, to control me. I asked Carraig Donn, pouring myself into it, to keep me safe.

That night she came to me. It was out of my own singing she came:

> *And the people were saying no two were e'er wed*
> *But one has a sorrow that never was said;*
> *And I smiled as she passed with her goods and her gear*
> *And that was the last that I saw of my dear.*
>
> *Last night she came to me, my dead love came in,*
> *So softly she came that her feet made no din;*
> *She laid her hand on me and this she did say*
> *It will not be long, love, till our wedding day.*

The hand wasn't dead, it wasn't deadly. It touched me at a depth too deep to be purely inward. It touched me at a depth deeper than where catastrophe is possible. And I didn't know about such a depth. Till now I didn't know. I didn't know till my dead love touched me.

How different my clothes felt, pulling them on. My shoes weren't heartbroken now.

Out through the door I went, following her.

It was a path used sometimes by otters I took.

I resisted an impulse to go back and look at myself in the mirror. I wanted to see how I'd changed.

The path was the same. The stones the same. The river and the mountains were the same. It was the world I had lived in I was in, but how changed it was, how strange, her voice going before me, calling:

> *It will not be long, love, till our wedding day.*

How strange the world was.

How escaped from old habits of seeing it was. 'Twas as if a veil had opened and now, for the first time in my life, I was looking at ordinariness. Was I able, I wondered, for such revelations of ordinariness? Ordinary mountains. Ordinary sheep. An ordinary river. An ordinary morning mirrored in it.

Yesterday, if I met a man going into those mountains and he told me he was going in to mine iron, I'd have thought that natural. That, I'd have thought, was reasonable. This morning, I would think it was reasonable if he told me he was going in to mine mind. Blocks of it. Blocks of gneiss mind. Blocks of schist mind. Blocks of blue-mountain mind to build sheep pens with.

It was into ordinariness she was calling me:

It will not be long, love, till our wedding day.

From beyond my own mountains I heard it:

Till our wedding day.

From beyond and beyond, and again beyond high horizons, I heard it:

Our wedding day,

Between streams I could easily ford I was frightened. The ash tree behind me had five crows' nests in it. This was it.

Reality wasn't exchangeable for anything else. Here wasn't exchangeable for elsewhere. I consoled myself, reminding myself that she had touched me at a depth deeper than where catastrophe is possible.

But was this so? Was I deceiving myself?

A fox dung I saw calmed me. It was dry, so I picked it up. Breaking it, I could see by the undigested fur in it that it was, most likely, a vole he had eaten.

Manageable as I imagined it to be, this familiar, small fact gave me the courage to go on.

Breaking spider threads and webs as I walked, the dew still glistening on them, I came to a lone whitethorn. My first response was a racial reflex. I was ritually reverent. But not for long. Some awful argosy of ordinariness in it struck me. The aghast, green ordinariness of it struck me. Or did it assault me, breaking up traditional sanities of seeing in me?

Something had happened. It had happened so suddenly I couldn't say what it was.

I sat on a rock. I looked at the bush, seeking moorings for my mind in exact observation. A tormented-looking thing it was. All its growings were cantankerous and yet, in all of them, it had flowed, however snarlingly, with the prevailing winds. And how unfailingly persuasive those winds up here could be was all too obvious. Even in my own thinking there was already a kind of procumbent conformity with the wind's way. But there it was, this tormented little thing, standing alone, or withstanding alone, in rough, thorny truculence.

But no, it didn't work.

My mind wasn't moorable now to accepted sanities of eye and ear. My defences had been swept away and there it was, the tormented little bush. It was a truculent, thorny theophany I was seeing. A godless theophany. A theophany of the Divine before all Gods, beyond all Gods. But no, no, there was no theophany. The bush wasn't usurped by a Divine that was other than it. The bush itself, its very thingness, was the Highest Divine. Ordinariness, bush ordinariness, rock ordinariness was the Highest Divine.

To seek elsewhere than in ordinariness for the Highest Divine would have seemed to me now, sitting on a rock in front of the bush, to be a betrayal.

A carnage of evening colours faded, in fatal spasms, from the sky and from the lake. Standing on a spur of rock I knew but I couldn't see that I was mirrored. Six mountains mirrored in it touched the pike depths and the darker eel depths of the lake with their soft summits.

Three nights later, asleep in high heather, I dreamed my father was perched precariously on top of a stone buttress built against a tower-like, high house. I was fearful, looking up at him that he would come tumbling down. He managed to get down onto his knees and sit back on his haunches. Now he was more secure. His right thigh was naked. In it, high up towards the groin, there was an infection. It was ingrown. It was lurid and sore. He had a black razor in his hand. I pleaded with him not to lance the ingrown, lurid thing. Wait and go to a doctor, I pleaded. Partly by accident and partly by design, he did lance it. Disentangling the emerging infection with both his hands he handed it down to me, together with the razor. I woke up. I re-entered and relived the dream. Getting the message, I didn't take it seriously, not until dawn, when, awake again, I found myself entering another dream: My father was hanging head down from a rafter in the cow-stall. It was from a noose about the ankles of his left foot he was hanging. His free right leg, bent at the knee, made a triangle with his left knee. He was dead, yet, turning him a little, in a little arc, I sensed he was alive in his deadness. My brother was there. Will he help me? I asked. He will, my brother said. Are you sure? I persisted. I'm sure, my brother replied, I'm sure your father will help you. I woke up. But it wasn't from dreaming I had awakened. And it wasn't to waking I woke up. I walked in the Big Inbetween. Maybe, I thought, I will never walk out of it.

My clothes were heartbroken.

My shoes were heartbroken.

I was walking on bridge timbers.

I was walking on gravel.

I walked into a house.

I sat by the fire.
I looked at the rafters.
I heard footsteps on the bridge timbers.
I heard footsteps on the gravel path.
Eel Person and Pike Person came in.
They sat down.
They looked at me.
Attempting to explain to them why I was here I sang the whole song:

> *My young love said to me, my mother won't mind*
> *And my father won't slight you for your lack of kind,*
> *She stepped away from me and this she did say,*
> *It will not be long love till our wedding day.*
>
> *She stepped away from me and she moved through the fair*
> *And fondly I watched her move here and move there,*
> *She went away homeward with one star awake*
> *Like a swan in the evening going over a lake.*
>
> *The people were saying no two were e'er wed*
> *But one had a sorrow that never was said*
> *And I smiled as she passed with her goods and her gear,*
> *And that was the last that I saw of my dear.*
>
> *Last night she came to me, my dead love came in*
> *So softly she came that her feet made no din,*
> *She laid her hand on me and this she did say*
> *It will not be long love till our wedding day.*

And now you believe, Pike Person said, his eyes, like his teeth, introverted, now you believe you've inherited your trouble. You now believe, don't you, that your father handed it down to you. You now believe he handed it down to you with your first razor at puberty.

And now you believe, Eel Person said, his fins fine-combing the firelight, now you believe that hanging head down into animal nature in you, your father will heal you. Heal pike-depths in you. Heal darker eel-depths in you.

I believe, I said. I believe, listening to lark song sometimes, I won't always be so dark.

I believe, I said. I believe that one day, like the lake, I will mirror six mountains. And however deep I am, I believe they will touch me that deeply with their healing, evening altitudes.

Believe this, they said, standing up to go, believe that heights in you need healing as much as depths in you do.

I heard the sound of their footsteps, first on the gravel, and then, muffled by rain, on the bridge timbers.

I had missed my chance.

Now that they were gone, I felt sure they had come to pray with me. But I hadn't been hospitable. I had talked only of healing heights, I hadn't talked at all of healing depths, of healing eel-depths and healing pike-depths.

I imagine it. Eel and Pike praying with me. Eel-me and Pike-me praying with me. I imagined their mantras. And Eel Person came and he asked, what is your mantra?

All matter is mantra, I said, that is my mantra.

And Pike Person came and he asked, what is your mantra?

All matter is mantra, I said, that is my mantra.

And we sang it all night. Eel-me and Pike-me and Me, we sang it all night. And when we fell silent, the mountains sang it, because that's their mantra. And listening to them now we knew that always, night and day, mountains sing the mantra they are made of.

And yes, I said, looking back at it, crossing the bridge the next morning, it looks like a house your unredeemed depths would pray with you in.

How like my own house, river-mirrored, it was.

And in the open bogland I turned aside to stand, surrendered and helpless, under a singing lark. It was more out of habit than out of need I did it. Also, this morning, it was more out of habit than need that I laid all awful regressions in me on the bright bird's shoulders.

It was good, and necessary maybe, to balance things, to weight the way up with the way down, to weight the soaring lark with the hanged man.

Standing there under the lark, I imagined him singing above my dreams, above my father handing down trouble, above him, hanging head down, in the cow-stall.

I imagined him singing, soaring as he sang, above mountains mirrored, summits down, in a lake.

But maybe I was too caught up in the terrors and wonders of up and down. Maybe neither up nor down, nor both together, was a way out for me. Maybe I hadn't the necessary gifts or the grace for up and down.

And now again, as if this sudden, almost accidental, realization had something to do with it, I heard her calling:

It will not be long, love, till our wedding day.

Having a head like mine means that the insurgent wonder of ordinary things is difficult to live with. Having a head like mine, a head prone to sudden return to old sanities, having that kind of head means that mind in Mother Goose mood, or world in Mother Goose mood, is hard to handle.

Threatened, I take refuge in some exact thing.

This time it was a dragonfly on an outcrop of mica-bright rock.

Needle-thin, her body was a succession of blue and black segments, the articulating black segments short, the blue long, the blue being the beautiful blue forget-me-not.

Cosmologies which aren't so blue, I thought, looking at her, cosmologies which aren't Admiral-butterfly red, which aren't brown trout brown with lovely stars, are a lie I thought. And this thought walked with me up and over and down the far side of a gap in the mountains.

It was a gap in the mountains. It looked like a gap in the mountains. So like a gap in the mountains did it appear to me that I took no particular or curious notice of it.

I had crossed it, but I hadn't come into the next valley.

Wide open before me, the next valley, in some wholly unobstructing way, was closed to me. I was in it, I could walk in it, I could build a house and settle down in it, but in some strange way I would never have come into it. Walking alone this time, having no elevating thought to lighten my climbing, I retraced my steps crossing back to the valley I had come from.

Coming through it this way, it was an altogether narrower gap than I had experienced it to be. There was anguish here. Anguish of dangerous height and depth here. Anguish of rocks I must walk around, of rocks I must walk between. Sounds above me stopped me. What can that be, I wondered, listening. A lone lame goat? A goat left behind, a goat with a broken leg crossing scree? I couldn't be sure. I couldn't see. I had seen the scree coming. A shout, I thought then, or a belling deer, would set it off, avalanching it down on top of me. And now, walking back, I was walking under it.

I sat down under the danger, but not deliberately. I didn't decide to do it. I just found myself doing it, and that is clean contrary to the kind of man I am. I don't look for trouble. But long before now I had good reason to know that mountains are dangerous. And not only dangerous. In lonely, unvisited places among them they are dangerously strange. They will sometimes seem to capture or command our wills. We do not what we came here to do. We do what they decide we will do. We do something unlikely. As I did now. I sat down under the danger.

It was echoes of your own loneliness and lostness you heard, she said.

I was talking to an old, old woman, if that's what she was.

She lived in a house here in the gap.

But how can it be? I asked. How can I not have seen your house when I first came this way?

You didn't see it. You couldn't. It was sitting where you sat all those days and nights, sitting there surviving your mind, that opened your eyes, she said.

And no, she said, no, there was no goat with a broken leg. She lifted her head and now for the first time I saw her face. A fistful of features it was. A fistful of fog.

More fog than features.

It was echoes of your own loneliness and lostness you heard, she said. And they were the loneliest and therefore the holiest sounds you have so far heard. They were the sounds of this gap opening, of your mind opening, of nature opening, letting you in.

There are valleys like that she said. States of nature like that. States of soul. It is walking away from them that we walk into them.

She was silent.

I hadn't asked her any questions, yet she answered the questions I'd have asked her. All except one. Had she given me leave, I'd have asked her about my father hanging head down in the cowstall. Times there had been when I had felt that his motionlessness and my movements were interchangeable. My movements and his motionlessness were the same journey. And yet, it was only because he had consented to be motionless that I could move, crossing the thresholds I had crossed.

Had she given me leave, I'd have asked her whether from now on I could claim the rights, and the rights-of-way, of the Hanged Man.

But now 'twas too late. She was and yet she wasn't there. Her appearance was there, but whether there was any reality behind the appearance I couldn't be sure. Sure I was, though, that this reality, whatever it was, didn't fit her appearance as snugly as my foot fitted my shoe.

Had she, I wondered, been enacting something that was happening to me? Had she enacted me to me?

And is that now how someone coming towards me would see me—a fistful of features, a fistful of fog? And the fist fog?

For an instant, an instant as deep as eternity, I didn't exist. But then again I heard them, the holy, lonely sounds, sounds of a goat with a broken leg crossing scree.

What a perfect little thing the wren was, and how delighted I was to see her turning a corner farther down the gap. A busy little syllogism she was, busy but perfect, proving something. Proving for me, at this companionable moment, that proof wasn't needed. This was a place of raucous rock savageries. Even the silence here was raucous. Cliffs, and again great cliffs, cold-shouldered all my thinking. Looking up from one small gorge I feared that my mind, like a lung, might collapse. It was hard going. Horizonless and hard. And now, as I was experiencing it, this gap wasn't only a rupture among mountains. It was a rupture, hugely rude and wild, in the reciprocal hospitalities of thing and thought. Mutuality wasn't a way of the world here.

I was having a bad time. I was blaming myself. I shouldn't have followed the call. But that's what I'm doing I thought, I'm following a call and I somehow knew that even if I walked away from it now I would still be walking towards it.

I walked on. Coming out into bushy, rough, open ground, there she was, the exact little splendour, her thatch of feathers so dainty and so trim. It wouldn't be at all odd to expect that she would look bedraggled and over bespoke, she, as I soon found out, being a mother of five greedy young ones who, hearing her coming, would erupt into screeching, reaching lust for life, doubling their weight every few days. But no. There was brisk and belligerent brightness of life in her. And just as the moon, otherwise dead and dark, catches fire and light from the sun, so did I catch fire and light from this little spark. For one perilous moment the little mum mothered me.

But it wasn't only old me that she mothered. As I was soon to find out, she had mothered dormancies of hearing and seeing and of soul in me.

Walking between them, I could hear the mountains chanting their mantra. Or was it their mantra that was chanting them? Looking at them, they appeared to me now to be densities, delighted densities, of that mantra. And soon, surrendering to it, this mantra that was chanting the mountains was chanting me. All day long that day I was one mantra with what is.

Slowly, like a tide, it ebbed, leaving me of one mind and of one musk with the seven red deer who were walking with me. Qualmless and perfect, their walking was lauds. Life, not the author of life, or the source of life, they praised. And such was the probity in them of antler and hoof, such was the probity in them of allowed, alert life, that I couldn't think of them as acolytes to something not yet. Life in them wasn't life in arrears of its earthly reach. Superb they were, and terribly well, delicately alert at nostril and ankle. I marvelled at them, every head held high, every head a trove of lovely sensings.

It wasn't until I had found it that I realized I had been seeking it. Lauds I had sought. Lauds life. And here it was. There were seven red deer walking with me and I was one mind, one musk with them. I was one lauds life with them walking between mountains, down towards a lake, a swan moving over it, and one star awake.

We walked through a fragment of lost conversation:

In the universe somewhere a sob, yes, that's what I'm saying.

A sob? A sorrow, a heave of deep sorrow, is that what you mean?

Yes, a sob. It's as big as our sun. Like our sun, it rises and sets.

On what does it rise and set? On an earth like ours?

Yes, and universes have condensed and dissolved around it. But during and in between universes it has been changing, becoming a jewel. A sapphire now, sun big, it sobs its redeeming, its reminding radiances into our world. Can't you see what I'm saying is true? Can't you see how blue our mountains are?

The deer who walked into it did not walk out of this conversation with me.

In it were ravishments.

In it were ecstasies, jewel-blue, into other worlds.

Hearing her call, so near at hand now, I walked past them. I came out.

At first I didn't recognize it. But then I was sure. I named the three near islands. It was to the shore of my own lake that I had come. There was smoke, billowing and blue, rising from the middle chimney of my house.

Out of habit, but happily, I rowed myself over to an island. Out of habit, yet happily, I lay down curling up foetally on the mouldering swan's nest. And now, as I so often had, I imagined the swan in the evening and the one star awake. I imagined me being swan born. For the next three days and three nights I imagined me being star born, eel depths, and pike depths coming to bless me.

Lark song above me, blessing me, releasing me, I rose up the next morning a man.

Crossing the threshold I knew, seeing her, it was I not she who had been dead, dead yet alive, hanging head down into awful acknowledgment of hurtful horn, hurtful hoof in me. Only so, it seemed, could I have learned tenderness.

It was late that night when we smoored the fire and went to bed.

CONNLA'S WELL

None of my friends knew that during all those years I was in Otherworld fosterage to Connla.

I cut turf with them. I milked cows. I ground corn. I played hurling, coming off the bawn sometimes as badly bruised as the toughest of them.

What I didn't know and what they didn't know is that this world and the Otherworld are one world. How we perceive and live in this one world is what makes the difference. The Otherworld is a way of hearing and seeing.

I would often wake at dawn and I'd lie there listening to herring gulls and herons and curlews down on the shore.

There was a big heronry, sometimes more than twenty nests, in the wood behind our house. Under it, the floor of the wood was white with their scour.

In spring, the smell of it would almost knock me, but I'd brave it anyway, for I loved to collect the turquoise shells or half shells they'd drop from their nests. The shells of herons' eggs were the only turquoise things in our world. Although sometimes, on a clear morning, the inlet of sea below our house, that too would be turquoise. But I couldn't collect that. A wind would be rising soon or the tide would ebb and I'd watch it fade.

How often I heard it, the screech and the croak of a heron flying over our house to her young at dawn.

A screech, a screech, a screech, a squabble of croaks, a dull croak.

Herons flying over our house to their nests.

The giving and the lurid, loud greed of those early disgorgings.

That's what I'd hear lying awake before dawn under our thatch.

One of them is king, my father said. One of them is the king heron. He's the one with the sea-blue voice.

Pigs, they used to say, can see the wind. Can my father see sound? I wondered. I asked him.

Yes, he said. It's like lightning and thunder. First I see the lightning and then, waiting awhile, I hear the thunder. I see the heron's screech before I hear it.

Light and sound, he said, are the stuff of all things. And the sound I heard out at sea one night, a sound I didn't hear with my hearing, the sound that isn't a sound of two things striking together, that's the seed sound, the source sound of the sun and moon and the stars. The sun and the moon and the stars are condensations of that sound.

It wasn't what my father said that was important. It was the ageless silence of his voice that awakened something in me, a yearning in me.

After that I played only one other hurling match. Surrendering to a need for solitude and silence, I'd go off alone into the woods or into the hills, sitting all night in the crotch of a tree, sitting sometimes all day by a corrie lake in the mountains.

On a calm day in the mountains, I postponed all purpose and allowed my spirit to be still. When I was as calm as the lake was I mirrored the mountains as serenely as it did. Mirroring them, I didn't modify them. No ebbing into self awareness shimmered them. Clear, like the lake, to my very depths, they touched the quick in me with their unperturbed, ageless summits. By nightfall there was no me. Where no perceiver was, where no organ of perception was, there was an eternal, serene perceiving.

Even tonight, overlaid though they be by self awareness and self purpose, that corrie lake and that calm perceiving are within me. Within me, imperturbably in my depths, are the summits, are the elevations of spirit, I sometimes need. More often than not, I don't have access to them when I need them, but I know they are there.

All of this wasn't something I did. All of this, when I surrendered to them, was something my surroundings did for me. It was with my surroundings that I walked into myself and found eternity.

I walked back out of eternity happily able to settle for less.

But was it less?

Seen in a mood we have sometimes access to, the least, little thing is in no way less than the Supreme.

But I did settle for less. I settled for selfhood and ordinariness.

My capacity for ordinariness grew with the years. Ordinary work. Ordinary things. Ordinary people. Ordinary ways with things and with people.

So deeply presiding in me did this capacity for ordinariness become that one day, it occurred to me, it had grown into its opposite. I would sometimes experience a kind of rapturous incapacity to move on or away from the presence of some ordinary thing that had caught my attention.

> Settling for less was a way to wonder.
> Settling for less was a way to Connla's Well.
> Connla and his well are within.

They are a mood, a way of seeing, that comes to the surface from within. And people who have found their way to that well, everything they say of it is true. It is an otherworldly well. That means it is a well of this, our ordinary world, when this, our ordinary world, is seen and perceived in that marvellous mood that emerges from within.

Growing in a shadowy cool arch, a hazel grows over it. All year round, but only now and then, a hazel nut falls onto it. Salmon who eat these nuts acquire the wisdom out of which all worlds are born. Returning downstream they carry it to the farthest reaches of the world's dreaming and waking.

And yes. It is true what they say: the rivers of Ireland have their source in this well.

And Connla? Who is he? He is you. He is me. At a depth of you, you are Connla.

At a depth of him also, my father was Connla. And, although I didn't know it, he wasn't only my natural father. In his ways and in his words, he was also my otherworldly father and, from the day I was born, I was in otherworldly fosterage to him. He nourished a way of seeing things in me. He nourished in me a way of being in the world.

When my father asked me how I was he didn't only mean how I was in this world, he was asking me how I was in all worlds. Was I the kind of person, he was asking, who would be welcome in all worlds? Were my feet philosophically fit to walk elsewhere?

And I knew what he meant: if you aren't philosophically fit to walk in the Otherworld you aren't philosophically fit to walk in this world. All other worlds and this world are one world. And the only philosophical words you need are wonder and wonder and again wonder.

As, at the end of their lives, some heroes of old sailed away in a crystal boat to the Otherworld so, at some depth of ourselves, did each of us come to this world, which we call ordinary, in a crystal boat.

There aren't many who know that these days, though. There aren't many who pass my house walking inland. There aren't many who know that the path to Connla's well is open. I know it.

As poet and philosopher, I walk the path to Connla's Well.

As poet and philosopher, it's my task to keep it open.

THE REALM OF LOGRES

The Realm of Logres, it is called, a name which suggests that it is a country, but that's not so. It might sometimes, as in England during Arthur's reign, coincide with a country, but, essentially, the Realm of Logres is a state of mind that comes to the surface in people and things. Sometimes it happens like this: a hero, born to the task, draws the sword of our Gorgocogito consciousness of it out of a stone, the stone becomes a shrine that houses a linga standing in a yoni, our Medusa mindset lies shattered at our feet, and then, for us and for all things, it is like waking up, it's an event as big as waking up, as stupendous as waking up, we wake up not to the old failures of mind and eye, we wake up in Logres.

In a Logres contemporary with Arthur's, the Earth itself was source and goal of a great quest. Particular men and women didn't choose this quest. It chose them, sometimes violently. Resisting it, once it had chosen you, was fruitless. And so it was that a man, under fierce and final duress, dropped the hind leg of a horse he was shoeing one day and walked away, not once looking back, not even at night. Other obligations, whatever they were, were ahead of him somewhere.

But where was it, that somewhere? Beyond how many rivers was it? Beyond how many otter territories, how many heron territories was it?

Catching up, however late, with yet another red, yet another suffocated, sunset didn't bring him any closer.

He gave up.

He came home, walking eastward into enormous mornings. Years later, an old man now, sitting by his fire, remembering, he heard the sounds of a horseshoe and a hammer falling onto a flagstone floor. It was the miracle of hearing he heard.

It was the sound of his Medusa mindset being shattered he heard. Having lived in it during all of his long life he had, now at last, reached Logres. And if, still in quest of The Grail, Sir Gawain rode one evening into his yard he would ask him, should it please him, to dismount, saying, here in this ordinary yard is the end of your seeking, here in this yard are The Hallows and The Hurt Man, healed as you see; here in this yard you can hear the sounds of a horseshoe and a hammer falling onto a flagstone floor.

MORGAN LE FAY, OUR MAYASHAKTI

It began as a yearning to grow in ways my culture didn't approve of. I couldn't, in turn, approve of what my culture was doing to me. I couldn't consent to what it wanted to make of me.

Scarlet and yellow toadstools in the wood were like her auspices. One day I called her, asking her to come out of seclusion.

> It was Morgan Le Fay I called.
> It wasn't into the wood I called.

An accomplice in this with the depths of our minds, the wood can condense into weirdness or wisdom as easily now as it always did.

Wodwo I might meet. A dry stick I trod on might snarl, not snap. But that mightn't be the stick at all. That might be an ancient, hidden impulse in me snarling. It might be that. Or it mightn't. It's often hard to tell. In a wood at night inside and outside are the same state of mind occupying the same place. A stick I have walked on breaking is my mind breaking. Sitting in a wood at night, I know that the subjective-objective divide is a superficial device. It belongs only to the condensed scum of the mind.

No. It was into my mind I called. Into those depths of it that hadn't been harnessed or harmed by my education. At the end of my education I knew there were depths of me that hadn't been conscripted.

Living from those depths I might meet Wodwo, almost all of him eclipsed by the fathom of sticks he'd be carrying. Living from them I might one day be a marvel. I might one day be marvellous enough to meet Morgan Le Fay.

Always at nightfall my house is as hospitable as a fairy story is to the wood's weirdness or wisdom. Often, indeed, after I've looked at the night and come indoors on a winter's evening, sitting in my house is like sitting in an old story. I expect strangeness. And if I hear a knocking at my door at night I don't only think of my neighbour from over the lake, because, until I've opened it, I don't know what class of being from what class of world might have come, attracted by the firelight in my window.

I knock on strange doors myself. Almost every night I knock on the door of some old story. Old stories shelter me.

The horses of Donn Descorach are my $E=mc^2$.

Stories I tell myself on a winter's night, stories I'm a listening reverent guest in, they tell me more about the universe than $E=mc^2$ does.

There's the story of Cuchulainn's encounter with the shape-shifting Morrigan. When I inhabit it, that story tells me more about the perceiver and the perceived than physicists in Copenhagen can. Taking me by the hand, it brings me into the mystery atoms are adumbrations of, and reality of.

Till I open it, I don't know what class of being has come to my door. It might be The Morrigan.

The Morrigan is any shape that pleases her. She is any shape that suits her in any situation. She is eel, she is she-wolf, she is hornless red heifer, she is red-mouthed scald crow.

Or it might be Donn Descorach. It might be Donn himself who has knocked. Like a summons to unearthly adventure that knocking would sound. And unlike Wodwo, Donn wouldn't be eclipsed by the fathom of sticks for your fire he'd be bringing.

Donn is red. And his horses are red. And we see them only, we hear the thunder and thud of them only in these moments of awful clarity when some great destiny or doom is shaping us for entry into great life.

Morgan Le Fay is great life.

Whenever, anywhere, a Galahad draws the sword from the scone, again releasing our ability to see the world's wonders, she reappears. First sight of her, at the beginning of a new and great antiquity for all things, is always the same.

By a lake that mirrors mountains and woods she walks. That one vision of her is all we need.

It was all I needed. Launching my boat that morning, I didn't know how many years of willing and able life I had left in me. But it didn't matter, I told myself. Beginnings such as these will find a way, if not in me, then in someone else.

How suave the water was. How suave the mirrored sky. How suavely it fell from the blades of my oars as I rowed myself over, over, over an endless water, the shoreline she walked on going from me like the horizon. Rowing, I realized, wouldn't get me there. I rowed home.

Coming through the wood I knew it: here, when you've seen her, is over there. The great over there, when you've seen her, is the great here-and-now where you are.

I didn't meet my Fata Morgana Mind in the wood that day. No. Not that day. No.

I'm an old man now. It is not only with my own old age that I'm old though. I'm old with my own old age but I'm old also with the new and great antiquity for all things that has been living itself in me.

Living alone in this wood. Living here this thirty-six years since I saw her. Can't you see it? Can't you see it in me, old man of the woods that I am?

The fathom of sticks I bring to your fire doesn't hide me. But don't look on me. Look at the new and the great antiquity for all things. Look at the great human future that can grow out of it. A great future for all things.

Maybe tonight. Beside me or inside me tonight maybe I'll hear the thunder and thud of the horses of Donn Descorach.

> In my Fata Morgana Mind I see them
> Not riotous. No. Not riotous.

Like summer mornings they are,

> Unreinable,
> Rearing to go
> And red.

THE MIND ALTERING ALTERS ALL, EVEN THE PAST

And Jacob went out from Beersheba and went toward Haran. And he lighted upon a certain place, and carried there all night, because the sun was set: and he took of the stones of that place, and put them for his pillows, and lay down in that place to sleep. And he dreamed and behold a ladder set up on the earth, and the top of it reached to heaven: and behold the angels of God ascending and descending on it. And, behold, the Lord stood above it and said, I am the Lord God of Abraham thy father, and the God of Isaac: the land whereon thou liest, to thee will I give it, and to thy seed: and thy seed shall be as the dust of the earth, and thou shalt spread abroad to the west and to the east and to the north and to the south, and in thee and in thy seed shall all the families of the earth be blessed. And, behold, I am with thee, and will keep thee in all places whither thou goest, and will bring thee again into this land: for I will not leave thee, until I have done that which I have spoken to thee of. And Jacob awakened out of his sleep, and he said, surely the Lord is in this place; and I knew it not. And he was afraid and said, How dreadful is this place! This is none other but the house of God, and this is the gate of heaven.

> A dream dreamed long ago.
> Dreaming itself even now through history.
> At work, even now, in territorial quarrels.

And when the choir of Canterbury Cathedral, an amazement of gothic daring, was being dedicated, it was with these, the amazed words of Jacob, that the tiered singers filled the vaults:

> How dreadful is this place!
> This is none other but the house of God,
> And this is the gate of heaven.

Doing so might be as arrogant and irreverent as wanting to redesign the choir of Canterbury Cathedral, but I sometimes find myself wanting to reimagine Jacob. In a vision I have of him, he is a Middle Eastern Aborigine, not a Bedouin. Having neither conscious direction or intention in it, his journey is a walkabout in the Dreamtime. And the stones he sets for his pillows, I think of them as Dreamtime stones: they dream his dream with Jacob, or, daring to say it, it is the same Dreamtime dream that is dreaming Jacob and the stones.

Sometimes I go all the way: the dreamers are being dreamed and the Dreamtime dream that is dreaming them is the stuff the dreamers are made of. That's how deeply surrendered they are on this first night of Jacob's journey.

Imagine it: Moses goes down into Egypt and, going in to him, he says to Pharaoh, let my people go.

Imagine it: Moses goes back into Old Testament times, into culturally Genetic times, and seeing them in hard bondage to their biblical biographies, Moses calls out in the desert, let Abraham go. Let Abraham, Isaac and Jacob go.

Imagine it: Abraham going out of his city. Abraham going out to go walkabout in the Dreamtime.

> Abraham going walkabout. Isaac going walkabout.
> And, in a world before Beer-Sheba was, or Haran was,
> Jacob going walkabout.

Imagine it: imagine Abraham, Isaac and Jacob to be Eternal Ones of the Dream, to be our Dreamtime Ancestors, to be Altjeringa Mitjina.

It is time to change our past. It is time, touching it with Aaron's wand, to turn it into an aboriginal past. It is time we had a Dreamtime past. It is time we had a Dreamtime past to which even now, being consecrated, we have sacred access.

To change our past is to change our present. To have lived differently in the past is to live differently in the present.

To couch the Old Testament with Aaron's wand is to touch the present. How glad we are, Ancestor, that you walked out.

It means that Gorgocogito won't have hegemony.

It means Uluru not Ulro.

It means the stone is enfranchised.

It means the dream is enfranchised.

It means that a latter-day Moses won't have to go in to Gorgocogito and say to her:

> Let Michelangelo's captives go.
> Let persons embedded in the Medusa mindset go.
> Let rivers go. Let rocks go. Let stars go.
> Let all things that are in hard epistemological bondage to our Gorgocogito perceptions and conceptions of them go.

How glad we are that the past can be changed, that a perilous present and future can be averted.

How exceedingly glad we are, Ancestor, that you went walkabout. That day long ago was Bastille Day for as Bastille Day also for star and stone. Bastille Day it was for perceiver and perceived. And the stone that Jacob set for his pillow, an a-stone-ishment it is turned inward into the vision it has and is of the House of God, the vision it has and is of the Gate of Heaven.

And Jacob rose up early in the morning and he took the stone that he had put for his pillow, and set it up for a pillar, and poured oil upon the top of it. And he called the name of that place Bethel [meaning house of God].

And the stone you set up for a pillar, this stone, which until now was an Ulro mullán, a Medusa mullán, what shall we call it? Looking forward to our Dreamtime, what shall we call it?

> Anantashaya Mullán

Looking forward to our future, what shall we call it?

> Mondukya Mullán

Mullán which, changing our past, changes our present and future.

Glory to God for this great day.
Bastille Day.

Bastille Day for rivers. Bastille Day for stars. Bastille Day for Medusa's, that is, for Michelangelo's Captives. Bastille Day for the 'naked shingles of the world'. Bastille Day for the ring of Darwin's geological hammer, that ring now becoming

Om
Om
Om
Aum
Aum
Aumen

MISSA IN NOCTE

It was a short dream, but how sure it was, how very sure it was, of what it wanted to say: I was walking with my mother in a featureless landscape. It was like walking through despair. Despair became wind, wet darkness, rustics, rain. We climbed a low hill and there it was, the loveliest countryside I had ever seen. Light in it wasn't light from outside it shining upon it. It breathed and lived and had its being in light from within itself, its own soul light. And yet, so ordinary was it, it wouldn't be out of place to sharpen a scythe in it, or sow oats in it. It wouldn't seem odd if, walking past the nearest low house in it, I heard someone singing Loch Shileann Side.

As we crossed into it my mother looked at me: they speak the native language here, she said. That was all. I woke up. But it wasn't my everyday eyes I opened. It wasn't to my everyday mind I returned. I no longer saw things as I used to see them.

Sitting by the fire that night I remembered my mother's funeral. It wasn't, as I'd have liked it to be, a ship burial. I had no boat to send her out of this world in. But I had a prayer, and, fixing the retaining scraws to the little earth mound, I prayed it:

> Go forth upon thy journey from this world, O Christian soul,
> In the name of God, the Almighty Father, who created thee;
> In the name of Jesus Christ, his Son, who redeemed thee;
> In the name of the Holy Ghost who sanctifieth thee.

> May thy guardian angel succour and defend thee;
> May the prayers of the blessed saints help thee;
> May thy Redeemer look upon thee in pardon and in mercy;
> May thy portion be peace;
> May thy rest be with him this day in paradise.
> Depart, O Christian Soul, out of this world.

So maybe, I thought, remembering the dream, maybe that prayer was enough. Maybe that prayer was her boat,

> Her Sutton-Hoo boat,
> Her Oseberg boat.

All burials, with or without a ship, are ship burials I thought. And our last breath, our death-rattle breath, maybe it fills the sails that carry us out, both sides of our ship being starboard now.

I relived the dream.

Maybe I thought, reliving it, there is no need at all for a boat. Maybe the journey we go forth upon isn't so long after all. Maybe we just wake up and find ourselves sharpening a scythe in the immortal elsewhere that is here where we are. Maybe it is like this: I am seed-sowing in my garden, I put my hand into my sack and, a missed heartbeat later, I broadcast the fistful of oats in paradise. And I haven't even died. I hear and call back to my wife who is calling me to dinner. All that has happened is that the blindness of everyday, anxious seeing has fallen from my eyes.

And the native language of paradise, the native language of the far side, which is the same as this side, our side, of the hill, what could that language be, I wondered.

> Sound of a scythe being sharpened?
> Sound of a woman calling her husband to dinner?
> Sounds of a salmon river, sounds of wind?

Sound of my turf fire? I didn't light the lamp. Firelight tonight was all I needed. It is Christmas morning in my nature now, I said. Imagining the sound of a scythe being sharpened, hearing it, I repeated it three times:

> It is Christmas morning in my nature now
> It is Christmas morning in my nature now
> It is Christmas morning in my nature now.

> In my eyes it is Christmas morning
> In my hands it is Christmas morning
> In my instincts and angers it is Christmas morning
> In my inner hells it is Christmas morning.

It is Christmas morning
It is Christmas morning
It is Christinas morning
It is Christmas morning in my nature now.

I sang the great Christmas Antiphons:

DOminus dixit ad me: Filius meus es tu, ego hodie genui te. Ps. Quare fremuerunt gentes: et populi meditati sunt inania?

TEcum principium in die virtutis tuae: in splendoribus sanctorum, ex utero ante luciferum genui te.

I sang them all night.
I sang them till dawn.
In the end, the sound of a scythe being sharpened was singing them antiphonally with me:

Tecum principium in die, virtutis tuae:
in splendoribus sanctorum ex utero ante luciferum
genui te.

Laetentur caeli, I sang.

Et exultet terra, the scythe sang, the skeleton sang.
The skeleton's exultet terra was my Oseberg boat.
My Oseberg boat, and my boat song.
It was bringing me back to my side of the hill.
It was bringing me back on Christmas morning to the paradise I had always lived in.

PARTHOLON

I know what my neighbours would say if I said I was the Dagda, if I said that, like the Dagda, I mated with river goddesses and was married to one of them, the willowy one, Boann of the Boyne.

I know what my neighbours would say if I said I was Midir of Brí Leith keeping my door open all day and all night for whoever might wish to come in, for Connla of Connla's well, for Dien Cecht and for Étain coming to me this time, drawn to my lamp, as a beautiful Burren moth.

There is, maybe, something worse I could say. I could say that I am who I have been for the past fifty years, and that means many things. It means our modern Western mindset. It means that, having been born into it, and having grown up in it, I inherited the modern consensus about Reality.

I had heard it said that God always forgives, human beings sometimes forgive, nature never forgives.

Nature in me didn't forgive me.

> Étain didn't come to my hundred-watt bulb,
> Dreams couldn't live in my hundred-watt mind.

I was in trouble.

In trouble by day. And as if the floorboards pulled their nails and folded upwards in the night, sleep was a Viking's ship burial. It carried me to savage shores, most of them within. It carried me to rebirth in a Navajo cradle:

> *I have made a cradleboard for you, my child.*
> *May you grow to a great old age.*
> *Of the sun's rays I have made the back,*
> *Of black clouds I have made the blanket,*
> *Of rainbow I have made the bow,*
> *Of high horizons I have made the side-loops,*
> *Of lightnings I have made the lacings,*
> *Of river mirrorings have I made the footboard,*
> *Of dawn have I made the covering,*
> *Of Earth's welcome for you have I made the bed.*

Coming like Partholon I came home bringing this cradle with me.

Should you wish to be born among us, Étain, we have the sun's rays and the rainbow. Should you wish to be born among us, Connla, we have the cradle and the song.

The Tuatha De Danann have four great treasures. But now, holding the great new treasure, the cradle, in common, all the peoples of Ireland, visible and invisible, present and past, can be one great people:

> The People of the Cradle,
> Tuatha an Chliabhain.

There is no need now to fight a Third Battle of Magh Tuired.

It isn't always from overseas that Partholon comes. He sometimes comes from among us. He comes when we've lost our way.

Wherever the cradle is, there is Uisnech.

Wherever any cradle like it is, there also is Uisnech and, invisible or visible, the five trees of the centre are there, the Tree of Ross and the Tree of Mugna and the Ancient Tree of Datha and the Branching Tree of Uisnech and the Ancient Tree of Tortu.

> It is Altjeringa in Ireland now.
> It is Dreamtime now among Tuatha an Chliabhain.

COMING FORTH BY DAY

I

As Ancient Egyptians practised it, mummification was as much a ritual as it was a physical work. This isn't surprising given that the purpose of the work was to reconstitute persons who had died so that, thus restored, and revived in their former identities, they might live immortally in an immortal elsewhere.

A ritual of particular importance was called Opening the Mouth. In a vignette of it in the funerary papyrus of Nakht, we see a falcon-headed God holding an adze towards the face of the deceased, and while this is being done we can imagine a lector priest speaking on Nakht's behalf:

My mouth is opened by Ptah and what was on my mouth has been loosened by my local god. Thoth comes indeed, filled and equipped with magic. And the bonds of Seth which restricted my mouth have been loosened. A turn has warded them off and has cast away the restrictions of Seth.

My mouth is opened, my mouth is split open by Shu with that iron harpoon of his with which he split open the mouths of the gods. I am Sakhmet and I sit beside Her who is in the great wind of the sky; I am Orion the Great who dwells with the Souls of Heliopolis.

As for any magic spell or any words which may be uttered against me, the gods will rise up against it, even the entire Ennead.

This ritual, it was believed, restored his faculties, dispersed or annulled by death, to Nakht. He wouldn't, as a consequence of it, arrive insensate and witless in the bright world he was being prepared for. Nor would he arrive there without his heart. Seat and source of physical life in him and of so much else that was essential to him, his heart also was ritually restored to him, so that he could sing.

My heart is mine in the House of Hearts, my heart is mine in the House of Hearts, my heart is mine, and it is at rest there. I will not eat the cakes of Osiris on the eastern side of the Gay-water in the barge when you sail downstream or upstream, and I will not go aboard the boat in which you are. My mouth will be given to me that I may speak with it, my legs to walk, and my arms to fell my enemy. The doors of the sky are opened for me; Geb, chiefest of gods, throws open his jaws for me, he opens my eyes which were closed up, he extends my legs which were contracted; Anubis strengthens for me my thighs, which were joined together, the goddess Shakmet stretches me out. I will be in the sky, a command shall be made for my benefit in Memphis, I shall be aware in my heart, I shall have power in my heart, I shall have power in my arms, I shall have power in my legs, I shall have power to do whatever I desire; my soul and my corpse shall not be restrained at the portals of the West when I go in or out in peace.

A mortuary song, a song a mummy sings, a song a corpse sings, saying rigor mortis shall have no dominion.

There is rigor mortis. There is rigor vitae. And as with Nakht in death, so with so many of us who are still alive: our senses and faculties have atrophied, have died. Or worse, they have turned malignant. Our ears are hammers and anvils. Our eyes are tumours of seeing. Looking at a tree we see timber. Looking at a cow we see kilos of meat. Looking at mountains we see our Medusa mindset.

Wordsworth describes the process:

> *Our birth is but a sleep and a forgetting:*
> *The Soul that rises with us, our life's Star,*
> *Hath had elsewhere its setting,*
> *And cometh from afar:*
> *Not in entire forgetfulness,*
> *And not in utter nakedness,*
> *But trailing clouds of glory do we come*
> *From God, who is our home:*
> *Heaven lies about us in our infancy!*

> *Shades of the prison-house begin to close*
> *Upon the growing Boy,*
> *But he beholds the light, and whence it flows,*
> *He sees it in his joy;*
> *The Youth, who daily farther from the east*
> *Must travel, still is Nature's priest,*
> *And by the vision splendid*
> *Is on his way attended;*
> *At length the Man perceives it die away,*
> *And fade into the light of common day.*

II

Earlier, by a century and a half or so, Thomas Traherne sang a great dirge for the lost Paradisal light:

All appeared new, and strange, at the first, inexpressibly rare and delightful and beautiful. I was a little stranger, which at my entrance in to the world was saluted and surrounded with innumerable joys. My knowledge was divine. I knew by intuition those things which since my apostasy I collected again by the highest reason. My very ignorance was advantageous. I seemed as one brought into the state of innocence. All things were spotless and pure and glorious: yea, and infinitely mine, and joyful and precious. I knew not that there were any sins, or complaints, or laws. I dreamed not of poverties, contentions, or vices. All tears and quarrels were hidden from my eyes. Everything was at rest, free and immortal. I knew nothing of sickness or death or rents or exaction, either for tribute or bread. In the absence of these I was entertained like an angel with the works of God in their splendour and glory. I saw all in the peace of Eden; heaven and earth did sing my creator's praises, and could not make more melody to Adam than to me. All time was eternity, and a perpetual Sabbath. Is it not strange that an infant should be heir of the world, and see those mysteries which the books of the learned never unfold.

III

The corn was orient and immortal wheat which never should be reaped, nor was ever sown. I thought it had stood from everlasting to everlasting. The dust and stones of the street were as precious as gold: the gates were at first the end of the world. The green trees when I saw them first through one of the gates transported and ravished me, their sweetness and unusual beauty made my heart to leap, and almost mad with ecstasy, they were such strange and wonderful things. The men! Oh what reverend and venerable creatures did the aged seem! Immortal cherubims! And young men glittering and sparkling angels, and maids strange seraphic pieces of life and beauty! Boys and girls tumbling in the street, and playing, were moving jewels. I knew not that they were born or should die; but all things abided eternally as they were in their proper places. Eternity was manifest in the light of the day, and something infinite behind everything appeared, which talked with my expectations and moved my desire. The city seemed to stand in Eden, or to be built in heaven. The streets were mine, the temple was mine, the people were mine, their clothes and gold and silver were mine, as much as their sparking eyes, fair skins and ruddy faces. The skies were mine, and so were the sun and moon and stars, and all the world was mine; and I the only spectator and enjoyer of it. I knew no churlish proprieties, nor bounds, nor divisions: but all proprieties and divisions were mine: all treasures and the possession of them. So that with much ado I was corrupted, and made to learn the dirty devices of the world. Which now I unlearn, and become, as it were, a little child again that I may enter into the Kingdom of God.

IV

The first light which shined in my infancy in its primitive and innocent clarity was totally eclipsed: insomuch that I was fain to learn all again. If you ask me how it was eclipsed? Truly by the customs and manners of men, which like contrary winds blew it out; by an innumerable company of other objects, rude, vulgar and worthless things, that like so many loads of earth and dung did overwhelm and bury it; by the impetuous torrent of wrong desires in all others whom I saw or knew that carried me away and alienated me from it; by a whole sea of other matters and concernments that covered and drowned it: finally by the evil influence of a bad education that did not foster and cherish it. All men's thoughts and words were about other matters. They all prized new things which I did not dream of. I was a stranger and unacquainted with them; I was little and reverenced their authority; I was weak, and easily guided by their example; ambitious also, and desirous to approve myself unto them. And finding no one syllable in any man's mouth of those things, by degrees they vanished, my thoughts (as indeed what is more fleeting than a thought) were blotted out; and, at last all the celestial great and stable treasures to which I was born, as wholly forgotten as if they had never been.

He having died, his senses and faculties were ritually restored to Nakht, so that now, and henceforward forever, he could live immortally in the immortal elsewhere as Egyptians imagined it.

Us also. We have died. Our birth was a dying, our growing a dying, into the light of common, commercial day.

After a bad education there are many of us whose eyes are the visible tumours of brains possessed and eclipsed in their deepest inwardness by the dirty devices of our builded world.

To open our eyes to the world is to open our tumours to it. And our telescope on Mount Palomar is but an extension of their tumourous range.

Ritually reconstituted, his faculties restored to him, Nakht announced that he was the Phoenix in Hermopolis, announced that the doors of the sky were opened to him.

Wouldn't it be wonderful if, ritually reconstituted, our pristine faculties restored to us, we too could announce that, not the doors to the sky but the doors to the earth were opened to us. Because what else but our pristine faculties is the third eye that Orientals talk about? Faculties with which we would see that, yes indeed, so it is, the corn is orient and immortal wheat.

What other purposes does our culture have but to help us, as Egyptian culture helped Nakht, to come forth by Day. And as dawn is daybreak to it, so also is nightfall daybreak to that Day. Its splendours are of the night and of the day. Great Day. Day we already walk in. The splendouring we walk in.

Are you there Nakht? And you Horakhty, are you there? Do you have the ancient adze? Have you Shu's harpoon?

Give us heart, Horakhty. And may it please Shu to open our mouths, with harpoon and with adze open them, so that we might see and speak the stupendousness of things.

SUMER IS YCUMEN IN

Up until the early decades of the last century, the peasants and villagers of Europe didn't wait passively for summer to come in. They brought it in, ceremonially. The following would be typical of what they did: the girls and boys would make a puppet of straw or of rags, calling it Death. Carrying it out to throw it beyond the boundaries they would sing: 'We carry Death out of the village.'

In some districts, they wouldn't just throw it intact across the boundary, nor would they be content to just throw it into a river asking the river to carry it out of their world: mocking it, jeering at it, they would tear Death asunder and, setting fire to it, they would dance boisterously, still mocking, still jeering, about the flames. This done, the youngsters would then go into a wood, they would cut down a green bough or a young green tree, and, adorning it, they would carry it into the village singing a song traditional in their district, for example:

> *We have carried Death out;*
> *We are bringing the dear Summer back*:
> *The Summer and the May*
> *And all the flowers gay.*

A charming custom. Not only charming, however. To someone who, with the Stoics, believes in the sympathy of all things, it is, also, a profoundly reasonable, even a profoundly inevitable, custom.

And yet I have difficulty with it. Bluntly: I am not sure that it is good practice to carry Death out of our village.

I can of course see why we would want to carry out a negative understanding of Death and throw it into a river that will carry it down into the swallowing, all-dissolving ocean. Having done this, though, it will then behove us to bring a new understanding of Death, opening our doors to it now as an essential leaven of intensest, mortal life.

There is, Macbeth. There is something serious in mortality. It is serious even when it is forgotten during Suso's noon of heavenly lightnings, during Pascal's night of fire.

We carry death out of our village. Yes, we carry out all cosmologies that hurt the scars, all cosmologies that deaden and make dead the intensely living, intensely intelligent stars. We carry out Big Bang.

We carry out winter. Yes, we carry out our Gorgon-Cartesian, our petrafying perceptions of things. We carry out all thinking of and from the limits of contraction and opacity.

And we bring in Summer. Culturally we must bring it in.

As Leonardo, putting the finishing touch to the chiaroscuro of Mona's mouth, is bringing it in.

As the monk who walks mountains searching for the herbs from which he will make the inks and dyes for the Book of Kells is bringing it in.

As the young woman who, in a pub in Galway, picks up her fiddle and plays a familiar tune on it is bringing it in. Her rich, black hair tumbling down into the Mason's Apron, as if to listen, is bringing it in.

A man who lives in, but isn't entirely of, the modern world is walking to work one January morning. He looks across the bay, and the bogs, to where the sun is coming over the horizon. He turns towards it and, raising his hands, as the green baboons of The Egyptian Book of the Dead do, he adores it. And he calls it by the name by which Nefertiti, standing in her mortuary chapel doorway, would have called it. He calls it Horakhty. Here on this wet, western road on a January morning, he speaks the brightest, divine name of the Brightest, Divine Being that Ancient Egyptians had experience of Destitute himself, he speaks the greatest word of an ancient religion. And, looking across the bay and the bogs to Horakhty, he cannot now see in our great word or formula the meaning Einstein intended for it. Illuminated by Horakhty, E means ecstasy, m means Moksha and c is a hieroglyph for the uraeus-ringed retina of Einstein's third eye.

Now carry we Death out of the village
And the new Summer into the village.
Welcome, dear Summer,
Sweet little corn.

Now carry we 'single vision and Newton's sleep' out of our village. Cogito consciousness carry we out. Commonage consciousness carry we in.

Sumer is ycumen in
Lude sing, cuccu!

Groweth seed and bloweth med
And springeth the wode nu.
Sing, cuccu!
Awe bleeteth after lamb
Lowth after calve cu
Bulloc sterteth, bucke verteth
Merie sing, cuccu!
Cuccu, cuccu.
Wel singes thu, cuccu;
Ne swink thu never nu!

Singing it, we bring the Mandukya Om into our village. Speaking them outside every door of our village, we bring new words into our village. Knowing new possibilities of summer understanding, of summer growing, in them, we sing them: Nirguna Brahman, Saguna Brahman, Shabda Brahman, Anantashaya, Shakti, Mayashakti, Kundalashakri, chakra, Bhakti yoga, Jnana yoga, Jivanmukta, Mahavakya, Mandukya Om.

Wel singes thu, cuccu;
Ne swink thu never nu!

And where do you come from? asks the young woman sitting beside me in the bus. From a place inside me I say. From a farm inside me. From a farm far away inside me called Fern Hill I say.

Your name, please? the man in the passport office asked me.

Honoured-among-wagons, I replied. That's my name on Monday. On Tuesday the blackbirds call me Prince of the apple towns. On Wednesday the geese call me Famous among the barns. On Thursday the owls who are carrying me away call me Nightly under the simple stars. On Friday morning coming home I am The Wanderer white with the dew, the cock on my shoulder. On Saturday alone on the hills I am the Farm forever fled. On Sunday, there it is, summer again, Fern Hill again, horses again, the spellbound horses walking warm out of the whinnying green stables on to the fields of praise.

Horses walking spellbound, constellations walking spellbound. Ursa, Aries, Capricorn, Cancer, Leo, Virgo walking spellbound, Taurus walking spellbound on to the fields of praise.

Dylan came singing summer. He came bringing a new first page for our Holy Book.

Like horses, we have all walked spellbound out of a whinnying green stable on to the fields of praise.

Wel singes thu, cuccu,
Ne swink thu never nu!

Words we bring: viksepa shakti, avarana shakti, adhyaropa.

Words from where words fall away: avarana, Klesa avarana, Jneya avarana, ashraya paravritti, padmasambhava, ratnasambhava, vajrayana, vajrasattva, prajna paramita.

Earth we call it. Tellurically, Earth. Chthonically, Earth. For us who live on it, it is or it should be Big Medicine. And looking at it from a distance, looking at it from the moon, it wouldn't be amiss to think of it as padmasambhava, Ratnasambhava. Looking at it from a wet, western road on a January morning walking to work, it wouldn't be amiss to call it Buddh Gaia.

From Once-Upon-a-Time we are, we sing, coming home to our village.

From a farm far away within we are, we sing.

From Buddh Gaia we are, we sing, the cocks whose crowing will awaken us awake on our shoulders.

And we are glad, because we who walked spellbound, walk wide awake now, in the fields of praise.

Ne swink ye never nu! Cucuricu, Cucuricu,
Crow ye nu
Cucuricu, Cucuricu, Cucuricu.

BEFORE SHEELA-NA-GIG WAS, DANU IS

That's what I dreamed, in a second dream. I dreamed that now we could begin again. It was a kind of exodus I saw, all the people of Ireland walking into Hallowe'en night. Walking into its terrors. Walking through them.

Into Tuatha De Danann sleep we walked. In darkness walked. We emerged into Tuatha De Danann dreaming. We emerged into Tuatha De Danann waking. And we were glad. We were living again in Ancient Ireland. Danu, her breasts plenteous, was our Goddess. Dien Cecht was our physician. And the path to Connla's Well was open.

Danu I saw.

As natural as nature itself is she.

A sense I had, looking at her, is that Mangerton cliffs share her heart beat with her. Like sea cliffs, her moods have caves in them. At dawn, her dreaming ebbed, she beachcombs her own inner shores.

No religion could hold her. No cult could claim her. And, still looking at her, I saw that it was only in Tuatha De Danann dreaming and walking that we could have second sight of her.

Tuatha De Danann dreaming, Tuatha De Danann waking, it was into them we had walked, and the long nights after Samhain were ahead of us, nights when the epochs and ages of willed, wide-awake history count for so little.

After a night of Tuatha De Danann sleep we awake to a neighing where no horse is.

And this little bush growing alone. Look at it, its tangle of anxieties flowing the prevailing way and yet, stark though it is, and starved, its constellations of haws are in the ascendant, existing it seems beyond it.

It was only when the exodus I had walked in walked me out of my self-willed way, only then did I meet him.

I met Dien Cecht, medicine man of the Tuatha De. As you'd meet a mountain ash in a lonely place I met him. I met him in a high place, both of us climbing. I met him only, I could only have met him, when waking in me was as hospitable to the strangeness of the world as dreaming is. I met him, I could only have met him, when, like the bush, I had learned to go and grow in the prevailing way, the Tuatha De Danann way we had walked into.

Beside him, climbing at nightfall into mist between The Paps, I knew that I was a latecomer. I was a Celt, a man, and so, if only in dreams I would never remember, I was Badb possessed, I was Sheela shocked. I must undergo cultural conversion. In my hands and my eyes I must undergo it. In waking and dreaming undergo it. I must undergo it in learning and lore. Culturally, I must have other, older origins. Tuatha De Danann dreaming and waking must generate me, must be beginnings of me.

Standing barefoot and naked in the streambed between her breasts, Dien Cecht, the medicine man of her people, presented me to Danu.

He gave me three rosaries of rowan berries, two of her Hindu breasts, one of her Hindu yoni.

MANDUKYA DAWN OVER DANU'S IRELAND

I

It was nature itself that shaped them, that moulded them. Given their perfection of form on an Irish horizon, it wouldn't be going too far to say that it was nature itself that sculpted them.

Nature wasn't in a hurry. It had time on its hands. It had long geological epochs and ages to work in. It worked with earth tremors and rivers. It worked with the big and the small rock fracturings of fire and ice. It worked with the erosions and corrosions of wind and rain. And there they are now, two hills, two perfect breasts on a horizon in Ireland. Having cairns for nipples, the old ceo draíochta veils and unveils them.

The Paps, they are called.

The Paps of Danu.

From of old, Danu was called the Mother of the Irish gods. And that's saying something.

That's saying she was mother of Lugh, the Sun God.

That's saying she was mother of Macha, the horse goddess.

That's saying she was mother of red-mouthed Morrigu, the battle goddess.

That's saying she was mother of Cúroi Mac Dara, the god in a grey mantle who one day picked up his own severed head and walked away.

That's saying she was mother of Midir and Manannan. Manannan was god of the sea, or a god who lived in the sea. Manannan only needed to shake his red and green cloak between his wife and her lover and never afterwards did they so much as remember each other. Never afterwards did they so much as catch sight of each other in a dream.

Being the mother of the Irish gods, Danu was mother of the salmon-god, all-seeing and all-wise in the Boyne, all-wise but blind in Assaroe.

A goddess of the Indo-Europeans, Danu migrated with her people. She migrated with those of them who eventually made it to India, and so it is no surprise to find that there are hymns to her in the Rig Veda. Also of course she migrated with those of her people who came into Europe. On her way west, she gave her name to three rivers, the Dnieper, the Don and the Danube.

And here on a horizon of Ireland's dreamtime are two holy hills.

When the mist disperses we see that their nipples are cairns.

II

How do I approach hills so holy? Do I do what his God commanded Moses to do, do I put off my shoes from off my feet?

I don't mean my physical shoes, my physical boots, the boots I bought recently in Stanley's in Clifden.

I mean the cosmologies I'm shod in.

My head shod, my seeing shod, my thinking shod, my talking shod. Shod in touch. In hearing shod.

So shod, I hurt the earth I walk on.

I hear a sheep farmer calling his dog. Whistling like him, calling as echoingly loud and long as he calls, I too should call, calling my cosmologies home from the universe.

Nights there are when I feel that all cosmological thinking about them hurts the stars.

So strangely near some nights are the Stars, so like next-door neighbours are they, that I leave my door open, expecting Virgo or Capricorn or Aquarius to drop in.

It would be wrong, wouldn't it, to walk cosmologically roughshod over them?

I will.

I'll put off my shoes from off my feet.

I'll put off all cosmologies from off my mind.

III

Dien Cecht, the healer among the Tuatha De, he came this way. Singing with it, singing its song of many sounds, he crossed this stream, leaving a scent not of this world in the heather. Getting that scent, a hare stopped in his tracks, a low, defunct lobe alive again.

A scent of Otherworlds. A scent of summer thunder. Coming home one night, Dien Cecht heard a howling high and far away. He looked around, Its mouth wide open, fiercely fanged and angry, the lightning struck.

For the very short while that he was on fire, he saw into all worlds.

In those few moments he was welcome in all worlds.

He heard their songs.

He saw our hurt.

Dien Cecht had no choice. Smelling of thunder, blackened and singed, his face and his hands peeling like birch bark, he was now a healer.

While he heals, singing the songs he heard, he is sometimes an ecstasy of fire, sometimes of ashes.

While he heals a howling, high and far away, is heard.

> He came this way.

In his footsteps, picking up the strange scent, I climb.

IV

To be mirrored in the little lake that mirrors the Paps—that is strange. It is like an invitation into a purer, clearer experience of ourselves. It is like falling asleep in one world and waking up in another.

It happens, doesn't it?

An old fiddler leaves a neighbour's house, and he walks towards home, his eyes as he does so getting used to the dark. But he doesn't walk in his own door that night. Not that night. Nor the next night. Nor the night after that.

Sight nor light of him there isn't, till nine nights later. Offering no explanation or excuse, he sits by the fire.

He needs time.

He needs to get used to things.

When he is sure of things he goes and takes down his fiddle and he plays the air he heard in the Otherworld.

His wife would hear it all over again.

He hesitates.

Play it, she says.

But how, he complains, how can he play an air of the Otherworld on a fiddle of this world?

Try it, she says.

Such airs, he says, must create their own instruments.

Such airs, he says, must create their own world. A world they can be played in. And hearing they must create. Hearing they can be heard with.

V

It isn't yet the tundra I'd expect it to be, this high ground between the Paps. After five or six hours sitting below thin little falls and cascades of water there is something I know. I know that my empirical mind is a third eye's blindspot.

VI

Sometimes it's us who are visionary.

Sometimes it's things.

This evening, here between the Paps, it's this autumn red rowan, red with red berries and a few red leaves.

Even if no one ever laid eyes on it, it would be a vision.

Even in a universe in which eyesight hadn't yet evolved, it would be a vision.

In its presence I'm embarrassed by eyesight. By the little self-serving efficiencies of eyesight.

After three or four hours in its presence I yet again know that there is a rare state of mind that makes my head obsolete.

VII

Climbing steeply, I come up onto a green flood-plain, its grass close cropped by the Paps' sheep.

Looking up at the high horizon round me now, a fear I had setting out deepens into trepidation.

I sit on the fallen wall of an old stone sheep-pen.

Remembering another day among other mountains, I don't need to be told that now again I have come up into a height where I am threatened by avalanche. Not a physical avalanche. Not an avalanche of snow or scree.

At worst, such an avalanche can only overwhelm us downwards into death.

Altogether more frightful is a spiritual avalanche. An avalanche set off by pride, by wilful self-promotion. An avalanche set off by our unreadiness for the heights we have come up into. Such an avalanche can carry us down out of the world altogether. It can carry us down, frightened and alive, into what at first contact will seem to be endless perdition in an endless vacancy.

Also there is an inner apocalypse, an apocalypse of insight that leaves us bewildered and desperate, knowing that conscious and unconscious psyche is the blind not the window.

Because, I suppose, of its association with sheep pens as forgotten and old as the one I am sitting on, I take refuge in a song called 'Dónal Óg'. It's the young woman who loved and still loves him who sings:

> *Do gheallais domhsa, ní ba dheacair duit,*
> *loingeas óir faoi chrann seoil airgid*
> *dhá bhaile dhéag de bhailte margaidh*
> *is cúirt bhréa aolta cois taobh na farraige.*
>
> *Do gheallais domhsa, ní nárbh fheidir,*
> *go dhabharfá laimhne de chroicean eisc dom*
> *go dhabharfá bróga de chroiceann éan dom*
> *is culaith den tsíoda ba dhaoire in Éirinn.*

Yes, ships of gold with masts of silver he promised her. Twelve market towns and a house by the sea he promised her. Gloves made by elves and shoes made in fairy forts he promised her. And, altogether more passionately to be desired, he promised that he'd be at the sheep croft:

> *Do gheallais domhsa, agus d'insis bréag dom,*
> *go mbeifeá romhamsa ag cró na gcaorach ...*

And she would be there. Whatever the weather, she would be there. A bull in a field she must cross, a flood in a river she must ford, three gaps and a fourth gap closed against her, nothing would stop her, she would be there because he would be there, a man of his word, at the sheep croft waiting.

Sheltering from this shower, sheltering here at this near gable, he'll surely be she thought, coming over the brow of the last ridge.

But no! No matter. It's lambing time and he's busy.

Only one more stream to ford, and two rising fields, and then he'll look round, and how glad he will be to see it's me who is there.

But no! Not in the pens.
Not in the near field. Not in the far field.
And the sheep not gathered.
She opens a door.
No. Not inside either.
And not in the hay loft.

Back on the ridge, the better to see, she looks down into the valley. She looks down, dumbfounded, into a dream dreamed three nights ago, Dónal Óg with his back to her, his belongings slung over his shoulder.

She whistles for Dónal. And she calls. Three hundred times she calls. But a lamb bleating, and he bleating weakly, is all she gets for answer:

> *do ligeas fead agus trí cead glaoch chughat*
> *is ní bhfuaireas ann ac uan ag meilig.*

Months later, her heart black as a coal on the floor of a forge, she sings, singing to him who isn't there;

> *Bhainis soir díom is bhainis siar díom,*
> *bhainis romham is bhainis im dhiaidh díom,*
> *bhainis an gealach is bhainis an grian díom,*
> *'s is ro-mhór m'eagla gur bhainis Dia díom.*

> You have taken my east from me,
> and you have taken my west from me;
> you have taken my before-me from me,
> and you have taken my behind-me from me;
> you have taken the moon and taken the sun from me;
> and 'tis my great fear
> that you have taken my God from me.

Dónal and Danu.
No sigh of Dónal at the sheep croft.
And, at the sheep pen here between her own breasts, no sign of Danu.

VIII

Night. Dark night.
Dark night outside.
Dark night inside.
But I praise you, Danu, that you will not condescend to sensory need.
I praise you, Danu, that you will not condescend to apparition.
Here between your breasts it is as absence that you are present.
That, or like Dónal Óg, your back is turned and your are walking away.
The lament of a woman for Dónal could be the lament of bhakta for Danu:

> *Tá mo chroise chomh dubh le hairne*
> *nó le gual dubh a bheadh I gcearta,*
> *nó le bonn broíge ar halla bána*
> *is tá lionn dubh mór os cionn mo ghaire*

> My heart is as black as the sloe,
> as black as a coal that you'd find in a forge,
> as black as the track of a shoe in a white hall,
> and suffocated by a blackness is my laughter.

And yet there they are, there between your breasts, Danu, are the four elevations of the mystical ascent to which you call us, the elevation of the lake, the elevation of the first flood plain, the elevation of the second flood plain and then, veiled by what we see, by vision veiled, the heights.

Often, by frightful but blessed reversal of expectation, it is the avalanche that carries us down into the depths that carries into the heights.

It is in an inner apocalypse, an apocalypse of divinely vouchsafed illumination and grace that a way is opened for us.

And so, getting to know you in a way that Hindus didn't know you, in a way that our ancestors in Ireland didn't know you, can we think of you, Danu, as the goddess we only see when your back is turned, as the goddess we only see when you are walking away.

That is your glory. And, even when our heart is as black as a coal on the floor of a forge, it is our glory.

I praise you, Danu, for not being at our beck and call.

I praise you, Danu, for your beneficent refusal to take up residence in our myths and stories about you.

I praise you, Danu, that you do not attempt to win favour with us by accepting a niche in a religion which, in its ignorance, would shorten the distance between the human and the divine.

I praise you, Danu, that it is above all when we yield to your highest aspirations for us that you are there for us.

And yet, in contradiction to all of this, there they are, two lovely hills in West Munster. They have cairns for nipples. The old ceo draíochta veils and unveils them.

Looking at them, we know how bountifully immanent in all things is the Transcendent Divine. As the breasts of the goddess Danu, it is bountifully immanent in stone and star. As the breasts of the goddess Danu, it is bountifully immanent in the herb that heals us, in the cancer that kills us.

Having wandered outwards into an illusory sense of existence in independence from the Ground that grounds us, we live and are lived by the contradiction.

For the transcendent way in which you are so mountainously immanent in sand-grain and galaxy, I praise you, Danu.

Of old, in Ireland, they called you.

Bandia an tSonusa
The Goddess of Prosperity.

But you are more, a goddess marvellously more, than your breasts here below suggest that you are.

You are Danu. Prayed to in India, prayed to in Ireland, who but you can sponsor and propose the Mandukya Upanishad as the meeting ground of East and West, of people praying by Galway Bay and the Bay of Bengal.

You are Danu.

IX

The rowan I remember.

The autumn red rowan growing between two cascades and falls of water.

Even if no one ever laid eyes on it, it would be a vision.

Even in a universe in which eyesight hadn't yet evolved, it would be a vision.

A red Rig Veda in Ireland it is,
A red Gita to Danu in Ireland it is,
A Mandukya dawn over Danu's Ireland it is,
This
Little Yggdrasil

And the berries I picked from the mosses beneath it—closing my hand on them they feel like a rosary.

A rosary of fallen berries.
Of berries fallen from the world tree.

And in the walk of her, walking to meet him, there were splendours of passionate life.

In the walk of her walking through fair and through field to meet him—in the walk of her walking to meet Dónal Óg, all our contemporary cosmologies were refuted.

SECOND COMING CHRISTIANITY

The Second Coming of Christ which Christians expect and await—it isn't a new or another coming. It is a mystical understanding of the First Coming.

Second Coming Christianity has been with us, waiting for us, since the beginning.

In Second Coming Christianity the Triduum Sacrum is a Quinduum Sacrum:

> Jesus Grand-Canyon deep in the world's karma.
>
> Jesus on the Hill of the Koshaless Skull.
>
> Jesu Apsusayin.
>
> Jesu Anadyomene.
>
> Jivanmukta Jesus preaching his first Evangelanta sermon.

Imagine it:

> Venus Anadyomene,
> Venus coming shorewards on a sea shell.

Imagine it:

> Jesus Anadyomene,
> Jesus coming shorewards on the Mandukya Upanishad.

Jesus coming shorewards on a Hindu interpretation of all that has happened to him.

A CEILING OF SIBYLLINE VISIONS FOR THE RUINED CATHEDRAL OF CLONMACNOISE

I
SEEING THROUGH TO GETHSEMANE I SEE

> A theranthropic Jesus,
> A theriomorphic Jesus.

A Jesus in the image and likeness of the Aztec Earthmother.

All that we inwardly are is religiously enfranchised.
All that we inwardly are is redeemed.

II

He being the primitive, club-wielding hero he was, Herakles couldn't even imagine this last labour. On the thirteenth day he rested, and he was well pleased, thinking that now, finally, culture could flourish. No Nemean lion would rise rampant against our citadel. We wouldn't wake one morning to find Hydra's nine heads hissing at us in our nine city gates. Neither would culture asphyxiate in its own Augean accumulations.

It was a troubled city we built.

Our King was club-footed. Even in our dreams we were club-headed, unable to see.

Soothseeing, I see hope. I bear hope. I hear a new hero. Him I hear saying:

> Put up your dragon-slaying
> sword I'll be the scabbard.

III

Vespers continuing, yet awhile, in his Theban Temple, Atum goes down into Manu, the Western Mountain.

Sitting amidships in the Duat, his Spear laid aside, the Night Sun sings, as Orpheus would, playing his lyre.

Brightened by his rising above Bakhu, the Eastern Mountain, six green baboons dance their morning greetings to

> Apophis-Horus of the Horizon.

IV

Behold a great wonder on Patmos:

Orpheus, he singing, surrounded by Tiamat, Apsu, Kingu, Zu, Labdu-Asag, Vritra, Makara, Mahisasura, Python, Leviathan, Apophis, Rahu, Draco, Drakaina, Phorkys, Echidna, Chimaira, Lamia, Yam, Mot, Minotaur, Typhon, Triton, Keros, Proteus, Cerberus, and still on their way, hearing the song, Fenrir, Faffnir, Grendel, and others, all of them, from all cultures, all our repressions, Dzoonokw, Hohokw, and Numxilexiu, he who throws a great wave before him, he comes, Great Jiakim comes, hearing the song, singing the song, drawn by the song, drawn into nine circles around it,

> Around Orpheus and his song,
> All their poisons hearing the song,
> All their poisons healed by the song,
> All of them singing.

And the singing saves,

> It saves,
> It saves,
> It saves.

> And all shall be saved,
> And all shall be saved,
> All our repressions shall be saved.

V

Not a voice calling out,

> Great Pan is dead.

A voice calling out,

> Pashupati lives.

And when you come opposite Europe tell them, calling out to them that:

> Pashupati lives.

VI

Soothseeing I see, a woodsman comes to Camelot. He draws the sword of our petra-fying perceptions of it out of a stone.

> The stone blossoms, gothically.

But don't call them windows.
When you walk the long aisle, walking between them, call them auroras.

> Auroras of Soul.

VII

In the far north-west on an ocean shore there I see a stone boat.

> I see voyages in it
> Yes,
> Yes,

> I see a way through.

> I see voyages to good ways of seeing things in it.

VIII

Our myths crossing the Kedron.
Our philosophies crossing the Kedron.

Our science crossing the Kedron.
Talk about Christ crossing the Kedron.

IX

Grand-Canyon deep in the world's karma, alone on a firefloor there, Jesus prays, but the chalice does not pass. His psyche comes to the boil. It boils over at femur and face. He is sore amazed.

On Golgotha, his kenosis complete, his hurt head fallen onto his chest, he hears and he sees Chandogya Good News in the Koshaless skull.

> Yatra na anyat pasyati na anyat srinoti na
> anyad vijanati, sa bhuma.

X

The Abyss I see. A Beginning I see. A new Dreamtime I see. I see

Jesu Apsusayin.

IMAGINE

Imagine another Patrick. A Patrick in our time for our time. A Patrick who not only seeks to bring a richer Christianity to Ireland, he seeks also to bring what is best in its Celtic and pre-Celtic inheritance to Ireland.

The Christianity he brings has crossed the Kedron. Watching with its founder, it has knelt Grand-Canyon deep in the world's karma. Watching with him, it has climbed the Hill of the Koshaless Skull.

The Christianity he brings isn't in thrall to the mythologies, theologies, philosophies and cosmologies of the eastern Mediterranean hinterlands.

Imagine him: a Patrick in whom the two extremities of the Indo-European migrations meet.

Imagine him: a Patrick who knows that until the Battle of the Boyne Ireland belonged to Asia.

Imagine him; a Patrick who longs for a day when Ireland will again belong to Asia.

Imagine him: a Patrick who speaks a Bhagavad Gita on the site where we fought and still fight the Battle of the Boyne.

Imagine him: a Patrick who knows that on her way west, coming with a people who worshipped her, the Goddess Danu gave her name to the Don, the Dnieper and the Danube. Two beautiful hills in Sliabh Luachra are said to be her breasts. The Paps, they are called. Dá Clích Danann they are called.

Imagine him: a Patrick who for forty days and nights practises jnana yoga between the Paps of Danu, Danu being a Hindu Goddess to whom one of the hymns of the Rig Veda is addressed.

Imagine him: in his vision of them, the Magi came from lands farther east than the Bible has heard of. The gifts they bring are the Mandukya Upanishad, the Tao Te Ching and the Heart Sutra.

Imagine him: a Patrick who believes that the Tao Te Ching is Old Testament, New Testament and Future Testament to the Sermon on the Mount.

Imagine him: a Patrick for whom Croagh Patrick is Cruachan Aigle, and on its summit, on Reek Sunday, he speaks six Upanishadic Mahavakyas to the assembled multitudes.

Imagine him: a Patrick who has a vision of Jesus Anadyomene, Jesus coming ashore on the Mandukya Upanishad.

Imagine it: an Ireland whose centre at Uisnech is

Mullán Om,
Mullán na Mireann,
The Mireann being: vaisvanara, taijasa, susupta and turiya.

Imagine it: an Ireland which, four times a year, is able for the silence after A, U, and M.

Imagine it: the numinous new chapters which might one day be added to our Lebor Gabála Erenn.

A chapter called

Mendukya Mullán

A chapter called

Mendukya Mórdháil

We have a centre that will hold.
We have a ceremony that will hold.

THE NEW GAE BOLGA

No willing suspension of disbelief was called for when, answering what seemed like a far-away knock on my door, I opened it, and there he was, his glittering eye clouded now by a kind of pleading. I was of course taken aback, but not for long, because it was for the likes of him, for Faust, for the Wandering Jew, or for some other great Transgressor, that I had always kept a chair at my fire.

It is a serious chair, I said, remorselessly, by way of challenge.

He didn't speak.

I made it myself.

I made it myself from an oak I uncovered six sods deep in a bog.

Bog-oak we call it.

He didn't speak.

Altogether more serious than the ship you sailed in is the chair you are sitting in.

Sitting in that chair, you are sitting six sods deep in yourself.

Sitting in that chair, you are sitting in the silence below history.

So it won't work.

Fixing you sea-grey eye on me won't work.

Nor will it work to sing the old Rime in the old riming way:

> *At length did cross the Albatross,*
> *Through the fog it came;*
> *As if it had been a Christian soul,*
> *We hailed it in God's name.*

The small light of the lamp didn't reach him. Loud by times, the light of the fire did, and it illuminated as much of him as I wanted to see, as maybe I dared to see.

He didn't only look like himself.

He didn't only look like a man gone wrong.

He looked like humanity gone wrong.

Or worse.

He looked like Nature's revenge. As if Nature had already decided it wanted us out of its way.

I didn't succumb to pity.

That would be to give in to the sea-grey eye.

I was fighting the sea-grey eye.

I'd defeat the sea-grey eye.

I did relent.

You are welcome to sit by my fire for a night, I said.

You are welcome to sit in silence below history.

Only this you must remember: my chair is also made of bog-oak. You will not dominate me into powerless listening.

Now I was the one who was staring.

I didn't go to sea, I said.

I didn't go to sea the way you went to sea. I stayed in the bogs I was born into. But don't think lightly of that. Any night you like, even now to night, I can meet your sea-grey eye with my bog-brown eye. My credentials in disaster, and in the insights that come with disaster, are no less that yours are. I demand good manners in my house.

He didn't speak.

I spoke: they don't live next door to me. Neither in time nor in space do they live next door to me. But Faust and the Wandering Jew are my next door neighbours. And if only you can learn to behave yourself, maybe we will accept you as a neighbour too. A neighbour in the ordinary, in the very ordinary dimension of this world that we call Purgatory.

He didn't speak.

I spoke.

Fend for yourself, I said. I'm going to bed.

Again, three nights later, I answered a far-away knock on my door.

Showing signs he was willing to meet me on equal terms, he came in and sat down.

And you thought you were the first, I said.

The first in what? he asked.

The first to be disastered into the great desolation:

> *The fair breeze blew, the white foam flew,*
> *The furrow followed free;*
> *We were the first that ever burst*
> *Into that silent sea.*

In what way were you disastered? he asked.

I hesitated.

He persisted.

I think of it as my Good Friday, I said. The veil of my mind was rent, and afterwards, for years, I was in the great dark, seeking but not finding God, a God too near to be experienced or known, so I had in the end to go beyond being an experiencer. In my quest for God, I had to leave me as an experiencer at home. An experience of God is but yet another eclipse of God.

And now?

Now, reaching down, God has drawn me up into respite.

Respite where?

Where I've told you. In the ordinary, in the very ordinary dimension of this world called Purgatory.

Is there fire in your purgatory?

Yes.

And it burns?

Yes.

What in you does it burn?

A will to what is impossible, a will to ontological apostasy, a will to existence in wilful independence from God as Ground.

That simple?

That terrible. It isn't only the Wandering Jew who has spat in God's face. It isn't only Faust who has sold his soul. And, repeating your fall, it isn't only you who has dropped below your eternal horizon. It isn't only you who has dropped below the light of the kirk and the light of the lighthouse.

And now, I said, now I'll outstare you: wandering the world telling your story gives you the illusion that you are doing something, that you are going somewhere. But of course you aren't. You are becalmed in your Purgatory. And to be becalmed in Purgatory is as little good to you morally and spiritually as it is to be becalmed at sea. This therefore is what you must do. You must ship with Ahab as his chief harpooner. But, blind in the typical way that we in the West are blind, that could mean that in three years time I will answer a far-away knock on my door and there you will be, the White Whale hanging from your neck. So, I am warning you: don't drink Ahab's sea-grey grog, for if you do you will surely repeat the old Mesopotamian mistake. And that is a serious mistake. And we should take it seriously. As seriously as the hunters of the Palaeolithic took it, enacting it tragically in the pit in Lascaux. There we see that Nature has pushed the birdman aside, saying in effect that it isn't now through humanity that it will or can evolve. But, in the faint hope that Nature's decision isn't irreversible, I'm outstaring you now, I'm outstaring your sea-grey eye with my bog-brown eye, and I'm telling you what to do. I am telling you to ship with Ahab, our mad captain. Ship with him as his chief harpooner, for where else but in the pit in Lascaux, where else but in Esagila, where else but on the quarter deck of the *Pequod*, where else but where we are most astray can we most effectively challenge our madness. Don't come home with evolution obstructed, with evolution run aground in humanity, hanging from your neck. Be a new kind of hero. Be the new harpooner. Be a harpooner evolution can work with. Be a harpooner who uses his harpoon in the way that a prospective Buddha uses his sword of discrimination. I will tell you what this calls for. What it calls for is action. When you have heard the mad captain's apocalyptic harangue, you will stand aside from your mesmerized mates, and you will say, I am now the *Pequod*'s harpooner, and then showing them your steel, you will say, the name of my harpoon is Ahimsa. It is with Ahimsa, it is in living and in being lived by the Sermon on the Mount, that we strike through—no—that we see through the world-illusion. And if, like Arjuna at Kurukshetra, your nerve should fail, remember this: behind the world-illusion is the world as it actually is, unworldly, wise in the way that minds can't be wise, and knowable naively in states of pure wonder.

That way the *Pequod* might be saved. That way, under full sail, top gallants and royals set, she might come home as Nave.

He didn't speak.

I spoke.

I've news for you, I said. Ishmael has already seen four spectres going aboard before him. That's Faust, the Wandering Jew, myself and—you, all four of us coming back into history, all four of us rejoining the Western voyage.

That's it.

Your destiny has come to find you in the Purgatory you have taken refuge from it in.

Good night, harpooner. I'm going to bed.

ENFLAITH THE BIRD REIGN OF THE ONCE AND FUTURE KING

I

Other boys had an ancestry, I had a pedigree, and my pedigree meant it was mostly through dreaming that I would know and deal with reality. Overflowing all inner and outer banks, dreaming would sometimes be an inundation, an outcrop of waking nowhere in sight.

Even when he was near me, talking to me, my father was far away. In birdform, among birds, their underwings raucously red, is how I remember him.

Meass Buachalla was my mother. She looked after a king's cattle. She had cures. And she crossed into Otherworlds as easily as someone who has slept all night crosses into waking. Sometimes a long sojourn in an Otherworld would fall between the two parts of a conversation I'd have with her.

The birds my father flocked with could, on occasion, be murmuringly savage. Mostly, though, they were as shy as geese. Only once did I ever come close to them. Which was my father I couldn't say. When they took flight, I saw again that underwing and underweb they were raucously red.

One evening, shortly before I'd have closed it, a hurt bird, a scald crow, flew through my door. Without thinking, I held out my hand, palm downwards. She perched on it. She looked at me. She squawked three times. Then she flew back out, leaving her hurt behind. I knew I would carry that hurt for the rest of my life. And I also knew that I wouldn't be a warrior, even though that's why I had been fostered out so young to my uncle, a wide man, a man of war, and famous, his hospitality talked of from sea to sea.

After seven years I had only my hurt to go home with.

And I didn't reach home.

The path I had taken was taking me nowhere. Mountains I had in mind, it hadn't in mind. 'Twas as if it were walked only by beings who had no knowledge or need of elsewhere. Are there such beings? I wondered. I was beginning to be frightened. Are there beings for whom all elsewheres are where they are? What kind of mind have they? What kind of eyes?

At the end of three vexed days, the sunset vexed and very red, I gave up. I sat on a rock. It was strange. These thoughts I was thinking didn't seem to be my thoughts. But whose thoughts were they? Were they the land's thoughts? It was an old, old land, older than human intentions and purposes. Human intentions and purposes were nowhere visible in it. Was it taking me over? Was it thinking through me?

Could it be, I thought, that I have walked into a mood of mind or a mood of nature in which there are no intentions? Could it be, I thought, that having intentions fences me in?

But thoughts like these couldn't be my thoughts.

Thoughts like these didn't fit my forehead. They didn't fit seed or sense in me. I was afraid. Had I walked into someone's dream of me?

I got up and walked on, looking for evidence of the everyday world.

It was everywhere in evidence.

Off the path, on a patch of wet grass, was a pair of snails. Copulating they were, their horns, all eight of them, withdrawn from the distractions of a world now not necessary.

In the lee of a shag of bushes, mostly blackthorn, not yet blossoming, was a ram. Lying there, his head high, he was chewing the cud and between his horns, leaning forward, a magpie was picking wool for her nest.

As I approached it, noisily, a stick breaking under my feet, a pair of mallard broke in a frightened confusion of forms from a cove of reeds and then, assuming distinct duck shapes, they turned south and the water drops that fell from them left trails of expanding circles on the candour of the lake.

> Three days became four days,
> Three nights became four nights.

After nine days and nights I knew that, disarmed as I was, I had met my destiny. The candour of the lake in front of me, that was it.

It was a temptation to something more dangerous than sanctity.

Leaving her hurt in me, the hurt bird had disarmed me of shield and spear and sword. Had disarmed me of high horsemanship, of a right, already won, to a high place at the warriors' table.

But now the lake was disarming me, not of accoutrements and acquirements, but of something I was. And nine years later, having lived since then in a restored crannog, a high island to the north of me, patches of reeds east of me, nine years later it would still, at odd moments, disarm me of all I self seekingly was.

I would see how unworldly the world was.

There were mornings, calm and clear, when the candour of the lake was candour of hand and eye in me.

The candour of its seeing would sometimes be my seeing, seeing the mountains without distortion.

> The distortion of greed.
> The distortion of anger.
> The distortion of love.
> The distortion of hope.
> The distortion of despair.
> The distortion above all of intention and purpose.

At night, delight was the light in my lamp, it was the light in me. And moths came.

A moth from Brí Leith.

It was her joy to find someone with whom she could be human. It was her joy to find someone who was able for the splendours of her needs at night. It was hurt in me that enabled me. We pitied the shining stars. But we knew, looking at them, that their night would come. It had come for us. All summer long all elsewheres were where we were. Tír Tairngí was in her hair. Magh Mel was in my eyes. We walked, whenever we walked abroad, in Emain Abhlach.

II

I dreamed: my house was my grave mound. I was desolate, groping carved walls in the darkness. I found the passage. I was walking, I hoped, towards dawn. A solstice spear, a sun-spear, speared me, tumbling me back.

I sat with the bones of my incarnations.

I ate the food of the dead. Bird food, boar food, horse food. Someone was there.

He was gathering the bones. Bones of the bird I was, of the boar I was, of the horse I was. Of creatures unknown that I was.

He heaped them together, boar bones at the bottom, bird bones on top.
Your bonefire, he said, setting fire to them.
He threw me into the flames.
I was sitting in ashes when I revived.
My first breath was a last plume of smoke.
Eat it, he said.

As I ate the ashes, I had visions. I was walking with animals. I was kind of their kind. I was mind of their mind. I woke up. I got up. Crossing the causeway I was when I realized I had the sun-spear in my hand. It would, I realized, be in my hand whenever I needed it.

III

In a wood a voice called out,

> You are now a people's dream of you. Walk in it.

Again, after a long while, it called,

> Walk in it.

Six mornings later before sunrise it called,

> Walk in the people's dream of you.

The last time it called the voice was an echo:

> Naked, it said, naked naked naked.

Naked, like a child not ashamed, I walked out of the wood. Ahead of me, on the rough sward, grazing it, were the birds my father flocked with.

I walked towards them. They took to flight alighting not far away. I kept walking. Again they took flight, and again they alighted. And so it continued till they came to the sea. There the one who was my father turned and, assuming human form, he came to me saying, Walk on as you are. Walk northwards naked to Tara. You will be king.

IV

He could escape into other species, she could escape into other worlds. I couldn't. Or rather I decided that even if I could I wouldn't. Smoke of a bonefire in my nostrils, Magh Mel long gone from my eyes, I would be loyal to the hurt human, the hurt bird. My reign would be a Bird reign.

Walking northwards naked to Tara, a sun-spear, spear of initiations, in my hand, that was my peoples' dream of me. That was Étain's dream of me. Throughout all my reign Étain was human. Étain was happy.

And Manannan Mac Lir, he was happy one night to find Ireland, not Tír Tairngrí, in Fand's hair.

EPILOGUE

THE LAST EUREKA

In the opening story of this book you assert, if that isn't too strong a word, that the only way back to our dreamtime is by rite of passage. Would you elaborate on this?

One day a friend of mine suggested that, since we were in the vicinity, we should go to Newgrange. Half an hour later, having paid whatever the fee was, the Irish Board of Works had given us permission to proceed towards the great megalithic entrance. On the way it occurred to me that this threshold we are thinking of crossing is a threshold between worlds, and with that I baulked.

No, I said to my friend, I cannot go in.

She looked puzzled.

I owed her an explanation.

Permission from this world, I said, showing her my ticket, isn't the same thing as an invitation from the Otherworld. I'll wait for you on the road outside.

Can I reflect with you on this little incident?

There are times when we must be content with our profanity. Given that we haven't undergone the enabling initiations and purifications, we must be content to remain in the *pro-naos,* in the yard in front of the holy place, in the yard outside the place of revelation, the place of sacred showing. It is a calamity of the modern world that so few of us experience our profanity in that literal sense of the word. And if we haven't experienced ourselves in our profanity then it is likely that we haven't experienced ourselves in the presence of the holy.

Think of Jacob on his way to Haran:

And Jacob went out from Beersheba, and went toward Haran. And he lighted upon a certain place, and he tarried there all night, because the sun was set; and he took of the stones of that place, and put them for his pillows, and lay down in that place to sleep. And he dreamed, and behold a ladder set up on the earth, and the top of it reached to heaven: and behold the angels of God ascending and descending on it. And, behold, the Lord stood above it, and said, I am the Lord God of Abraham thy father, and the God of Isaac: the land whereon thou liest, to thee will I give it, and to thy seed. And thy seed shall be as the dust of the earth, and thou shalt spread abroad to the west, and to the east, and to the north, and to the south: and in thee and in thy seed shall all the families of the earth be blessed. And, behold, I am with thee, and will keep thee in all places whither thou goest, and will bring thee again into this land, for I will not leave thee, until I have done that which I have spoken to thee of. And Jacob awaked out of his dream, and he said, surely the Lord is in this place; and I knew it not. And he was afraid, and said, how dreadful is this place! this is none other but the house of God, and this is the gate of heaven ...

Imagine how quaint it would be if, arriving at this gate, I presented a ticket issued to me by the Irish Board of Works.

Or just as bad: imagine that I arrive at the gate of heaven and having greeted the Angel of Final Assize I take the initiative saying, hang on there now till I seek in my rucksack for a book I would read to you from. By none other than Tom Paine, it is a book we are very proud of, and it is called *The Rights of Man* ...

Please though, don't misconstrue what I am saying here. Our rights as citizens, won over a long time and at frightful cost, are a singularly great if also a much threatened inheritance. But we aren't only citizens signing up to a social contract. Or, as Emerson would remind us, we aren't only what we sociologically are:

It is the largest part of man that is not inventoried. He had many enumerable parts: he is social, professional, political, sectarian, literary, and in this or that sect and corporation. But after the most exhausting census has been made, there remains as much more which no tongue can tell. And this remainder is that which interests.

It isn't with banners flying and singing the battle song of our republic that we cross into that remainder. And, again, how quaint it would be to charge that remainder under one or another of the amendments to our constitution. How quaint it would be to bring the Night Mare, Fuseli's Night Mare, before the European Court of Human Rights. How quaint it would be to arraign our own depths, to charge them with anarchy, to charge them with having waged a life-long campaign of intimidation and terror against us. How quaint it would be to charge them with all those wicked dreams that so abuse our curtained, or uncurtained, sleep.

There is more to human inwardness than Freud found in it. Than Freud, relying on cause and effect explanation, found in it.

There is more to the universe than Einstein found in it. Than Einstein, relying on what is mathematically possible and respectable, found in it.

For me the word Fódhla has inner psychological as well as outer cosmological reference. Fódhla is a mood of mind, is a mood of the universe, that isn't mathematically mirrorable.

To cross into this mood of mind and of universe, to cross into Fódhla, is to cross into our Dreamtime.

At the borders of Fódhla I am aware of rite not right.

At the borders of our Dreamtime, seeking entrance, I look not to my ticket from the Irish Board of Works but to the Ces Noidhen.

As I seek to inherit it in this book, the Ces Noidhen is a blessing not a curse. Indeed, far from it being an impassable frustration, it is a way through. It is a rite of passage in which, with her divine favour, we suffer her labour pains with the Celtic Horse Goddess.

In this we see that the invitation to suffer with the divine One, with the human-divine One, didn't come first into Ireland with Christ.

It is, however, a matter of historical fact, isn't it, that the Celtic Ces Noidhen gave way to the Christian Passion?

Yes, but to me that only means that the Cross of the Scriptures belongs as much to our Dreamtime as does Brugh na Boinne, it means that the Passion narratives belong to it as much as does the Wasting Sickness of Cuchulainn.

Also, whereas the Celtic Ces Noidhen and the Christian Passion suggest the possibility of safe if frightful transitions, the ticket of admittance issued by the Irish Board of Works suggests ignorance and therefore trespass.

Think of the necropolis seal on the subterranean door to Tutankhamen's tomb. Think of how alive with withering, killing spells it was. And yet we broke it, opening a way for the terrors of the Egyptian underworld to emerge and plague us.

And this of course was just a precedent for breaking the sanctuary seal of the atom, and the people of Hiroshima know and the people of Nagasaki know that the mushroom we thereby let out was anything but an hors d'oeuvre delicacy.

That's us. We are the species that has broken the seal.

And Colin Clout has come home again.

And Colin reports that high in the hills above his house a sheep has given birth to an afterbirth only.

Is it any wonder therefore that this book begins where it does, with the Ces Noidhen? In a phrase of George Steiner's, is it any wonder that now again in our times Pastoral has become Paschal?

Even in your benign interpretation of it, surely the day for the Ces Noidhen is past. Past for a people cut off from wild nature, from wild animals and the wild earth.

I gather from your question that I might have given a false impression. So let me be clear on one thing. In the book I have written I at no point imply or intend to imply that the Ces Noidhen might one day take over from the Triduum Sacrum. And as for the day of the Ces Noidhen being past, I both do and don't agree with you. In this our century we didn't only go with Yeats to watch or maybe perform a purifying fire-dance on the pavement of a holy city, we went with him also to watch, or maybe perform, a hawk-dance at the Hawk's Well.

Given that, like Yeats himself, most of us aren't yet ready to set all our minds upon *the steep ascent,* upon *the winding stair,* isn't it *behovabil,* as Dame Julian might say, that we find a way of sanctifying our life in nature. By telling, and therefore in a sense by ritually enacting, six native American stories, I've attempted to address this need, if need it is, in another book. But, intending no violation to Yeats's play, maybe something as sacredly simple as a hawk dance at the Hawk's Well would do. As I've been saying, given the kind of universe we live in, we need threshold rituals. But don't we also need rituals in which we can sacredly acknowledge and sacredly incorporate the theranthropic. Rituals in which we sacredly acknowledge that within my more evolved brain is the old smell brain. Rituals in which we sacredly acknowledge that the hands with which we play the Kreutzer Sonata are still structurally analogous to the fins they have evolved from. So catastrophic now is our isolation from nature that we need to in some way acknowledge and enact our affinity with it. We need, if only with every new moon, to be as Franciscan as St Francis was.

We need, if only with every new moon, to live from commonage consciousness.

We need, if only with every new moon, to dance the dance of commonage consciousness.

And maybe they will, maybe the bison of the Pleistocene will come back and teach us that dance.

Maybe the few remaining bears or the few remaining eagles will teach it to us.

Maybe a hawk hovering above a dry Hawk's Well will teach it to us.

And maybe then, maybe when we sing the song and dance the dance of commonage consciousness, maybe when we sing the song and dance the dance of our Franciscan fraternity with the sun, of our Franciscan sorority with the moon, maybe then the stones in the well will moisten, maybe then the deep well waters will flow, bringing newness of life to our Waste Land.

That's why, somewhere at the heart of this book, we bring a Navajo cradle into our Dreamtime:

> *I have made a cradleboard for you, my child.*
> *May you grow to be a great old age.*
> *Of the sun's rays I have made the back,*
> *Of black clouds I have made the blanket,*
> *Of rainbow I have made the bow,*
> *Of high horizons I have made the side-loops,*
> *Of lightnings I have made the lacings,*
> *Of river mirrorings have I made the footboard,*
> *Of dawn have I made the covering,*
> *Of Earth's welcome for you have I made the bed.*

This cradle suggests an affinity with nature, a trust in nature.

Indeed, it might even suggest the possibility of fraternity with nature, of sorority with nature.

How rich we are! We have the cradle and the canticle.

Laying her in the cradle we can sing the canticle to Lucy.

To Lucy who lives in us all we can sing:

> *Laudato si, Misignore, per fratre sole ...*
> *Laudato si, Misignore, per sora luna et le stelle ...*
> *Laudato si, Misignore, per sor aqua ...*
> *Laudato si, Misignore, per sora nostra matre terra ...*

Song in which we learn to say, Brother Sun.

Song in which we learn to say, Sister Moon.

A song to come ashore with.

A safer song to come ashore with than the song of almost insane self-exaltation that Amhairghin Glungheal came ashore with:

> *Am Gaeth i muir*
> *Am tonn treathain*
> *Am fuaim mara*
> *Am dam seacht ndreann*
> *Am seg for ail*
> *Am der ngrene ...*

> I am wind on sea
> I am ocean wave
> I am roar of sea
> I am bull of seven fights
> I am hawk on cliff
> I am dewdrop ...

So, as I see it, this book doesn't settle for the Ces Noidhen. Nor does it recommend that we enact it as the ritual last act of a Celtic Holy Week. I placed it at the beginning of the book for the same reason that the people who supply us with electricity place the lightning sign, the warning sign, on their poles and pylons. Acutely aware as we nowadays are of our human rights, many of us think that, merely by passing through a turn-stile operated by a government employee, we can walk back into the thing we call Celtic consciouness. In their warriors the Celts were head-hunters. Nor for them to make do with the scalp. In their druids, or in some of them, the Celts practised the most killing kinds of magic. Think of how Balor came to have his evil eye, his *suil mildagach*. Clearly, it wasn't always pure pork-broth that bubbled in the Celtic cauldron.

> *Fillet of a fenny snake*
> *In the cauldron boil and bake:*
> *Eye of newt and toe of frog,*
> *Wool of bat and tongue of dog,*
> *Adder's fork and blind worm's sting,*
> *Lizard's leg and howlet's wing,*
> *For a charm of powerful trouble,*
> *Like a hell-broth boil and bubble.*

In Australian Aboriginal terms, some of these druids knew how to point the bone.

And, their interests in any way threatened, they had no compunction about pointing it.

Little wonder St Patrick was so careful to put on the whole armour of his god, leaving no think for the evil to enter:

> *Crist lim, Crist reum, Crist im degaid,*
> *Crist indium, Crist issum, Crist uasam,*
> *Crist dessum, Crist tuatham,*
> *Crist illius, Crist isius, Crist inerus ...*

Aware of the forces ranged against him in a way that Macbeth wasn't, St Patrick survived.

So, this book isn't in the business of indiscriminately praising the world that Macbeth so calamitously went astray in. And was led astray in.

Speaking for myself, I am not so sure that I have got what it takes to stand in her world with Ceridwen, to spend a night in his wood, in his Birnam Wood, with Mac Cuill.

And yet, because of great need, I wait for an invitation that might one day come to me out of Fódhla.

Because of great need, I wait for an invitation to walk in our Dreamtime. This book doesn't claim to be anything more than a propaideutic.

In this book we don't only suffer her labour pains with the Horse Goddess. We also suffer her death and rebirth pains with the Corn Mother. Graphically, we suffer at the harvesting edge of scythe and sickle and then again, come Spring, we suffer inhumation under plough and harrow. And, since there is no growing without growing pains, we know why Eliot will have said that April is the cruellest month. All of this, if it can be called such, is participation mystique *with a difference isn't it?*

Years ago, living as I then was in Connemara, I moved house. It was all of five or six weeks later that I had reason to open a cupboard in the kitchen. On a shelf of it were some potatoes that the previous occupant had left behind. Drawing only upon their own energies, these tubers had sprouted so naturally and so self-sacrificially as it were that now they were withered and shrivelled, and cut off as they were from soil and sun, the spouts were long and ghostly, almost transparent.

Desperately, they needed inhumation.

Desperately also, does modern humanity need to find ways, ritual ways, of living and expressing its affinity with nature. With Stoics, I believe that there is a *sumpatheia ton hollon,* a universal sympathy, that runs through all things, that connects all things with all things, and it would I believe be good for all things, including ourselves, if we lived from that sympathy.

In this we might need a little of what Karl Marx was pleased to call the idiocy of rural life.

Unafraid of such aspersion, we might carry out Death and bring in Summer.

Refusing the destination proposed to us by dialectical materialism, we might carry out all dead metaphors, all dead or killing cosmologies and bring in the green Yggdrasil branch.

Deciding to live in nature as well as in history, we might even suffer, if only ritually and vicariously, with the Corn Mother, or, as Robert Burns would probably have it, with John Barleycorn:

> *There was three kings into the east,*
> *Three kings both great and high,*
> *And they had sworn a solemn oath*
> *John Barleycorn should die.*
>
> *They took a plough and ploughed him down,*
> *Put clods upon his head,*
> *And they hae sworn a solemn oath*
> *John Barleycorn was dead.*

But the cheerful Spring came kindly on
And showers began to fall;
John Barleycorn got up again
And sore surprised them all.

The sultry suns of Summer came,
And he grew thick and strong,
His head weel arm'd wi' pointed spears,
That no one should him wrong.

The sober Autumn enter'd mild,
When he grew wan and pale;
His bending joints and drooping head
Show'd he began to fail.

His colour sicken'd more and more,
He faded into age:
And then his enemies began
To shew their deadly rage.

They've ta'en a weapon, long and sharp,
And cut him by the knee:
They tied him fast upon a cart,
Like a rogue for forgerie.

They laid him down upon his back,
And cudgell'd him full sore;
They hung him up before the storm,
And turned him o'er and o'er.

They filled up a darksome pit
With water to the brim,
They heaved in John Barleycorn,
There let him sink or swim.

They laid him out upon the flow,
To work him farther woe,
And still, as signs of life appeared,
They toss'd him to and fro.

They wasted, o'er a scorching flame
The marrow of his bones;
But a miller us'd him worse of all,
For he crushed him beween two stones.

> *And they hae ta'en his very heart's blood*
> *And drank it round and round;*
> *And still the more and more they drank*
> *Their joy did more abound.*
>
> *John Barleycorn was a hero bold,*
> *Of noble enterprise,*
> *For, if you do but taste his blood,*
> *'Twill make your courage rise.*
>
> *'Twill make a man forget his woe;*
> *'Twill heighten all his joy,*
> *'Twill make the widow's heart to sing,*
> *Though the tear were in her eye.*
>
> *Then let us toast John Barleycorn,*
> *Each man a glass in hand,*
> *And nay his great posterity*
> *Ne'er fail in old Scotland.*

Given the kind of thinking that has come to prevail among Europeans since the seventeenth century, it must now be acknowledged that John Barleycorn has in fact failed, failed totally, and not just in Scotland. And for want of the ritual recognition and honour once accorded to him, John himself, the hero bold, has died. And this reminds me of one of the stranger moments in the history of the ancient Mediterranean, that moment when a voice comes over the water saying, Great Pan is dead. This incident I've already rehearsed in the text but since on this occasion the context is different it might be no harm to let it pass before us again. As recorded for us by Plutarch in his work *De Oraculorem Defectu*, it is a certain Philip who speaks:

As for death among such beings [i.e., deities] I have heard the words of a man who was not a fool nor an impostor. The father of Aemilianus the orator, to whom some of you have listened, was Epitherses, who lived in our town, and was my teacher in grammar. He said that once upon a time, in making a voyage to Italy, he embarked on a ship carrying freight and many passengers. It was already evening when, near the Echinades Islands, the wind dropped and the ship drifted near Paxi. Almost everybody was awake, and a good many had not finished their after-dinner wine. Suddenly from the island of Paxi was heard the voice of someone loudly calling Thamus, so that all were amazed. Thamus was an Egyptian Pilot, not known by name even to many on board. Twice he was called and made no reply, but the third time he answered; and the caller, raising his voice, said, 'When you come opposite to Palodes, announce that Great Pan is dead. On hearing this, all, said Epitherses, were astonished and reasoned among themselves whether it was better to carry out the order or to refuse to meddle and let the matter go. Under the circumstances Thamus made up his mind that if there should be a breeze, he would sail past and keep quiet, but with no wind and a smooth sea about the place he would announce what he had heard. So, when he came opposite Palodes, and there was neither wind nor wave, Thamus, from the stern, looking toward the land, said the words as he had heard them: 'Great Pan is dead.' Even before he had finished, there was a great cry of lamentation, not of one person but of many, mingled with exclamations of amazement.

Two of Europe's saddest annunciations, surely.

The death of Pan announced from a ship becalmed before Palodes.

The death of John Barleycorn announced from a ship becalmed between the Western Isles.

The death of Pan is the death of our ability to look with a kindly, acknowledging eye on all that we phylogenetically are.

The death of John Barleycorn is the death of our ability to live the *sumpatheia* which at some level exists between all things. Which, at some level, exists between predator and prey.

To live that *sumpatheia* with one other thing, to live it with the sown and mown wheatfield, is to live it with all things:

> *And night after night*
> *We heard the same hooves:*
> *The hoarse horse*
> *We had dreamed of had died.*
>
> *But our love was still a eucharist*
> *Because long before Christ was crucified*
> *We reaped the stubble after Death*
> *And drank the icor on his scythe*

In itself the death of Pan is a Götterdämmerung, because with him died all the theranthropic divinities of the ancient world.

In itself the death of John Barleycorn is also a Götterdämmerung, because with him died all the nature spirits our ancestors had and hadn't names for. Could it be though that these divinities haven't in fact died? Could it be that, looking into the future and foreseeing the chainsawing savagery that would one day destroy their world, they have merely withdrawn into dimensions of reality beyond our destructive reach?

Either way, the sheer enormity, in its consequences for consciousness and culture, of the disappearance of John Barleycorn can be gauged by bringing it into association with a theory which has suggested that the origins of Greek tragedy are to be found in 'the agon of the Fertility Spirit, his Pathos and Theophany'. Add to this Nietzsche's reminder that 'in its earliest form Greek tragedy had for is sole theme the sufferings of Dionysus and that for a long time the only stage hero was Dionysus himself'.

The sufferings of Dionysus and the sufferings of John Barleycorn.

How well, in brisk, ballad form, does Burns describe them:

> *They've ta'en a weapon, long and sharp,*
> *And cut him by the knee;*
> *Then tied him fast upon a cart,*
> *Like a rogue for forgerie.*
>
> *They laid him down upon his back,*
> *And cudgell'd him full sore;*
> *They hung him up before the storm*
> *And turn'd him oe'r and oe'r...*

In one form or another, these verses are among the first and oldest sediments of Western consciousness.

Whether as Demeter or Dionysus, whether as Corn Maiden or Corn Caillech, John Barleycorn was with us setting out.

For reasons all too evident, he isn't walking with us now.

Relying, like the tubers in the cupboard, on our own withering energies, we are walking alone.

We are in trouble.

As I've said, Colin Clout has come down from the hills to tell us of the dreadful eclogue that has enacted itself in the heathers up there.

Pastoral must become Paschal.

And, if there is to be one, the legend of the next great age must be.

SUMPATHEIA TON HOLLON

Are you suggesting that like the tubers in the cupboard we are in danger of being left behind by evolution? Are you suggesting that we, like the tubers, need inhumation?

Yes, we need inhumation altogether more than we need to go to the Moon or Mars. Going to the Moon or Mars is naked ape stuff. It is a refusal if not also a betrayal of the last great steps in evolution which have already taken place here at home.

So yes, we are in danger of being left behind. It might even be that no Piers Plowman will come and open the door of the grotty little cupboard we call the space age, the age in which, almost universally, we abandoned *advancement essential* for *advancement local.*

Has it occurred to you that to be as totally opposed to space travel as you are might also be a betrayal?

You misunderstand me or rather you haven't yet heard me out on this. I am not in fact opposed to space travel. What I'm opposed to is space travel by technogical means. By Asuric means. By Titanic means. Any voyage that begins in Titanic blast-off isn't going to bring us anywhere worth going to. It isn't going to bring us to Fódhla. It isn't going to bring us to Beulah. It is only going to bring us to Ulro elsewhere. What is the big difference between being a Michelangelo captive on Mars and being a Michelangelo captive here on Earth? We should, I believe, wait upon the further evolutionary emergence of shamanic powers, of shamanic flight. We should wait on the further evolutionary emergence of world-soul telepathy, of world-soul clairaudience and clairvoyance. We should wait upon the evolutionary emergence of clairvoyaging, of voyaging without material means. That way our Titanism might die out at source. That way the Ulro-roar of our constructed world mightn't have a chance to spread much farther than our own solar system.

Talk to me about what you mean by inhumation?

At the end of his awful safari into phylogenetic inwardness and outwardness, Job shook dust and ashes on his head. I wish, though, that it was a scruple of soil that he had shaken on it, because in this way he would be indicating to himself and to us, that he had now at last accepted that he wasn't only a citizen who had signed up to a social contract. With this simple gesture he would be indicating that he wasn't only on the earth but that he was also of it. With it he would be indicating that he was in some sense telluric, in some sense chthonic.

What I am saying is this: given that we aren't only of the polis, it is as important that Job should have sprinkled an acknowledging scruple of soil on himself while he was still alive as that Antigone should have sprinkled a similar acknowledging scruple of it on her brother when he lay there dead but unburied outside the seventh, fratricidal gate of what was once so hopefully called the City of Man.

It sounds like a primitive baptism, doesn't it? Or worse. It sounds like a baptism into what is primitive in us, and if that is so, then better by far that we should shrivel in the grotty cupboard.

As I see it, it is a baptism of simple acknowledgment, of acknowledgment in hope not in despair. And as for what is primitive in us—well, we are altogether more primitive now, aren't we, than we were in the Pleistocene? We are altogether more primitive now, aren't we, than we were at any time since we came down from the trees? The fact that our primitivism is now equipped with Boyle's Law and $E=mc^2$ doesn't make it any less primitive, only more powerful. And that is why this book hasn't settled for a dreamy Dreamtime. That is why it hasn't settled for the Ces Noidhen. That is why it hasn't settled for the pathos, kathodos and anodos of the Fertility Spirit.

I will put it this way. I imagine Jesus making the *abhaya mudra,* that supreme, divine gesture which, when Shiva makes it, says, fear not.

Making it after his anodos, the hand with which Jesus makes this fear-not gesture is pointing at once in two directions. It is pointing introvertedly at the fin, out of which it has itself evolved and, in correlative acknowledgment as it were, it is pointing extrovertedly at Bright Angel Trial.

So Jesus is Lord of the Trail, is he?

Yes. Having allowed evolution to find a way in him, Jesus is Lord of the evolutionary Trail, he is Lord of the Evolutionary Aisle.

And so, on a calm evening, coming towards us over the water from Paxi, that is what the voice will say:

Thamus. Thamus, when you come opposite Palodes call out to the red and green beachcombers, saying:

> The new Lord is Lord of the Trail.

And when they've exulted, call out to them saying:

> Shining with a brightness brighter than the star brightness,
> brighter than mind brightness,
> the Earth is already an evolutionary success.

Do I correctly conclude that for you Fódhla and Logres are states of mind more than they are countries—more than they are realms some people have and some people haven't access to?

They are states of mind, yes, but they are also states of things, states of the universe.

It is hard to explain.

There are days when the world comes out of concealment. Coming out from behind the eclipse of perceiver and perceived, what is Is. No longer sundered into subject and object, what is Is.

And sometimes, after sitting all day by a stream in the mountains, there is something we know. From experience we know that there is a rare state of mind that makes the head obsolete. And that, Sir Gawain, is what you should be seeking. To seek for the Grail as object is a vulgarity. Seek it and find it as rare state of mind and then every sand grain is Grail.

Drop down but a little from this state, down but a little towards what we call normality, and now you are walking in Fódhla, in Logres. You aren't elsewhere than where you ordinarily are when walking in Logres, in Fódhla.

You can see, can't you, that England is the Hadrian's Wall we have built against Logres, that Ireland is the Hadrian's Wall we have built against Fódhla, that the modern world is the Hadrian's Wall we have built against the Day, the Great Day, that Ancient Egyptians so wished to come forth into?

Between Ancient Egyptians and that Day there were twelve gates. Twelve underworld gates. At every gate, whether silent or growling, a most menacing challenge.

Sety I, a Pharaoh, was buried in a sarcophagus of white alabaster. Inside and outside, that sarcophagus was incised with a text that we call The Book of Gates. In the thinking of the time, that meant that he was buried in a sacramental enactment of his journey through those gates. Quite simply, the text he was buried in would see him through.

I expect that on the spiral path to the heart of Newgrange I too will come to twelve gates. And there is one thing of which I am sure: a ticket from the Irish Board of Works won't open them for me.

So, as the Ghost of Christmas Past, long past, might say, God bless us everyone, for our comb walls have no glyphs and our coffin boards are bare.

We have substituted rights for rites of passage.

So ask not for what the bell tolls.

In particular, it tolls for an age of archaeological sacrilege.

In general, it tolls for our way of being in the world.

From atom and tomb it is our own destruction we have released.

And yet, apparently in the shadow of such doom, you have written a book that attempts to carry out Death and bring in Summer. Is that not odd?

Every year, after all, at the winter solstice, the light does enter the heart of our darkness.

Entering, it illuminates us working away in what Blake has called our dark Satanic mills.

But we shouldn't be too hopeful, for maybe the light finds it easier to ascend the passage in Newgrange than it does to ascend the passage we call Wall Street. And maybe the dead in Newgrange can be revivified in a way that the living in Wall Street cannot. Only Anubis, the morgue god, knows.

Think of him. Think of Anubis.

In the underworld Anubis is a black jackal.

And there he is, crouched and alert, and watching us, as we push open the door of Tutankhamun's tomb.

The creak of that door, that now is the signature tune, the Underworld signature tune, of our age.

But there he is, watching us.

Watching us from within the cell, watching from within the atom, watching us from within all those places into which we have trespassed.

It is against him, it is against Anubis, god of our mortuary slab, that we have most seriously sinned.

Before anything else, we need to appease him.

And in this there is hope: foregoing the invitation that comes with prayer, we broke into the atom and released that explosion of rays which to us are death-rays, but only because we haven't over aeons had any good reason to adapt to them. Having a sense of sacred threshold and having a sense of trespass, the peoples of medieval Europe prayed—in their crypts they prayed, with their spires they prayed—and the atom revealed itself to them as a rose window.

And the suggestion here is that until the rose window is retina and lens to our naked eye, until it is retina and lens to our microscopes and telescopes, we won't be seeing the world as it is?

Yes. This book is one long Battle of Magh Tuired and that, as you know, was and is a battle against the evil eye, against the *suil mildagach,* in us all. It is a battle against that eye doing what it does to reality in Medusa, doing what it does to reality in Descartes. In Medusa and Descartes it turns the living, dreaming rock into a *res,* it turns Uluru into Ulro. The book is a battle against that eye as protruding brain tumour, blue or green or brown or black. That's the eye that commodifies everything, that looks at a cow and sees gallons of milk, that looks at a tree and sees cubic feet of timber.

The Battle of Magh Tuired is the Irish version of the old Indo-European battle between rival pantheons, between Gods and Antigods, between Gods and Titans, between Gods and Giants. In India it is the battle between the Devas and the Asuras, in Greece it is a battle between an older generation of Gods led by Cronus and a younger generation of Gods led by Zeus, in Nordic countries it is the battle between the Aesir and the Vanir, and in Ireland it is the battle between the Tuatha De Danann and the Fomorians. Essentially though, in Ireland, it is a battle between Lugh and Balor, between Good and Evil. And in an account of it in Old Irish we read of that central encounter:

> *Imma-comairnic de Luc ocus di Bolur Birugderc esin cath.*
> Lugh and Balor of the piercing eye met in the battle.

A little further on we read:

> *Tocauhar a malae dia deirc Baloir*
> The lid was raised from Balor's eye.

Raised then in Ancient Ireland and raised again I believe in modern, Cartesian Europe.

For three centuries this *derc Baloir* has been turning the world into a Waste Land.

Dreamtime fights that eye. It fights Balor in us, it fights Medusa in us, it fights everything in us that is perceptually and conceptually hurtful to star and stone. It fights old myths and metaphors in so far as they have become forms of our sensibility and categories of our understanding. It fights the *it-world* we project into the living world. And in that fight its motto is:

Animam debes mutare non caelum

It is yourself as perceiver of the world, not the world, that you should be attempting to change.

To this end, it dares, at one level, to mount a challenge to the whole sensory-intellectual tool-kit of Europeans, or should I say, of Ulropeans.

Challenging our sense of the inalienable interdependence of fixed identity and fixed form, the book rehearses the shape-shifts of Fintan Mac Bóchra, the Fox Woman and red-mouthed Badhbh.

Regarding time, the book has it that 'all time is once-upon-a-time'. Regarding space, it says, 'all elsewheres, supernatural and natural, are where we are'. Regarding inertia, acceleration and motion, it offers the spectacle of Rhiannon's riding. Regarding causality, it draws attention to the marvellous kind of seeing that occurs when 'cosmologies of cause and effect fall from our eyes and lives.' Something Shakespeare says in *All's Well That Ends Well* is relevant here:

> They say miracles are past, and we have our philosophical persons, to make modern and familiar, things supernatural and causeless. Here it is, that we make trifles of terrors, ensconcing ourselves into seeming knowledge when we should submit ourselves to an unknown fear.

It isn't only supernatural things that are causeless. There are days when, emerging out of Tao, all things are causeless. It is a *mo-wei* world we live in and, however evanescently, Nietzsche knew it:

> Here is a musician who, more than any other musician, is a master at discovering the tones out of the realm of suffering, depressed, tormented souls and at giving speech even to tormented animals. Nobody equals him in the colour of late fall, the indescribably moving happiness of the last, very last, very briefest enjoyment; he finds sounds for those secret and uncanny midnights of the soul in which cause and effect appear to be unhinged and any moment something can come into being 'out of nothing'.

Much earlier, he had drawn out attention to what he called

> a profound illusion that first saw the light of the world in the person of Socrates: the unshakable faith that thought, using the thread of causality, can penetrate the deepest abysses of being ...

Nowadays in the West we are, quite literally, corrupted by a lust to explain things. Our lust to explain things veils things. Think of the Buddha's Flower Sermon. Water isn't H_2O. It might be composed of H_2O, but it isn't only what it is composed of. Once it has come into existence it is no longer composed. It isn't a compound. And water in the Owenmore river is entirely different from water in the Owenglin river. Just look and you will see. Be true to your eyes, not to the desiderata of science or language. Zen Buddhists know it: there is a seeing that is the same thing as satori.

In its opening movements, the piece called 'Shaman' enacts a kathodes into the deepest spit of mind in us—knowing nothing down here of the subjective-objective divide, we dream their dreams with mountain and star. And then, cutting this catalogue short, there is the piece called 'Stone Boat'—a challenge to our sense that gravity, as Newton described it, is coterminous, inwardly and outwardly, with our universe. Could it be, we wonder, sitting amidships as we sail in a stone boat between Ireland and Fódhla—could it be that, even in its tendencies downward, the universe is an Ascension Thursday? And could it be that, themselves ascending, the laws of gravity are its acolyte angels?

Can you imagine it?

> Sety's sarcophagus
> Sety's stone boat
> Boat that is Book of Underworld Gates

Boat that will ferry us beyond our Gorgon cosmologies. Boat that will ferry us among the unwearying stars. And who knows, maybe one night we will all of us experience those stars as Sety, having come forth into the immortal world, experienced them, as The Woman Who Rode Away, facing death, experienced them:

This at length became the only state of consciousness she really recognized: this exquisite sense of bleeding out into the higher beauty and harmony of things. Then she could actually hear the great stars in heaven, which she saw through her door, speaking from their motion and their brightness, saying things perfectly to the cosmos, as they trod in perfect ripples, like bells on the floor of heaven, passing one another and grouping in the tameless dance with the spaces of dark between.

Imagine it:

> Opening it in a dream. Sir Isaac sees that his *Principia* has become a Book of Gates.

Imagine it:

> Dreamed by an Ancient Egyptian dream, Sir Isaac sails celestially in Sety's stone boat.

Imagine it: In the course of his celestial sailing, Sir Isaac comes across Li Tieh-Kuai, one of the Pa Hsien or Eight Immortals of Taoist lore. Li was lame. Lao Tzu gave him an iron crutch. Sometimes, without warning, Li would hurl that crutch into the air, it would become a waterfall, and looping onto it he would sail away.

Imagine them: Those dimensions or moods of our universe whose symbol and sign is Li Tieh-Kuai's iron crutch.

Like Bernice's hair, this crutch might one day sail away and become a constellation—the Crutch Constellation—and there it is, Magi walking with it, Newton, Descartes and Bacon walking with it, to where it stands still above what Wallace Stevens has called a new intelligence.

Imagine it: A vision of the universe in which the stone boat and the iron crutch are principia. Principa to which we accord as much recognition as we already do to the laws of gravity. There are dimensions and moods of the universe, dimensions and moods of our own minds, to which, one day most graciously, we will all be admitted. At a depth of ourselves we are all of us Taoist Immortals. At a depth of itself it is with the Great Imagination that the universe is coterminous. At the end of the day it is with Nirvikalpa Samadhi that it is coterminous, which means of course that inwardly and outwardly there is no terminus. Everything is Divine Ground and is out of Divine Ground, but being out of Divine Ground does not mean being outside of Divine Ground. When, eventually, we arrive home how astonished we will be to discover that we never left home. And this brings us to one of the generating intuitions of *Dreamtime*: so strange and so marvellous is the universe that it justifies the folk-tale as much as it justifies science, it justifies the fairy-story as much as it justifies maths-physics, it justifies the Upanishad and the Parana as much as it justifies the General Theory of Relativity. *Dreamtime* attempts to let the fairy-story and the Upanishad take us by the hand. It could be that standing on the sea-shore Newton himself would have been willing to listen to Upanishad and Purana:

> I do not know how I may appear to the world; but to myself I seem to have been only like a boy, playing on the sea-shore, and diverting myself, in now and then finding another pebble or prettier shell than ordinary, while the great ocean of truth lay all undiscovered before me.

Could it be that the boy who puts the pretty shell to his ear might be willing in later life to put the Mandukya Upanishad to his ear. The woman who, seeking the great world, rode away. The mystic who, seeking greater gods, sailed away. Tell us about it, Eva:

> *Lying at ease in the dark ship*
> *I watched the last pale night depart,*
> *I dreamt I saw blue shadows slip*
> *O'er the white snowfields of my heart;*
> *And the world had grown so wide*
> *There was room for all mankind—*
> *The icebergs round about the Pole*
> *Crashed in the silence of my soul*
> *And hemmed me in on every side.*

Our quest for the greater world is a quest for, a greater vision of the world we already live in.

Our quest for greater gods is a quest for the northern lights of the soul, auroras of soul, in which to see the gods we already know.

It is an apocalypse of mind and eye we need, an apocalypse that opens the veils of mind and eye, not an apocalypse that pulls down the stars, that obliterates the sea.

That's the apocalypse, the Ragnarok, that Fjalar, Goldcomb and Rustred are crowing for.

Can you hear them?

> Goldcomb crowing in the birdwood.
> Fjalar crowing on the crossbeam of a gibbet.
> Rustred crowing at the bars of Hel.

> Ride on, Rhiannon
> Sail on, Sety.

We must keep the adventure, the immram, afloat.

From the titles of two of its pieces, I gather that your book is a weave of songlines. Am I correct in this?

In this book, the word songline doesn't carry quite the same significance that it does for Australian Aborigines. It will I think be obvious from very early on that the songlines of our Dreamtime are not concerned to celebrate or re-enact a sequence or suite of events in the creation of the geophysical world. Instead, they celebrate a journey from one to another way of being in a world that already exists. With Job we journey downwards onto the savannah beneath our city streets. With Aeschylus we journey to Areopagus Rock. With Sophocles we journey to Colonus. With Pwyll we journey to Gorsedd Arberth. With the one who will be shaman we journey down into the deepest spirit of mind in us. With Ollamh Fódhla we climb and spend a summer between the Paps of Morrigu, and following in the footsteps of Dien Cecht we ascend to a place and state of mystical elevation between the Paps of Danu. And so on. And so on.

In this sense of the word, the Triduum Sacrum is a songline. It celebrates our journey, in identification with Christ, into newness of life.

And at the end of the book there he is, the Once and Future Kynge, walking naked to Tara with a sunspear in his hand. That spear replaces the bleeding lance, it replaces Cuchulainn's Gae Bolga. Elsewhere in the book it is called Ahimsa.

If he has to, he will launch it. But never in anger. Never in the interest of self-advancement.

There is the story of the samurai who, in a state of serene detachment, sets out to kill the killer of his Lord. Within a few days he has tracked him down and cornered him and is about to run him through but, at that moment, knowing the mind of his opponent, the killer spits at the samurai, aiming it so that it lands right on his mouth. This angers the samurai who, being true to his code, must now sheath his sword and walk away.

The reasoning here is that if he were to slay him now he would do so in anger and that would be bad for his own soul. So he must desist and wait for another day.

By this same code must Conaire, bearer of the sunspear, live.

The question for Conaire is: how, without becoming evil, can he take on evil? How, without becoming a Balor, can he take on Balor?

Cuchulainn learned nothing of this from Scathach and it is therefore sad that, in their different ways, both Yeats and Pearse should have enlisted him into their more or less common cause, the one on the Abbey stage, the other on the floor of the General Post Office.

Wise in the ways of the world, Conaire knows that however often he is killed, Balor will re-emerge. In that case, this man who once pursued the birds his father flocked with, will not hesitate. He will stand where Lugh stood. He will launch Ahimsa, and he won't, in doing so, damage his own soul or the soul of his people.

In the meantime, he is walking to Tara where he will be crowned.

A Kynge in whom nature and culture are working together, he will inaugurate the Birdreign, and in so doing he will be reuniting what fell asunder in the pit in Lascaux, in the pit of our ancient, Western mind.

Let us listen to Ingcel and Fer Regain talking about that reign:

Cid ahe libse a flaithius ind fir sin I tir nErenn? or Ingcel,

Is maith a flaith, ol Fer Rogain. Ni taudchaid nel tar grein o gabais flaith o medon erraich co medon fogmair, ocus ni taudchaid banna druchtae di feor co medon lai, ocus ni fascnan gaemgaeth cairchech cetrae co nonae, ocus ni foruich mac tibhri ina flaith tar ag fireand cacha indise on chind mbliadne co araill ocus ataat seacht meic thiri I ngiallnai fri raigid ina thigseom fri coimet in rechtai sin ocus ata culaitiri iarna cul. i. Macc Locc ocus is e taccair tar a cend hi tig Conaire. Is ina flaith is combind la cach fer guth araili ocus betis teta mendchrot ar febus no cana ocus in tsida ocus in chainchomraic fil sethau na Herind. Is ina flaith ataat na tri bairr for Erind.i. Barr des ocus barr scoth ocus barr measa.

What is his reign in Ireland like? asked Ingcel.

A good reign it is, replied Fer Regain. Since he became Kynge no cloud has covered the sun from the middle of spring to the middle of autumn, and not a drop of dew evaporates from the grass till midday, and no gust of wind shakes a cow's tail till evening, and in any one year a wolf will take no more than one bull calf from the enclosure, and guaranteeing this agreement seven wolves remain as hostages by the wall of his house, and by way of additional assurance, Mac Locc pleads their case in Conaire's house. To his neighbour each man's voice is as melodious as the voice of the harp, and that because of the excellence of law, of peace and of good will that obtains throughout Ireland. It is in Conaire's reign that we have the three crowns of Eriu, the crown of corn, the crown of flowers, and the crown of acorns.

It is as if the prophecy in Virgil's fourth eclogue had now at last been realized:

Ultima Cumaei venit jam carminis aetas;
Magnus ab integro saeclorum nascitur ordo.

In nature and name, Conaire's Birdreign reverses the overthrow of commonage consciousness in the pit at Lascaux.

In nature and name, Conaire's Birdreign reinaugurates a way of being in the world that gives the world a chance.

Would you say something about the heart bird that comes through Conaire's door while he is still in fosterage with his uncle?

He is, I think, the bird of the bird-staff in the pit in Lascaux. And the wound he brings is at once the wound of the Bull and the wound of the Birdman. Here an unconscious impulse is coming to consciousness and, in enduring it to redemptive denouement, Conaire is pharmakon to the Fisher King in us all, to maimed royalty in us all.

In Conaire, Western humanity goes free from the terrible consequences of the dolorous stroke.

Having read the story, I know who Conaire is genetically. But who he is archetypally, I am not so sure I can say.

Conaire's parents were, in the metaphoric sense of the word, amphibious. They could slip in and out of different worlds. In this, Conaire is like them. Only in his case the Otherworld isn't elsewhere. Tír Tairngrí is in his eyes. It is a way of seeing what others of us call ordinary things. Seeing things the way he does, he cannot possibly abuse or misuse them.

His is the wonder-eye, the opposite in every way of Balor's evil eye.

In Fódhla the wonder-eye is a blessing. In the everyday world where we constantly encounter the abuse and misuse of things it can be an affliction.

Conaire is hurt.

He is the one who offered his hand as a perch for the hurt bird.

An accomplice unconsciously with what was happening, the hurt of the hurt bird, the hurt of the hurt bull, the hurt of the hurt world, settled on him, and so his life ever afterwards will be characterized more by pathos than by ergos, more by passion than by labour.

Emerging from his passion and death, from the bone-fire of self-will, he is carrying the sunspear by which he himself has been killed. It is with the blood Balor in himself that it bleeds. When he has to, therefore, he will not launch it in the way that Cuchulainn launches Gae Bolga.

Given his state of mind when he launches Gae Bolga, Cuchulainn only adds to the evil he is combating.

With Conaire, as with Christ, heroism has changed.

With Conaire, as with Christ, the archetype has changed.

Walking with Conaire to Tara, we all might change.

But surely not everyone will walk with Conaire to Tara?

Wise in the way that he is wise, no one knows that better than Conaire.

But Conaire keeps on walking.

Naked and with a sunspear in his hand, Conaire keeps on walking to Tara.

And, whether we like it or not, whether we accept the challenge in it or not, we will this day hear the screech of axle-iron in Ireland.

Hearing that screech, we will know if we are true.

Can I conclude that in all of this you aren't just talking about the external king of an external realm?

Yes. No matter how much it might have faded from the surface of our lives, there is something right royal in us all. There is in us something that has never been corrupted by what Traherne has called the dirty devices of our everyday world. And that's what I'm talking about. Seeking in so doing to give no offence, the story is telling you that Magh Mel is in your eyes, that Tír Tairngrí is in your hair.

Seeking in so doing to give no offence, the story is telling you: walk naked to Tara and people bringing you your royal robes will come out to meet you.

That's what the story is saying:

> Walk naked to Tara and inherit your royalty.

The screech of axle-iron in Ireland, the screech of the hawk at the Hawk's Well, the creak of a door pushed open into the Underworld, a sheep giving birth to an afterbirth only, a hand held out to be a perch for a hurt bird, Magh Mel in our eyes, Tír Taingrí in our hair—you think in images. Is there a philosophical reason for this?

There are days when I look at the mountains and I think, there is nothing more ultimate than what I am seeing. This, though, does not mean that I wish to deny the existence of ultimate reality. What I am saying is, the metaphysical isn't meta-aesthetic. Today it isn't. Today among these mountains the transcendent isn't trans-sensory.

But where does that leave Tenebrae—the ritual in which we consent to an extinguishing of our senses and faculties?

It leaves it where it is, and where it should be, at the mystical heart of Christianity, and, if it doesn't sound too imperious to say so, at the mystical heart of every religion. Nothing that I am saying puts compromising pressure on what the Kena Upanishad avers:

There goes neither the eye, nor speech, nor the mind; we know it not, nor do we see how to teach one about it. Different it is from all that is known, and different from the unknown it also is.

Nothing that I am now saying derogates in any way from something said elsewhere in the book, that on Good Friday European philosophy moved house, moved that is from metaphysics to metanoesis. If, as Nietzsche insists, there are abysses of being before which cause-and-effect explanation recoils, then, who knows, maybe we will one day accord as much scientific respectability to the tenebrae harrow as we now do to the test tube.

Resolve the contradiction for me.

Zen Buddhists resolve it by saying, first there is a mountain, then there is no mountain, then again there is a mountain.

Second time around among the mountains, on Easter morning maybe, the Divine Ground of things is the radiance of things. Today the transcendent isn't trans-sensory.

> Invisible, we view Thee
> Intangible, we touch Thee

And this I suppose is as good a reason as any for thinking in images and not in abstractions.

In this book, for instance, we talk about soul not as Descartes would but as Ollamh Fódhla would. Where Descartes talks about *res inextensa* Ollamh Fódhla has this to say:

My house is mirrored in Linn Feic.

In a sense therefore I sleep in Linn Feic, I dream in Linn Feic.

At a sleeping depth of me that I'm not aware of, maybe I am a salmon in Linn Feic, and maybe I swim upstream every night, all the way up into the Otherworld, all the way up into Nectan's Well. At that depth of myself maybe the shadows of the Otherworld hazel are always upon me. Are always upon all of us, letting wisdom and wonder drop down into us.

Dreamtime is as much about a way of thinking as it is about things thought. A metaphysics that isn't in every sense sensuous is a lie.

Are you saying the medium is the message?

No. But I am saying that a primary message from the Primary Ground of things will be sensuous.

As sensuous as Fan Kuan's revelatory painting called 'Travellers among Mountains and Streams'.

As sensuous as the second movement of Mozart's Concerto for Flute and Harp.

As sensuous as some poems by St John of the Cross.

It is a lot to ask of people, isn't it? It is a lot to ask of people who, like Michelangelo's captives, are embedded in Ulro.

Well, the sword has been drawn from the stone. The sword of our petra-fying perceptions of it has been drawn from it, so now again Ulro is Uluru. Now again we can look at the world with Australian Aboriginal eyes. Looked at in this way, The Blockhead is our Indjuwanidjuwa. He is getting ready to set out on his Dreamtime walkabout.

Helping to structure it, his songline runs through the book. It runs through Ulropeans, the naked shingles of the world, Altjeringa Rock, rock that turns into an old woman driving a cow, rock that is *res extensa*, rock that we blitz with metaphors. Medusa Mullán, Sety's sarcophagus, sword in the scone, stone boat, stone egg, stone that is a-stone-ishment, stone that is Jacob's pillow and pillar, Plymouth Rock, Rock in Red Lily Billabong, Linga Fáil, and finally, at Uisnech, the centering stone. Stone about which all things are a Mandukya Mordháil. Carraig Om, Om na Mireann, Mullán Om, I call it.

As Hindus know it and chant it, Om is the first sound out of Brahmanirguna. Not being the sound of any two things striking together, it is a metaphysical sound and as such we cannot hear it in our everyday ordinary hearing.

The universe is an elaboration of Om, a blossoming of it, and so it is that the Chandogya Upanishad advises us to

Revere the sun up there which radiates heat as the syllable Om; for on rising it sings aloud for the sake of all creatures; on rising it strikes down darkness and fear. So too shall he who knows this smite down darkness and fear. (1, iii)

Characterizing space as the first manifestation of Om, it says:

To the extent that this supremely desirable manifestation of the syllable Om shall be known among your offspring, to that extent will they enjoy a supremely desirable life in this world and an exalted state in the next. (1, ix)

In the West, sadly, we only hear a Big Bang. But if we are to have a worthwhile future, if indeed we are to have any kind of future at all, it is incumbent upon us, most dreadfully now, to choose between the Om that Hindus hear and the Big Bang that Ulropeans hear.

Listening to the Ulro roar of shingles on Dover Beach, Arnold isn't a 'vast image out of Spiritus Mundi', he is an empirical person in an empirical place, but how portentous he is. In him is a recoil altogether more awful than the recoil that Nietzsche imagined. In him the modern adventure has run aground.

Meanwhile, waiting for us at Uisnech,
Mullán Om
Om na Mireann

Can you hear it?

The stone that is Om
The Om that is stone

Stone in the presence of which Medusa is Sibyl.
Sibyl of Uisnech
Singing she sees
Mandukya Messiah coming shorewards towards us.
Mandukya Morning coming over the Paps.
Let's sing them with her,
Let's sing with the Sibyl of Uisnech

Laetentur Caeli
et
Exultet Terra

Let's sing with the singing stone

Om
Om
Om

> Aum
> Aum
> Aum

Can you hear them? Speaking from their motion and their brightness, saying things perfectly to the cosmos.

> Om they say
> Om they are
> Om Om Om

We don't need to travel to the stars to be near the stars. We only need, sitting singly or in constellations here on Earth, to sing their song with them.

> Om
> Om
> Om
> Aum
> Aum
> Aumen

The Chandogya Upanishad is right. The universe is a mantraverse and that means that we can be in consonance, in con-son-ance, with it, not just as it is but as it has been and will be. Here we are talking about con-son-ance between us and the stars, about us and the stars sounding the same sacred sound together. We are talking about sounding and being sounded by the continuing first sound out of Divine Ground. And this suggests that, come the next clear night, Kepler should go out of doors and sing their mantra with the stars. That way he might find a remedy for his horror. That way also Pascal might find a remedy for his terror, Coleridge might find a remedy for his dejection, and Arnold might find a remedy for his recoil.

Astra-onomy is mantra-onomy, it is the naming and knowing of Om in its stellar and interstellar efflorations.

A planet in con-son-ance with all that astronomically is, is healthy.

A planet that has fallen out of con-son-ance with all that astronomically is, is sick.

So what we now need on Earth is that a critical number of people would leave the bubonic noise of our time and go aside to live in small monastic communities, each with its own pure bell calling them to con-son-ance with, star and stone, calling them to con-son-ance in plainsong and silence.

Given that, our planet might still have a chance. Given that, it might continue to be the evolutionary success it already is. In all of this I am of course hoping that the hundredth monkey is not so fantastical as phlogiston turned out to be.

Are you saying that we should go back to Dover Beach and relaunch the adventure?

I am saying that where Arnold heard the Ulro roar someone else has heard the Mandukya Om. I am saying that where Gamow heard a big bang someone else has heard the anahata shabda, the sound that isn't the sound of any two things striking together. And so, instead of talking about relaunching the human adventure, I'd prefer to talk about going back into the universal adventure, and that I think is what Mona is doing.

Looking at her walking ever more deeply into the mountains she has for so long eclipsed, we ask, where now is Kepler's horror? Where now is Pascal's terror? Where now is Coleridge's dejection? Where now is Arnold's recoil?

It would, I think, be wise to assume that they are walking with her, for, given how we are constituted, it is likely that, in one form or another, horror and terror and dejection and recoil will wait upon those who, in their day, respond to the call to keep the adventure afloat.

It is one thing to challenge the sensory-intellectual tool-kit of Europeans. It is another thing altogether to ask Newton to imagine himself sailing in a stone-boat among the unwearying stars, to ask Darwin to adopt the mutations of Aaron's wand as a Kantian category of his understanding, to ask Einstein to take account in his cosmological thinking of a new constellation called the Iron Crutch, to ask us all to expect that at Samhain, some year soon, an old woman will drive her white cow in through the front door and out through the back door of our cause and effect thinking, to ask us to think of our deepest inwardness as an Otherworld well with an Otherworld hazel growing over it, to ask us to think of the earth as Buddh Gaia, to think of the universe as a mantraverse, to ask us to sometimes let the rocks and the trees do our thinking for us, to ask us to be happy to hear that there is a rare state of mind that makes the head obsolete, to ask us to be happy to hear that it is crediting ideas such as these, that it is singing ideas such as these, that Mona would lead Western humanity back into the mountains, to ask us to walk this new songline with her—you don't expert, do you, that academic philosophers will trade tenure for this?

All of this and more comes from our having pulled the sword from the stone. To pull the sword from the stone is to pull our Medusa perception of it out of it and that is a renaissance altogether greater than the Italian Renaissance, that is a revolution altogether greater than the French Revolution. Having done it, we are free, in a phrase of Wallace Stevens, to make a new intelligence prevail. Or better perhaps, to let a new intelligence emerge.

Sometimes when I look out through my window and I think of the sensory-intellectual tool-kit with which we attempt to describe what I am seeing, then I think that I am not the only one who needs to lower his head down in the hare's form in the heathers of the Roundstone Bog.

That done, your question concerning method in philosophy has value only in so far as it provokes a more aggressive question in response.

Why, I would ask you, why in order to be respectable must philosophy conduct itself as logical argument, as dialectics? Why must philosophy always read like Aristotle's *Metaphysics?* Why can't it sometimes read like a choric ode from the *Bacchae* by Euripides? If the universe is lyrical, how can it be philosophically improper to be lyrical with it? 'Perhaps there is', Nietzsche says, 'a realm of wisdom from which the logician is exiled.' And maybe Aristotle himself wasn't always as Aristotelian as we imagine him to have been. He did say, didn't he: 'The more solitary and retired I become, the more I love the myth.' He even coined a new word, *philomythos,* meaning lover of myth. And in doing so he wished to suggest that the philo-mythos, the lover of myth, can as surely reach ultimate Truth as can the philo-sophos, the lover of wisdom. If it can be said of Dreamtime that it is philosophical, it is philomythically that it is so. It is philomythically that it would draw close to the genius of the universe.

Can you imagine it? Aristotle sitting in his house with Fintan Mac Bóchra. Fintan Son of the Sea. Fintan who, when he wished to survive the Flood, turned himself into a salmon. Fintan who, as hawk overflying it, came to know and remember all that was done and said by the Dreamtime peoples of Dreamtime Ireland. Fintan who, every May Eve, suffered her labour pains with the Celtic Horse Goddess.

Fintan would have seen Conaire, son of the Birdman, walking naked to Tara. He'd have seen Étain loosening her hair at the well in Brí Leith.

Imagine it: Aristotle looking at the world through the eyes of Fintan Mac Bóchra.

Imagine him discovering that the principle of non-contradiction and the principle of the excluded middle are laws of Aristotelian thought, not laws of nature.

Imagine it: looking at the world through Fintan Mac Bóchra's eyes, Aristotle discovers that there are no laws of nature, only surprises of nature, miracles of nature.

Every *fód* of Fódhla is potentially a *fóidín mearai.* When, going out to round up my cows, I set foot on such *fód,* my journey becomes an immram. When, coming home from a neighbour's house, I set foot on it, my journey becomes an eachtra.

Haldane was right: the universe is queerer than we can even imagine. It is certainly more of a wonder than we are ordinarily able for. In its ordinariness more of a wonder.

Don't call it a universe at all.

Call it *Thaumophany*.
Call it Wonder-Become-Manifest.

We merely need to recall a moment in Black Elk's clairvoyaging:

> I looked about me now and the horses of the west were thunders
> and the horses of the north were geese.

Give the universe land, Aristotle. Give it land, lots of land, don't fence it in. And the Bay Horse, Albert! And the Horsehead Nebula! They won't be corralled, Albert. They won't be cosmologically corralled. Neighing to each other, they won't be stabled in $E=mc^2$. Throw Aaron's rod on the ground. Hurl Li Tieh-Kuai's iron crutch into the air. The rod and the crutch are as true of the universe as are the laws of gravity. That's why we must not concede to science sole responsibility for talking about the universe. We must continue to give lore a look in. Gorsedd Arberth is as important as Mount Palomar. Fern Hill is as important as the Nuffield Neurological Centre.

And so I imagine it: empty handed and weary, and looking like an old Naskapi hunter, Einstein walks home through the fields one evening. How surprised he is to see smoke rising from his chimney.

There you have it: Newton and the seashell, Einstein and the Foxwoman.

Picking up the seashell, Newton puts it to his ear and hears the Mandukya Om.

Having gone bush for a year and having lived for much of it with the Foxwoman, Einstein now accepts that the folk-mind has its reasons. He now accepts that a mind to which the fox-pelt is cortex has its reasons.

Deliberately limiting itself, this book is content with two ways of doing philosophy, the Celtic way and the Christian way. Call them, if you wish, the Dreamtime way and the contemplative way.

The task of the Celtic philosopher-poet is to keep the path to Connla's Well open.

The task of the Christian philosopher is to cross the Kedron and watch with Jesus.

It isn't lightly that anyone will consent to cross the Kedron with Jesus. To do so is to consent to a totemic assimilation of your life to the life of the Lamb of God in his Passion and death and, if God is gracious, in his Resurrection. To do so is to consent to the possibility that European philosophy might move house in you, might move, that is, from metaphysic to metanoesis. Ordinarily, this crossing over will not take place in us without awful trouble: dark night of the soul trouble, passive dark night of the spirit trouble, darkness of Good Friday on Golgotha trouble.

> Cup of trembling trouble
> Wine of astonishment trouble

Psychologically, the highest word that is given to us to speak is

> Gethsemane

Epistemologically, the highest word that is given to us to speak is

> Golgotha

Cosmologically, the highest word that is given to us to speak is

> Easter

Rolling from the door of his tomb, Medusa Mullán becomes what it always was

> Mandukya Mullán
> Mullán Om

Surely now you can hear the great stars in heaven.

Now that your Medusa mindset has rolled from your mind, rolled from your eyes, rolled from the soles of your feet, surely now you can hear them.

Speaking from their motion and their brightness, saying things perfectly to the cosmos.

> Om they say
> Om they are

Let's sing with them.

Marx said that the purpose of philosophy is not to interpret reality but to change it. What I am saying, what Mullán Om is saying, is: don't, to begin with, be overconcerned either to interpret reality or to change it. Be concerned only to sing with it. Be delighted, and lighted, to sing with it.

> Singing with it, you will come to see.
> Singing with it, you will come to know.

> So let us sing with it.

> With sister moon sing,
> With brother sun sing.

Sitting singly, or in constellations, let us sing with the great stars in heaven,

> Om
> Om
> Om

> Aum
> Aum
> Aum

That's your song, Amhairghin Glungheal. That's a song to come ashore with:

> Om
> Om
> Om
> Aum
> Aum
> Aum

Poor Tom is not so cold.
We are not so unaccommodated as we thought we were.
We have a centre that will hold.
We have a ceremony that will hold.

> Om
> Om
> Om

We belong to a universe that is out of Divine Ground.
We belong to a universe that we can sing with.
And that's not all.

When, in a dream sent to us from within the atom itself, we unstitch its ultimate particle, then we will find what Pascal's housekeeper found when she unstitched the lining of his waistcoat. We will find a memorial of its Night of Fire:

> *Depuis environ dix heures et demie du soir*
> *jusques minuit et demie*
> *Feu*

And that will be it. That will be the last discovery of science. That will be its last eureka.

And we will sing it, that last eureka. With the singing atoms we will sing it. With the singing stars we will sing it. We will sing it with the singing universe.

> *Depuis environ dix heures et demie du soir*
> *jusques minuit et demie*
> *Feu*

Depuis environ dix heures et demie du soir
jusques minuit et demie
Feu

Depuis environ dix heures et demie du soir
jusques minuit et demie
Feu

Depuis environ dix heures et demie du soir
jusques minuit et demie
Feu

GLOSSARY

Abhaya Mudra: In the Hindu tradition, mudra denotes meaningful gesture, the hand and finger gestures of a dancer. The Abhaya Mudra is the fear-not gesture of Shiva Nacaraja, Among the catastrophes it invites us to think of with equanimity is the end of the world.

Adhyaropa: Removing the projected illusions, removing all that we have falsely superimposed upon the true nature of reality.

Advaita vedantins: In Hindu tradition, persons who subscribe to a doctrine of radical monism. For them, reality is Divine Reality, and it is one only without a second.

Advaitally: An adverb formed from the Sanskrit advaita—a-dvaita meaning not-two, non-dualism. Advaita Vedanta is a doctrine of radical monism. It insists that multiplicity is an illusion. Only the Divine One is.

Aes Sidhe: The faery people.

Ahimsa: A Sanscrit word used by Buddhists to denote their doctrine of non-violence.

Aill na Mireann: Also called Carraig Choitrigi (*q.v.*). Located at Uisnech, the traditional centre of Ireland, it literally means the stone of the divisions, the divisions in this case being the provinces of Ireland.

Al Hallaj: Muslim mystic crucified in a square in Baghdad in 922.

Altamira: Limestone cave near Santander in northern Spain containing palaeolithic paintings, *c.* 13,500 BC.

Altjeringa, or Alcburunga: The Dreamtime as Australian Aborigines understand it.

Arnold, Matthew (1822-88): English poet, critic, essayist and educationalist.

Ammit, Apep, Sobk, Mafdet, Wepwawet: Monstrous beings of Egyptian Underworld or Duat.

Anadyomene: Greek mythology tells of a war between Titans and Olympians. The Titans were the old, established gods. The Olympians, a new generation of gods, challenged them for supremacy. In the course of the ensuing conflict one of the Titans was castrated. Thrown into the sea, his testicles were carried out by the still-potent primordial waters, where they underwent a transformation into Venus, the Goddess of love. And Venus came towards us out of the sea. And Venus coming towards us out of the sea is called Venus Anadyomene.

Anagnorisis: A Greek word. A word that Aristotle uses to describe the moment of self-recognition in Greek drama.

Anantashaya: Ananta is a Sanskrit word meaning endless or infinite. In this context it signifies the infinite abyss pictured as a snake upon whose coils the recumbent God Vishnu dreams the universe.

Angakok Bear: The great bear encountered by an Inuit shaman.

Ani: An Ancient Egyptian official whose funerary papyrus is one of the most important editions of The Book of the Dead.

Animitta: A term occurring frequently in Mahayana Buddhism. Literally, the signless. In European philosophy, the undifferentiated would probably be the nearest equivalent.

Anodos: The way back up from the Underworld. Opposite of Kathodos *(q.v.)*.

Aodhagán: Aodhagán Ó Rathaille (?1670-1729). Sliabh Luachra poet from north Kerry who lamented, and bore witness to, the passing of Gaelic Ireland (see *Owen Roe*).

Apophis: The great and terrible serpent of the Ancient Egyptian Underworld with whom the sun god, journeying through it, must do battle.

Apoptai: Beholders of the vision in Eleusinian mysteries.

Apsusayin: Jesu Apsusayin: Jesus recumbent on the coils of Apsu, thought of here as the great serpent of the Abyss. The Hindu prototype is Vishnu Anantasayin: Vishnu recumbent on the coils of Ananta. Ananca means endless or infinite. In this present context, it refers to the infinite, primordial waters in serpent form. Recumbent and asleep on the coils of this serpent, Vishnu *(q.v.)* dreams the universe into existence. The universe is his dream. The dream of Vishnu on the coils of Ananta, or by extension into our tradition, the dream of Jesus on the coils of Apsu.

Archaeornis: Literally, ancient bird; bird just evolved from a reptile.

Asraya-paravritti: A revulsion, a turning away from the world-illusion at the root or source of consciousness.

Assam: Famous waterfall of the blind salmon on the Erne at Ballyshannon, Co. Donegal.

Asuras: The anti-gods in Hindu mythology.

Athanor: Vessel in which alchemical transformation of base metal to gold takes place.

Athena: Patron goddess of Athens, she is owl-eyed and therefore theranthropic.

Atreidae: Atreus and his descendants, the doomed royal family of Mycenae in Ancient Greece. A protarchosate, a primal act of madness, in one generation worked itself out destructively in succeeding generations.

Atreus: King of Mycenae, a lion-gated citadel of the Argolid in the Peloponnese. He and his descendants were known as the Atreidae, a family terribly troubled and doomed in its generations. Aeschylus, Sophocles and Euripides tell the story, or portions of the story, in their tragic dramas.

Atum: A name of the Egyptian sun god.

Aua: One of the Eskimo or Inuit shamans Rasmussen *(q.v.)* met.

Autochthonus: In origin, of the local earth, of the locality, not a stranger, not an invader.

Avaranashakti: The veiling power, the power by which we veil the true nature of reality. See the parable of the snake in the rope in Inis Fáil.

Bacon, Francis (1561-1626): Elizabethan writer and philosopher, his *Novum Organum of 1620* set out his 'true directions concerning the interpretation of nature'.

Badb or *Badhbh* (pronounced 'Bav'): The Celtic war-hag, who could appear as either woman or scald-crow. One of the shape-shifting beings *of Dreamtime* (see Morrigan).

Bakhu: In Egyptian mythology, mountain on eastern horizon from which the sun rises.

Belle Verriere: A famous stained-glass window of the Virgin Mary in Chartres Cathedral.

Berkeley, George (1685-1753): Irish philosopher and bishop, for whom *esse* is *percipi*.

Beulah: A phase of the Fall in William Blake's cosmology. See Isaiah 62:4.

Bhairava: The terror form of Shiva, a Hindu god.

Bhairavi: The terror form of Devi, a Hindu goddess.

Bhakta: A person whose yoga is a passionate devotion to a god or goddess.

Bhuvanubvar: A temple complex in the state of Orissa in eastern India.

Bigged: An old English word meaning built.

GLOSSARY 267

Bird reign: Conaire Caomh, a king of Ireland, reigned from Tara in early mediaeval times. His reign is known as the Bird reign, Enflaith in Gaelic, for the simple reason that his supernatural father appeared to Meass Buachalla, his mother, in the form of a bird. Taking off his bird form, he lay and mated with her in human form.

Black Elk (1862-1950): Native American medicine man of the Great Plains Oglala Sioux.

Blake, William (1757-1827); Poet, artist and mystic, born in London to an Irish hosier. His *Songs of Innocence and Experience* and *The Marriage of Heaven and Hell* appeared between 1789 and 1794, and 'Jerusalem' in 1804-8.

Boann: The river Boyne conceived of as a goddess.

Bodhi Tree: The tree under which Gautama, the Buddha, won enlightenment.

Bodhisattvas: In the Buddhist tradition, a Bodhisattva is, literally, an enlightened Being, a being whose essence is enlightenment or transcendental wisdom.

Boehme, Jacob (1575-1624): Peasant mystic and philosopher from Gorlitz in Germany.

Book of Gates, The: Ancient Egyptian book containing the spells and words of power that enable the soul to pass safely through the twelve pylons or gates of the Underworld.

Brahmanirguna: A Hindu word meaning the attributeless Brahman. The ultimate divine reality out of which universes emerge and into which they return.

Britadananyaka: One of the major upanishads.

Brí Leith: The *sídhe-* or fairy-mound of Midir, his otherworldly residence, imagined to be located in present-day Co. Longford.

Brontë, Emily (1818-48): Yorkshire-born poet, novelist, stoic and mystic.

Browne, Sir Thomas (1605-82): English physician and author of *Religio Medici* (1635). 'We carry with us the wonders we seek without us: there is all Africa and her prodigies in us; we are that bold and adventurous piece of nature, which he that studies wisely learns in a compendium what others labour at in a divided piece and endless volume.' (Everyman edn 1969, p.17)

Bruno, Giordano (1548-1600): Italian mystic (Joyce's 'the Nolan') burnt at stake in Rome.

Brugh: Gaelic word meaning hostel. Almost always in the old stories, Brugh is synonymous with the otherworld.

Cadmus: Semitic for 'man of the ease': an Asian who, following a cow, came into Greece and founded Thebes (*q.v.*) in Boeotia; a city troubled and plagued in its generations.

Carraig Choitrigi: Stone at the centre of Ireland on the hill of Uisnech, Co. Westmeath.

Carraig Donn: Originally 'Carrigdhoun', a famous song, commonly believed to be about the flight of the Wild Geese, composed by Cork barrister Denny Lane (1818-95).

Ceo Draíochta: Magic or marvellous mist.

Cernunnos: Antlered, and therefore theranthropic, god of the Celts.

Ces Noidhen: Literally, the pangs of childbearing (found in Táin Bó Cuailnge).

Chakral: Of, or having to do with, the chakras—centres or lotuses of awareness-energies, of non-ordinary consciousness in our subtle bodies.

Chalcedon: Small town on the Bosphorus, where a Christological definition about Jesus's two-natures-in-one person was elaborated at a Council of the Church in AD 451.

Chandogya: One of the major Upanishads.

Cheophoros: A Greek word meaning the libation-bearer.

Chonyid: In The *Tibetan Book of the Dead,* the antaribhava, or state between death and rebirth, is thought to fall into three bardos or stages: the Chikhai bardo, the Chonyid bardo, the Sidpa bardo. In the Chikhai bardo, we 'experience' the clear light of the Void. In the Chonyid bardo we experience our karmic propensities dawning upon us as peaceful and wrathful deities. In the Sidpa bardo we experience yearning for rebirth and yielding to it, if that's what we do, we approach a womb-door.

Claidheamh solais: Sword of light.
Coatlicue: The Aztec Earth Mother.
Colin Clout: The piping shepherd in Spenser's 'The Shepherd's Calendar'.
Con Céad Chathach: Con of the Hundred Battles, a hero in Celtic mythology.
Connla: In Irish mythology, he is associated with an Otherworld well in which the rivers of Ireland were thought to have their source.
Curoí Mac Dara: God and gatekeeper of the Celtic Otherworld. A great shape-shifter; among the most uncanny of Celtic gods. In one of his apparitions, he is a great churl, wearing a grey mantle. In another, he is known as Terror, son of Great Fear. He lived in a high cashel called Temair Luachra in Kerry.

Dagda, The: A god of the Ancient Irish.
Demeter: A horse-headed, theranthropic goddess among ancient Greeks; goddess of corn.
Descartes, René (1596-1650): French rationalist philosopher and mathematician. In this book he is thought of as the plenipotentiary of Gorgon among us.
Dhyani Dien Cecht: A Dien Cecht Buddha seen only in contemplation.
Dien Cecht: The physician among the Tuatha De Danann, the people of the goddess Danu, who are thought of as yet another people who came to Ireland but are, in fact, euhemerized gods and goddesses of the Celts.
Dionysus: God of wine and the orgiastic rites associated with it in Ancient Greece.
Donn Descorach: Lord of the Dead. To his Tech nDuinn, House of Donn, the dead came.

Eachtra: An adventure to or from the Otherworld of mythic, or of near-mythic, strangeness. (See also *Immram*.)
Eckhart, Meister (1260-1327): Rhineland mystic and teacher.
Emain Abhlach: Emain of the Apples, a paradisal Celtic Otherworld.
Enkidu: The hairy wild man of the steppes. Until Gilgamesh befriends him, corrupting him with corrupting consequences, the wild animals are his only companions. While Gilgamesh represents civilization and culture, Enkidu, in The Epic of Gilgamesh, represents the uncivilized, the wild.
Epona: The Celtic horse goddess. Her Welsh name is Rhiannon, her Irish name is Macha.
Erinyes: In early Greek mythology and literature, the terrible furies who pursue murderers of kith and kin.
Étain: The one-time wife of Midir of Brí Leith (*q.v.*), subject of an old Irish story called The Wooing of Étain. Overpowered by a jealous rival at one stage in her career, she undergoes transformation into a beautiful fly.
Eumenides: In the *Oresteia*, a trilogy of plays by Aeschylus produced in 458 BC, the Erinyes are converted to benevolent beings called Eumenides or well-wishers.
Evangelanta: A word newly coined. In Hinduism there are collections of sacred texts called the Vedas. They are, so to speak, a first revelation, heard in times long past, heard and remembered. Other texts, constituting a further 'revelation', were written later. These are the Upanishads, and the many developments of, and from, them, continuing to this day. Collectively, these latter texts are called Vedanta. The word Vedanta is a compound of veda and anta. Anta means after. So, Vedanta literally means after the Vedas. Texts written after the Vedas. In Christianity, we have the initial Good News. The Greek word for Good News is Evangel. As in Hinduism there is Veda and Vedanta, so in Christianity is there Evangel and Evangelanta. Coming as they do, after the Evangel, the writings of the Christian mystics constitute evangelanta.

Fand: Wife of Manannan Mac Lir, the Ancient Irish sea god.
Fata Morgana: Illusions associated with Morgan Le Fay.
Fénelon, Francois de (1651-1715): Prelate, educator and author *of Dialogues des morts*.
Fenrir- or fenriswolf: The malevolent wolf, who, at the beginning of Ragnarok *(q.v.)*, bursts his chains and runs free. So great is his gape that he can swallow the sun.
Fern Hill: The farmhouse that gave its title to a famous poem by Dylan Thomas.
Fintan Mac Bóchra: There is a largely fictitious history of Ireland which claims that the first people to come to this country were a band of fifty persons, mostly women, led by a woman called Cessair. Fintan Mac Bóchra was one of the few men among them. They came in antediluvian times. Fintan survived the Flood by becoming a salmon. He lived on into several later ages. Becoming a hawk, he would sometimes overfly the whole country, witnessing everything that was going on. In the end he was, as it were, the memory of the race.
Fjalar, Goldcomb, Rustred: Three cocks whose crowings announce Ragnarok.
Fódhla: An old name for Ireland. In this book it is a name for Dreamtime Ireland.
Frazer, James George (1854-1941): Glaswegian, social anthropologist, classicist and folklorist, taught at Cambridge and Liverpool. His most famous book is *The Golden Bough* (1890, re-written in 12 vols, 1911-15), named for the sacred grove at Nemi.

Gae Bolga: The name of Cuchulainn's most famous spear.
Gamow: The Russian scientist who proposed the Big Bang theory.
Ganesha: An elephant-headed god in the Hindu pantheon. He is a remover of obstacles, an opener of ways. Son of Shiva *(q.v.)* and Parvati *(q.v.)*. *Gautama's Udana*: The poem spoken by Gautama, the Buddha, on the morning of his enlightenment.
Gilgamesh: Legendary Sumerian hero-king of the third millenium BC. The story of his exploits was popular for centuries in Mesopotamia and beyond. This Babylonian poem is called in English 'The Epic of Gilgamesh'.
Gnothi seauton: The famous Socratic dictum, 'Know thyself'.
Gore-Booth, Eva (1870-1926): Irish feminist, pacifist, poet and Christian mystic.
Gorgocogito: A compound word conjoining Gorgo and cogito. Descartes, the French philosopher, sought to display and elaborate all knowledge as a totally deductive system. To this purpose he started with an indubitable first statement, *Cogito ergo sum* (I think, therefore I am). The word Gorgocogito implies that our thinking is Gorgo thinking, turning everything that we think about and look upon into stone.
Gorgon: In Greek mythology, a being so terrible in appearance that anyone who looked at her turned to stone. Her Abyssinian desert homeland was littered with the petrified people who came her way, equated here with the *res extensa (q.v.)* universe that Descartes, Cartesians and Ulropeans *(q.v.)* perceive. See *Medusa*.
Goshen: Land of Goshen from which Moses led children of Israel. Synonym for Egypt.
Great Herne or heron: A god in bird form, from Yeats's play *The Herne's Egg* (1938).

Hanuman: The monkey king in whose breast is a shrine to Rama, an incarnation of the god Vishnu, and Sita, his consort. See *The Mahabharata*.
Hagia Sophia: A church, reverted to being a mosque in Constantinople, or present-day Istanbul.
Hapiru: The Ancient Egyptian name, it is thought, for Hebrews.
Hathw: Theranthropic cow goddess of the Egyptians.
Hawk's Well, At the: Play by W.B. Yeats *(q.v.)* first put on in 1916; well of healing waters.

Heimarmene: A Greek word meaning fate or necessity. As used by the Gnostics, it referred to the vast oppressive system that the universe is.

Hill of the Koshaless Skull: Golgotha. In Hebrew the word Golgotha means place of the skull. Here it is taken to mean place of Adam's empty skull at the foot of the cross. Being empty, a Hindu might say of that skull that it is koshaless, meaning it is without the veiling or obscuring power of our senses and faculties. Kosha is Sanskrit for veil or obscuration. As Hindus think of them, our senses and faculties do not reveal ultimate reality, which for them is divine. Rather, they veil it or obscure it. That is why, seeking the divine, we must practise being beyond them, as Adam's empty skull at the foot of the Golgotha cross is beyond them.

Hopkins, Gerard Manley (1844-89): English-born Jesuit priest and poet.

Hoplite: Ancient Greek foot-soldier armed with spear and sword.

Horakhty: In Egyptian religion, Horus of the horizon. The sun god in his morning form, rising above the eastern horizon.

Horemheb: One of the pharaohs of Ancient Egypt.

Horus: The Egyptian sun god in his morning appearance. He is often depicted as a falcon with the sun-disc on his head.

Idola tribus: Literally, idols of the tribe. Bacon suggested that in our search for the truth, there are four types of idol or illusion we must guard against: *idola specus, idola tribus, idola fori, and idola theatri*—idols of the cave, the tribe, the market-place and theatre.

Imbas forosnai: Method of divination practised by seer-poets of Ancient Ireland.

Immram: Tale in which one or more characters voyage to the Otherworld, usually by water of mythic or of near-mythic strangeness.

Injuwanidjuwa: In Australian Dreamtime, one of the Altjeringa Mitjina, an Eternal One of the Dream, who went walkabout, creating the landscape as he did so.

Jesu Apsusayin: As Hindus imagined Vishnu recumbent on the coils of Ananta so might Christians imagine Jesus recumbent on the coils of Apsu. Recumbent on Apsu, Jesus dreams a new universe. Recumbent ourselves, we can dream his Dreamtime dream with him. Prototype and patron of our Dreamtime.

Jtivanmukta: A Sanskrit word signifying a person who is liberated in this life.

Jnana yoga: A yoga in which we progress by means of intellectual insight. The Sanskrit word is related to our Greek word gnosis, meaning knowledge, insight, wisdom.

Kandariya Mahadeo: One of the temples at Khajuraho, in Madhya Pradesh in central India, whose architecturally integrated sculptures show strong Tantric inspiration.

Kanthaka: Name of the horse Buddha rode out on seeking enlightenment.

Katagogia: A Greek word meaning return, especially the return of a god.

Kathodes: Road going down, or the way down, or journey down, into the Underworld.

Kedron: The stream on the outskirts of Jerusalem which Jesus crossed on his way to Gethsemane. See The Gospel According to St John 18:1.

Kepler, Johann (1571-1630): astronomer, teacher and author of *Harmonice Mundi* (1619).

Kierkegaard, Sören (1813-55): Danish philosopher and existentialistic religious thinker.

Kosha: A Sanskrit word meaning veil or obscuration. According to Hindus, our senses, our minds and our passions are veils, veiling ultimate divine reality from us.

Kunapipi: In the Australian Dreamtime, she was one of the Altjeringa Mitjina, one of the Eternal Ones of the Dream, who went walkabout.

Kundalashakti. The coiled power in the muladhara chakra at the base of the spine. The power we seek to awaken in Kundalini yoga. Ultimately, Kundalashakti and Mayashakti are the same.

Kuruksetra: Scene of famous battle in *The Mababharata*, the great Hindu epic of 110,000 couplets dating back to the first millenium BC, in which Lord Krishna, in the guise of charioteer, spoke the Bhagavad Gita to the warrior prince Arjuna.

Kwakiutl: Indigenous peoples of Vancouver Island and environs on the Pacific Northwest coast, famed for their lavish tribal potlatch, or gift-giving, ceremonies.

Labdacidae: Laius and his royal descendants, of Thebes, a troubled city.

Lebor Gabála Erenn (Book of Invasions): The origin myth of the Irish contained in the Book of Leinster, a twelfth-century Irish manuscript anthology, edited by Professor R.A.S. MacAlister (Irish Texts Society, London 1939).

Lapsit Exillas: In Wolfram Von Eschenbach's *Parzival* (a thirteenth-century epic-poem, source of Wagner's libretto), the Grail is a stone, not a vessel, called Lapsit Exillas.

Lascaux: A cave at Montignac, Dordogne, south-western France, in which there are paleolithic paintings, *c.* 15,000 BC.

Lauds and Nones: Traditionally; in a Christian monastery, there were, each day, seven times of formal prayer: matins, lauds, terce, sext, nones, vespers and compline.

Leroi-Gourhan, André (1911-86): A French palaeontologist and anthropologist.

Leviathan: 'On that day the Lord with his sore and great and strong sword shall punish Leviathan the piercing serpent, even Leviathan the crooked serpent, and he shall slay the dragon that is in the sea', Isaiah 27:1. Not to be equated with anything biologically alive in our oceans today. A great and terrible sea monster.

Lingaraja Temple: One of the temples, in a complex of temples, at Bhuvaneshvar in India. Its innermost chamber is called the Garbhagrisha, the womb-chamber, and it houses a lingam standing in a yoni. The lingam symbolizes, and ritually is, the generative organ of the God, and the yoni symbolizes, and ritually is, the vulva of the Goddess.

Mabinogion, The: Collective name for eleven medieval Welsh prose tales commemorating ancient strata of Celtic myth and history, first published in English 1838-49.

Magh Mel: Literally, Plain of Honey, a paradisal Otherworld in Irish mythology.

Magh Tuired: In Irish mythology, there are accounts of a first and a second battle of Magh Tuired. In the first, the Tuatha De Danann fought the Firbolg. In the second, they fought the Fomorians. Both were fought to decide which of the peoples involved would possess the land of Ireland. Since the three peoples represented three different stares of mind, the issue on both occasions is as much philosophic as economic.

Magma: Geological term for lava outflow that has solidified.

Mahavakya: A great Upanishadic saying, such as *tat tvam asi* (that thou art). The canonical number of such sayings is six.

Malory, Sir Thomas (1415-71): A Warwickshire knight of uncertain identity, author of *Morte d'Arthur,* translated and compiled from Old French in London's Newgate Prison, where he died. These Arthurian tales were first printed by William Caxton in 1485.

Mandukya Upanishad: Canonical Hindu text from which philosophical monism derives.

Manu: In Egyptian mythology, Manu is the western mountain into which the sun descends, beginning its Underworld journey, every evening.

Mayashakti: A Hindu goddess, the source of the world-illusion.

Maymed Kynge: The wounded king, the Fisher King, king of the Grail Castle, wounded in the thigh (sexually wounded) as a consequence of a dolorous stroke. (See *Malory*.)

Medusa: Chief of the three Gorgons of Ancient Greece, who, when she looked at anything, turned it into stone. The only one that was mortal, slain by Perseus.

Megalonyx: One of the large fossil animals that Darwin discovered at Punta Alta *(q.v.)*.

Merlin: A magician, a woodsman. The wood he is a woodsman in is mostly an externalization of the human unconscious, the earth's unconscious. This book thinks of him as the last inheritor of Nordic and transnordic shamanism.

Metanoesis: As metaphysic means beyond the physical, metanoesis means beyond mind.

Miriam the prophetess: Hebrew prophetess who took a timbrel and danced and sang having come through the Red Sea.

Moksha: A Sanskrit word meaning liberation, a goal of spiritual endeavour.

Mordháil Uisnig: Dáil means assembly. The great assembly of people from the four quarters or provinces of Ireland at Uisnech, the ritual centre of Ancient Ireland.

Morgan Le Fay: A euhemerized goddess, in this book equated with Mayashakti. *(q.v.)*.

Morrigan: One of the trinity of Celtic war-hags. (See Badb.)

Mount Palomar: Observatory site of the five-metre Hale reflector telescope in southern California.

Mucalinda Buddha: A Buddha about whom the serpent king, Mucalinda, is coiled. Coiled about him not to constrict or kill him, but to protect him from the assaults of Kama Mara. In contradistinction to this Buddhist image, there is the Christian image of Mary standing on the head of the serpent to crush it.

Nemglan: One day Conaire was riding in his chariot towards Ath Cliath. Seeing a flock of huge white speckled birds in front of him, he gave chase, but no matter how hard and fast he rode the birds continued always a spear-cast ahead of him. Dismounting from his chariot, he pursued them on foot all the way into the sea. There they took off their bird-masks and turned on him with spears and swords. One bird protected him, saying, 'I am Nenaglan, king of your father's bird-troop. You are forbidden to cast at birds for, by reason of birth, every bird here is kin to you.' (From *Togail Bruidne Da Derga*, The Destruction of Da Derga's Hostel, E. Knott (ed.) [Dublin 1975])

Nierika: Huichol Indian for doorway or way between ordinary and non-ordinary reality.

Nietzsche, Friedrich (1844-1900): German philosopher born to a Lutheran pastor.

Niffari: An Egyptian Muslim mystic.

Nirguna Brahman: The Brahman who is without attributes.

Nirvikalpasamadhi: A contemplative state from which awareness-of-self-and-other-than-self has disappeared. A state of consciousness in which there is no object of consciousness.

Orpheus: A Greek hero or god in the presence of whose music and song, savage animals became peaceful and mild.

Oseberg boat: The famous boat, now in Oslo's Viking Museum, in which Queen Asa was buried *c.* AD 850 on the west coast of the Oslo fjord.

Osiris: Egyptian God of the Fields of Yaru, an otherworldly replica of this world.

Owen Roe: Eoghan Rua Ó Súilleabháin (1748-84). Kerry poet and amorist, who after the Cromwellian depradations wrote a type of poem called 'aisling', meaning a dream-vision, in this case a dream vision of the restoration of Gaelic Ireland (see *Aodghán*).

Padmasambhava: Lotus-born. Born purely of the lotus. The lotus, like our own water-lily, has its roots in the mud (of the passions), has its stem in the lucent water, and has its flower, fully opened, in pure sunlight.

Pan: Another theranthropic god of the Greeks. In Pan the *ther* is goat.
Paps of Danu, The: Breasts of Danu, an Indo-European goddess who, on her way West with her people gave her name to the Don, the Dneiper and Danube. Two hills at Sliabh Luachra in Kerry are known as her paps.
Paraclete: In Christianity, the Holy Spirit, pictured sometimes as a descending dove.
Paramahansa: Sanskrit word for wild gander, symbol of the liberated soul in Hinduism.
Paravritti, Asraya-paravritti: In Mahayana Buddhism, a profound revulsion or turning away at the foundations of consciousness, from the world-illusion and its source in our own asravas or outflows of gross desire, ignorance and will to live.
Parousia: In Christianity, the Second Coming of Christ in judgment and glory.
Parvati: Goddess daughter of Himalya and wife of the god Shiva in Hindu tradition.
Pascal, Blaise (1623-62): French mathematician, theologian and man of letters, champion of the Jansenists against the Jesuists; his *Pensées* appeared posthumously in 1670.
Pashupati: The horned divine Lord of Animals.
Persus: The Greek hero who slew Medusa using Minerva's shield, rescued Andromeda from the sea-monster and married her. (After death she was placed among the stars.)
Phlogiston: A gas posited by scientists to explain certain chemical phenomena; it was later shown not to exist.
Pleroma: Greek word for the fullness of Divine reality in the Godhead.
Porete, Margeurite: Mystic from Hainoult in Belgium, burnt at the stake in 1360.
Prajna paramita: A concept in Mahayana Buddhism meaning the wisdom that has gone beyond, the wisdom of the farther shore.
Pralaya: The state of uneventful, undifferentiated recumbence and prostration into which, at the end of its four great ages, a universe returns.
Propaideutic: An introductory teaching.
Psyverse: Compound word, psy(che) and (uni)verse, suggesting the universe is a psyche.
Ptah: An Ancient Egyptian god. Memphis was his cult centre.
Punta Alta: In geological times, for about seventy million years, the North and South American land-masses were separated, and during this time their faunas evolved in isolation from each other. When the land-bridge was restored, the great predators that had evolved in the north moved south, and events ominous unto extinction for many wiped out whole species, among them Megatherium, Megalonyx, Scelidotherium, Toxodon, Mylodon and Machrauchenia. Fossils of these animals Darwin found in and at the base of a cliff called Punta Alta on the coast of Argentina.
Python: A dragon with a lair in Delphi, where Apollo slew him and established an oracle.

Quondam Rex Rexque Futurus: The Once-and-Future King. It refers to King Arthur.
Quetzalcoatl: A Toltec-Aztec god of air and water. His name means the feathered or, plumed serpent. As such, he is, and represents, the union of opposites.

Racine, Jean (1639-1700): French tragic dramatist. *Phèdre* (1677) was based on *Hippolytus* by Euripides and tells of Theseus's wife Phèdre's guilty passion for her step-son.
Ragnarok: In Nordic mythology, Ragnarok is the name given to the cataclysms, upheavals, wars and conflicts in and through which a universe comes to an end.
Rasmussen, Knud (1879-1933): A Greenlander (born of Danish and Eskimo parents), explorer and ethnologist, who crossed Arctic North America (from Greenland to the Bering Strait, 1921-4), and wrote extensively on Eskimo culture.
Ratnasambhava: Jewel-born. As there are beings who are biologically born, so are there beings who are jewel-born.

274 GLOSSARY

Res Extensa: Literally, extended matter. In the seventeenth century philosophers and scientists distinguished between primary and secondary qualities, the former being extension and motion, the latter touch, taste, colour and smell. Only the primary qualities belonged to reality. All else was projection.

St John of the Cross (1542-91): Spanish mystic.
Saguna Brahman: The Brahman endowed with attributes, as opposed to the Brahman without attributes (*Brahmanirguna*).
Samadhi: Sanskrit word meaning contemplation.
Samsara: In Buddhism, the illusory world in which we are subject to death and rebirth.
Sety: A pharaoh.
Shabda Brahman: The Brahman of sounds. Brahman as he exists in mantras and hymns.
Shakti: Sanskrit word meaning energy or power. Personified, it is always female.
Shaman: Siberian term now adopted to denote a medicine man or woman.
Shantih: Sanskrit word meaning peace.
Shiva: Third person of Hindu Trinity, representing the destructive, and regenerative, principle.
Shu: Air, thought of as a god by the Ancient Egyptians.
Síolradh Ir is Eber: Descendants of Ir and Eibhár, two Celtic ancestors. The Irish people.
Sila Ersinarsinivdluge: An Eskimo phrase that translates as 'Don't be afraid of the universe'.
Silam Inua: An Eskimo or Inuit concept signifying something like the world soul as Plato or Plotinus understood it.
Simhanada Avalokteshvara: Avalokteshvara is a Bodhisattva (*q.v.*) who looks compassionately down on all suffering worlds. Entering these worlds, he roars a great lion roar, a Simhanada, seeking to awaken every being in them from illusion.
Sleagh solais: Spear of light.
Sorca: The Otherworld, not always thought of as an Underworld, in Irish mythology.
Spakona: Seeress or sibyl in Nordic mythology.
Stasimon: A song of the Chorus in Ancient Greek tragedy.
Stevens, Wallace (1879-1955): Pennsylvania-born insurance executive and poet.
Sugata: Well-gone, gone beyond world-illusion and the consciousness giving rise to it.
Sushummas: One of the nerve-lines in the subtle body along which chakras are located.
Suso (The Servitor) (*c.*1295-1366): Dominican, a disciple of Eckhart (*q.v.*) and, with the latter and Tauler, one of the three great medieval Rhineland-German mystics.
Susupta: The state of dreamless sleep.
Sutra: Sanskrit word meaning thread. Ancient aphoristic manuals with rules for systems of philosophy and grammar, directions for religious rituals and ceremonial customs. In Buddhism, any book containing or believed to contain teachings of the Buddha.
Sutton-Hoo: Site of a Saxon ship-burial (in East Anglia).
Syege Perelous: The perilous chair at the Round Table.

Taijasa: The state of dreaming.
Takanakapsaluk: One of the most sacred and famous Eskimo stories describes how she became the mother of sea-beasts—of seals, walrus, dolphins, porpoise, whales. She lives on the floor of the ocean.
Taliesin (*fl.* 550): The most archetypal bard in Welsh mythology.
Tao Té Ching: Translated by Arthur Waley (1934) as *The Way and its Power*, a Taoist sacred text attributed to Lao Tszu (*c.*604-523 BC) consisting of eighty-one short chapters of

poetry and philosophical reflection—profound and beautiful, sometimes paradoxical. It proposes a view of life equivalent to the lily-of-the-field section of the Sermon on the Mount in the Bible.

Tathata: A word often come across in the writings of Mahayana Buddhism. 'Suchness' is a common translation. The undifferentiated reality behind the world-illusion.

Tehom: Hebrew word for the Great Deep.

Thebes: A city Cadmus (*q.v.*) built, a troubled city; site of the Oedipus cycle, north of Athens.

Theranthropic: From two Greek words, *ther,* animal; *anthropus,* human. Used descriptively of beings who, anatomically, are an organic conjunction of animal and human parts. Anubis, for instance, the mortuary God of the Ancient Egyptians, has a jackal's head but is otherwise human in form.

Thesus: Greek hero who slew the Minotaur.

Tiamat: In Babylonian mythology, Tiamat is the primordial female monster of the Abyss. Marduk, a God held in highest esteem by the citizens of Babylon, did battle with her. Slaying her, he sliced her down the middle, elevating the upper fillet so that it became the sky, spreading out the lower fillet so that it became the Earth.

Tír Tarngrí. Land of Promise, a paradisal Celtic Otherworld, ruled over by Manannán Mac Lir in Irish mythology.

Tohu-Wavohu: The Hebrew word for chaos, the waste of dark, destructive waters against which the biblical God set up constraining bars and doors.

Triduum Sacrum: The three sacred days. Holy Thursday, Good Friday and Easter Sunday.

Traherne, Thomas (1637-74): English mystic and poet, born to a shoemaker in Hereford. His *Centuries of Meditation* were discovered in 1896-7 and first published in 1908.

Trois Frerès, Les: A paleolithic cave in southern France, famous for its prehistoric art.

Tsleg boi ac Lug: Spear of Lugh, a sun god of the Tuatha De Danann.

Tula: Meso-American city Quetzalcoatl (*q.v.*) purportedly built in pre-Columbian central Mexico, *c.* AD 750-1168, when the Toltecs dominated prior to the Aztecs.

Turiya: According to the Mandukya Upanishad (*q.v.*) this whole universe is Brahman. The innermost core of our being, called atman, that too is Brahman. This atman, which is Brahman, has four states: the waking state, the dreaming state, the state of dreamless sleep, and also a state called Turiya, a Sanskrit word that means the fourth. (As a river is absorbed, losing its identity in the ocean, so, in this fourth state, is the individual soul absorbed into Brahmanirguna. The Tehom we are biblically in dread of is the Turiya that we upanishadically yearn for.)

Uffington Horse: A great white horse 'etched' into a hillside at Uffington, in Oxfordshire.

Uisnech: Ancient ritual centre of Ireland, a hill in Co. Westmeath east of the village of Ballymore.

Uluru: Mountain in Dreamtime Australia; white people call it Ayer's Rock.

Ulro-/Ulropeans: The Fall, which the poet William Blake envisaged as a descent through four distinct states of mind: Eden, Beulah, Generation and Ulro. The latter is our condition.

Ungrund or Urgrund: A German mystical term denoting the divine no-ground that grounds. It arises in Boehme's (*q.v.*) attempt to explain the origin of things, especially the existence of evil.

Upanishads: Sanskrit for a sitting down (at another's feet); sacred Hindu texts on the nature of man and the universe, part of Vedic writings dating back two and a half millennia.

Urddhva Vahini: In Hindu Tantra, She Who Ascends; ascends, as Kundalini ascends through the chakras.
Uruk: City Gilgamesh built in Sumer, north-west of Ur.

Vaisvanara: The waking state.
Vajrasattva: Whose essence, like the thunderbolt, is indestructible and pure; a concept in Tibetan Buddhism.
Vajrasattvic: Adjectival form of the noun vajrasattva, a being or thing whose essence is diamond or adamantine, and therefore indestructible. Common in Tibetan Buddhism.
Vajrayana: A form of spiritual practice in Tibetan Buddhism.
Valhalla: Hall of the heroes in Nordic mythology.
Vates: Latin term meaning one divinely inspired; a prophet-poet, a Roman sibyl, hence 'vatic'.
Vedas: The four sacred books of the Brahmans (*Rig, Yajur, Sama* and *Atharva*), collections of prayers and hymns of ancient scripture; *veda* means knowledge in Sanskrit.
Viksepashakti: The projecting shakti, or power. The power by which we project a multitudinous universe into the One.
Vishnu: Major Hindu deity, the second member, with Brahma and Siva, of a triad of gods manifesting cosmic functions of the Supreme Being. A preserver of the universe and embodiment of goodness and mercy, his descents (*avataras*) include appearances as Rama and Krishna.
Vishvarupa: The Hindu god Vishnu (*q.v.*) when he is seen to contain within himself all the myriad forms of reality.
Voluspo: Norse poem in which Volva describes the cataclysmic end of an old world and birth of a new world. The best account of Ragnorok.
Volva: Seeress or sibyl in Nordic mythology.

Well of Connla: An Otherworld well. The rivers of Ireland are said to have their sources in it. A hazel grows over it. The nuts that fall into it have wisdom in them. Eaten by salmon, this wisdom is carried downstream to all parts of the country.
Wodwo: A being that Gawain met in the forest on his way to the Green Chapel.
Wordsworth, William (1770-1850): A Cumbria-born poet, his 'Ode on Intimations of Immortality from Recollections of Early Childhood' first appeared in *Poems in Two Volumes* (1807).

Yatra na anyat pasyati, na anyat srinoti na anyad vijanati, sa bhuma: (Where one sees nothing else, hears nothing else, knows nothing else, that is fullness.) Chandogya Upanishad, VII, XXIV.
Yeats, William Butler (1865-1939): Dublin-born poet, playwright, founder of the Abbey Theatre, senator, and winner of the Nobel Prize for Literature in 1923.
Yggdrasil: In Nordic mythology, the World Tree. It was believed to have nine worlds in it, some under its roots, some on its branches.